NORTHERN CALIFORNIA COAST BEST PLACES

Best Places Destination Guides

NORTHERN CALIFORNIA COAST BEST PLACES

A Destination Guide

*By Matthew R. Poole and the **Best Places** Editors*

SASQUATCH BOOKS
SEATTLE

Printed in the United States of America.

Cover design: Karen Schober
Cover map: Rolf Goetzinger
Foldout map: Dave Berger
Interior design adaptation and composition: Fay Bartels, Kate Basart, and Millie Beard
Interior illustrations: Greg Churchill

Library of Congress Cataloging in Publication Data

Poole, Matthew Richard.
Northern California Coast best places : a destination guide / Matthew Poole and the Best places editors.
        p. cm. — (Best places destination guides)
        Includes index.
        ISBN 1-57061-051-7
        1. California, Northern—Guidebooks. I. Title. II. Series.
    F867.5.P666   1996
        95-54205
    917.94—dc20

Sasquatch Books
1008 Western Avenue
Seattle, WA 98104
(206)467-4300
books@sasquatchbooks.com
http://www.sasquatchbooks.com

Sasquatch Books publishes high-quality adult nonfiction as well as children's books, all related to the Northwest (San Francisco to Alaska). For information about our books, contact us at the above address, or view our site on the World Wide Web.

CONTENTS

ACKNOWLEDGMENTS

The *Destination Guides* couldn't have been produced without the countless contributors to our *Best Places* and *Cheap Sleeps* series; however, if anyone deserves credit for creating this beast, it's my poor little Subaru. Together we literally drove to the Oregon border, flipped a U-turn, and made every right turn we could find that headed toward the sea. And through it all—the mud, the sand, the bone-jarring backroads—she never once let me down.

Next in line for recognition is Mona Behan, from whom I pilfered a sizable amount of her flawless reviews published in Sasquatch Book's *Northern California Best Places* (hey, if it works, don't fix it). Other contributors include writer/reviewers Rebecca Foree, Mary Anne Moore, and Maurice Read, as well as my ever-supportive editors, Joan Gregory and Stephanie Irving, the latter of whom decided childbirth was less painful than editing my work and punted the job to Joan mid-way through (and a nice catch it was).

Finally, I would like to thank everyone who housed, fed, informed, and befriended me during my journeys along the coast. Don't let anyone convince you that mankind is a selfish lot: the warmth, hospitality, and genuine selflessness I encountered from friends and strangers during my travels was constant and unwaivering.

To all of you—and Stephanie's baby—I dedicate this book.

—Matthew Richard Poole

PREFACE

The Sasquatch Books *Best Places* series is unique in that the guidebooks are written by and for locals—which makes them coveted by visitors. The books are designed for travelers who enjoy exploring the bounty of the region, who like out-of-the-way places of high character and individualism, and who take the time to seek out such places. Best Places inspectors travel anonymously and accept no free meals, accommodations, or other complimentary services. Our forthright reviews rate establishments on a scale of zero to four stars and describe the true strengths, foibles, and unique characteristics of each.

Our *Destinations Guides* are written for those who have always trusted the restaurant and lodging reviews in our *Best Places* series (such as *Northwest Best Places* and *Northern California Best Places*), but who longed for additional suggestions on what to do between dining and reclining. For each destination, we've provided Best Places selections for restaurants and lodgings. To give you more lodging options for your money, we've included recommended bargain lodgings from our *Northern California Cheap Sleeps*. Then we had our inspectors research each destination thoroughly, consulting myriad regional spies and sources, and collecting local knowledge about the best the area has to offer—from galleries to beaches, concerts to parks. The *Best Places Destination Guides* are designed to be chatty and easy to browse, with icons to help you locate your favorite activities.

We like to think the *Destination Guides* are the next best thing to having a friend on the Northern California Coast.

—*The Editors*

HOW TO USE THIS BOOK

RECOMMENDED RESTAURANTS AND LODGINGS

At the end of each town section you'll find restaurants and lodgings recommended by our *Best Places* editors.

 Restaurants

 Lodgings

Rating System: Establishments with stars have been rated on a scale of zero to four. Ratings are based on uniqueness, enjoyability, value, loyalty of local clientele, excellence of cooking, performance measured against goals, and professionalism of service. In addition, we've included recommended bargain lodgings— the best place for the best price. These are usually $60 or under for one night's lodging for two.

(*no stars*)	Worth knowing about, if nearby
☆	A good place
☆☆	Some wonderful qualities
☆☆☆	Distinguished, many outstanding features
☆☆☆☆	The very best in the region
Unrated	New or undergoing major changes

Price Range: When prices range between two categories (for example, moderate to expensive), the lower one is given. Call ahead to verify.

$$$ Expensive. Indicates a tab of more than $75 for dinner for two, including wine (but not tip), and more than $90 for one night's lodging for two.

$$ Moderate. Falls between expensive and inexpensive.

$ Inexpensive. Indicates a tab of less than $25 for dinner, and less than $60 for lodgings for two.

THE
MONTEREY
COAST

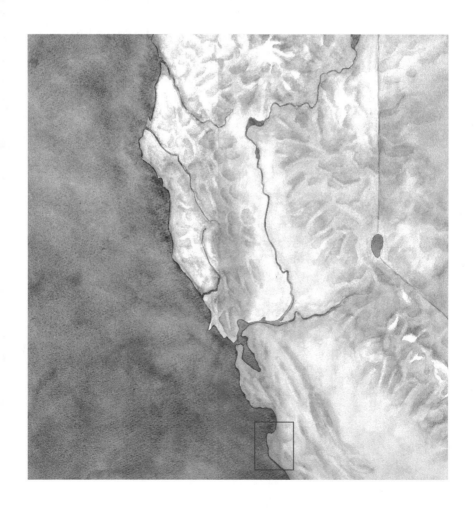

THE MONTEREY COAST

A south-to-north sweep of the Monterey County coastline, beginning in Big Sur and ending just north of Monterey at Castroville.

For the last 20 years, the Monterey coast has maintained a split personality. The handful of families who own most of the land south of Carmel—i.e., Big Sur—have endeavored to keep the area as indigenous and unpopulated as possible (in fact, Big Sur sustained a larger population at the turn of the century than it does today). The coastline north of Carmel, however, has become so saturated with homes, hotels, and tourist attractions that antidevelopment folks have coined the term "Carmelization" to describe the region's fall from grace; try to find free parking or affordable lodging on a summer weekend, and the issue becomes readily apparent.

Problems aside, no one can dispute that the Monterey coast is a land of superlatives. It has one of California's most renowned scenic thoroughfares (17-Mile Drive), a slew of internationally known golf courses, the most popular aquarium in the nation, and even the most famous ex-mayor in America (Clint Eastwood). Combine all this with truly incredible coastal vistas—particularly around Big Sur—and it's not hard to see why the Monterey coast's 8 million annual visitors don't mind paying a little to park.

BIG SUR

There isn't exactly a Big Sur in Big Sur . . . not a town by that name, anyway. Spanish settlers referred to the 90 miles of rugged, impassable coastline between Carmel and San Simeon as *El País Grande del Sur*, or "the big country to the south" (that is, south of their colony at Monterey). Proving that there's nothing the English language can't butcher for the sake of brevity, El Sur Grande eventually mutated into Big Sur, an appellation that still does little to convey the unbelievable beauty bestowed on the land by Madre Nature. Mist-shrouded forests, plunging cliffs, cobalt seas, and nary a Starbucks or Taco Bell account for one of the most beautiful coastal drives in the country, if not the world.

Despite Big Sur's popularity—summer weekends are unkind to the two-lane highway—the area has remained sparsely populated. Most visitors are day trippers vacationing in the Monterey area, who come to see what all the fuss is about. The rest, aka those in the know, journey here for a few days of camping, backpacking, or luxuriating in the elegant (and exorbitantly priced) resorts. If you're only visiting for the day, here's a few words of advice: start early, fill your tank, take a camera and binoculars, bring a jacket, wear comfortable shoes, drive slow, take a hike, then turn around at Julia Pfeiffer Burns State Park and do it all over again.

ACTIVITIES

 Point Lobos. Whether you're in Big Sur for a day or for a week, spend some time in the gorgeous 1,304-acre Point Lobos State Reserve (on Highway 1, 4 miles south of Carmel; 408-624-4909). More than a dozen trails lead to ocean coves, where you might spy sea otters, harbor seals, California sea lions, large colonies of seabirds, and between December and May, migrating California gray whales. Wherever you trek through Big Sur, however, beware of poison oak (remember: leaves of three, let it be; leaves of four, give me some more).

 Bixby Bridge. That magnificent arched span crossing over Bixby Creek Canyon is the Bixby Bridge, aka the Rainbow Bridge. At 268 feet high, 739 feet long, with a 320-foot arch, it's one of the world's highest single-span concrete bridges and a favorite stop for camera-wielding tourists. Photo tip: For the best shooting angle, drive a few hundred yards up the dirt road at the north end of the bridge (Old Coast Road).

Lighthouse. South of Bixby Bridge is the Point Sur Lighthouse, built in 1889 and towering 361 feet above the surf atop Point Sur, a giant volcanic-rock island easily visible from Highway 1. Inexpensive (though physically taxing), 2½-hour guided lighthouse tours—some by spectacular moonlight—are offered on weekends year-round and on Wednesdays in summer. Call for schedule information. Off Highway 1, 19 miles south of Carmel in Big Sur; (408)625-4419.

 Andrew Molera S. P. A popular retreat for hikers and bicyclists is the 4,800-acre Andrew Molera State Park, the largest state park on the Big Sur coast. More than 15 miles of trails zigzag through grasslands, redwood forests, and along Big Sur River. A mile-long walk through a meadow laced with wildflowers leads to a 2-mile-long beach

The only two naturally growing stands of Monterey cypress trees remaining on earth are at Point Lobos State Reserve and Pebble Beach on 17-Mile Drive.

Skip the $6 parking fee at Point Lobos State Reserve by parking alongside Highway 1 and walking (or biking) in. It's not only legal, the rangers recommend it.

harboring the area's best tide pools. On Highway 1, 21 miles south of Carmel; (408)667-2315.

 Old Coast Road. Across from the entrance to Andrew Molera State Park is the southern access point to Old Coast Road, a well-maintained (though bumpy) dirt road that passes through 10 miles of dense redwood groves and chaparral-covered ridges—with spectacular views of the coast—before exiting back onto Highway 1 at Bixby Bridge. A four-wheel-drive vehicle isn't necessary for the hourlong mini-adventure, but this isn't for the lion-hearted, either.

 Hiking. One thing Big Sur isn't short of is hiking trails. Pfeiffer–Big Sur State Park has dozens of trails—many with panoramic views of the sea—that crisscross the park's 810 acres of madrone and oak woodlands and misty redwood canyons. The Big Sur River meanders through the park, too, attracting anglers and swimmers hardy enough to brave the chilly waters. For overnighters, Pfeiffer–Big Sur offers ultracivilized camping facilities that include showers, a laundry, a store, an amphitheater for ranger-led campfire talks, and (bless 'em) flush toilets. Make reservations through Destinet at (800)444-PARK; park information, (408)667-2315.

 Beach. Though entrance to Pfeiffer–Big Sur State Park costs a hefty $6, the park's best attraction is free. Exactly 1$\frac{1}{10}$ miles south of the park's entrance on Highway 1 is the unmarked turnoff to Sycamore Canyon Road, a narrow 2$\frac{1}{3}$-mile paved road (motor homes can forget this one) that leads to beautiful but blustery Pfeiffer Beach. Even if the sun's a no-show, it's still worth a trip to marvel at the white-and-mauve sands, enormous sea caves, and pounding surf.

 Gallery. Three miles south of Nepenthe Restaurant is the Coast Gallery, a showplace for local artists and craftspeople featuring pottery, jewelry, and paintings, including watercolors by author Henry Miller, who lived nearby for more than 15 years. The gallery's casual Coast Cafe has a great view of the ocean and offers simple serve-yourself lunches of soup, sandwiches, baked goods, wine, and espresso drinks; Highway 1, Big Sur; (408)667-2301.

The Big Sur-prize. If you only have the time or energy for one short hike while touring Big Sur, head for the secret cove at Partington Canyon. Don't bother looking for it on the map; it's not there. Instead, park at the 37.85 mile marker (2 miles north of Julia Pfeiffer Burns State Park), walk down the canyon toward the ocean (ho hum), turn right at the "Underwater Forest" display (la-di-da), then left across the footbridge (boooring), and suddenly it's *"Whoa!* Where'd *that* come from?" A raging non sequitur in this remote valley, this 100-foot, handcarved, timber-reinforced tunnel leads to a dazzling hidden cove. Story goes John Partington built the tunnel for his tan-oak cutting and shipping operation, where sleds filled with tanoak bark were pulled down the mountain and loaded onto ships anchored in the placid cove.

Regardless of how Hollywood heartthrob Michelle Pfeiffer pronounces her last name, Big Sur's founding Pfeiffer family keeps the f silent and the p hard. Say Pie-fur and you're halfway to becoming a local.

 Julie Pfeiffer Burns. At the southern end of the Big Sur area is Julia Pfeiffer Burns State Park. With 4,000 acres to roam—and a less-crowded feel to it than the region's other parks—you'll find some excellent day hikes here. If you just want to get out of the car and stretch your legs, take the ¼-mile Waterfall Trail to the 80-foot-high McWay Waterfall, one of the few falls in California that plunges directly into the sea. Keep an eye open the for sea otters that play in McWay Cove; (408)667-2315.

Dipping Your Skinny. Most folks pay over 100 bucks to soak their bods in the hot springs overlooking the ocean at Esalen Institute, the world-famous New Age retreat that's renowned for its self-help workshops and body massages. The poorer sore, however, can relieve their aches for a mere $10 if they're willing to visit in the wee hours. How wee? Between 1am and 3am, any day of the week (and reservations are recommended even at those hours); (408)667-3023.

RESTAURANTS

CAFE KEVAH ☆☆

 If your idea of communing with nature is a comfy chair in the shade, a leafy salad, and a view of the rugged coast, then grab a seat on the deck of the Cafe Kevah, located one flight of stairs below the fabled—and absurdly

Just beyond Nepenthe Restaurant on the east side of Highway 1 is the nonprofit Henry Miller Memorial Library, a small wood cabin exhibiting the writer's entire collection of works (which are for sale); (408)667-2574.

overpriced—Nepenthe Restaurant. Not only is the food wonderful (e.g., Australian lamb skewers with couscous, green mint pesto, and garlic toast; grilled salmon over tossed greens with a papaya vinaigrette; buttermilk waffles and fresh vegetable omelets), it's inexpensive, too—all plates are under $10. The clincher, though, is the location: perched 800 feet above the glimmering Pacific, the cafe's deck has a phenomenal view of the Big Sur coastline. *On Hwy 1, 3 miles south of Pfeiffer–Big Sur State Park, Big Sur; (408)667-2344; Hwy 1, Big Sur; beer and wine; AE, MC, V; no checks; breakfast, lunch every day;$.*

LODGINGS

POST RANCH INN ■
SIERRA MAR RESTAURANT ☆☆☆☆

Travel & Leisure magazine has hailed the 98-acre Post Ranch Inn as "the most spectacular hotel on the Pacific Coast," and that might not be hyperbole. Discreetly hidden on a ridge in the Santa Lucia Mountains, its deceptively simple exteriors are meant to harmonize with the forested slopes, while windows, windows everywhere celebrate the breathtaking vista of sky and sea. Inside, the lodgepole construction and a wealth of warm woods lend a rough-hewn luxury to the rooms: earth tones, blues, and greens predominate, extending the link between the buildings and their environment. "Environment," in fact, is a word you'll hear a lot around this place: the Post Ranch Inn is one of the new breed of "eco-hotels" where the affluent can indulge in sumptuous luxury and still feel politically correct. For example, six of the units (known as the Tree Houses) were built on stilts to avoid disturbing the surrounding redwoods' root systems; other units are sunk into the earth and roofed with sod. The water is filtered; visitors are encouraged to sort their trash; and the paper upon which guests' rather staggering bills are printed is recycled.

Despite this more-ecologically-correct-than-thou atmosphere, the designers of the Post Ranch Inn didn't forget about the niceties of life. The 30 spacious rooms have spare—but by no means spartan—decor, including fireplaces, king-size beds, and sideboards made of African hardwoods (nonendangered, naturally). Plush robes hang in the closets, Jacuzzi tubs for two grace the well-equipped bathrooms, and stereo systems fill the air with ethereal New Age music. A continental breakfast and guided nature hikes are included in the room rates; the massages, facials, herbal wraps, and yoga classes are not. The Ranch also boasts a gorgeous, cliff-hugging restaurant that has been hailed as one of the best on the Central Coast. The Sierra Mar serves a sophisticated brand of California cuisine—roasted Guinea fowl with potato gnocchi, grilled rabbit with smoked bacon and sage—in a serene expanse of wood and glass that lets you drink in the incredible views along with the costly wine. *On Hwy 1, 30 miles south of Carmel; lodging (408)667-2200 or (800)527-2200, restaurant (408)667-2800; PO Box 219, Big Sur, CA 93920; full bar; AE, MC, V; checks OK; lunch Sat and Sun (reservations required for nonguests), dinner every day; $$$.*&

Post Ranch Inn architect Mickey Muennig supposedly camped out on the property for five months before setting pencil to paper for his design.

VENTANA COUNTRY INN RESORT ■ VENTANA RESTAURANT ☆☆☆☆

 If one casts the Post Ranch as the brash newcomer, the Ventana must be the revered granddaddy of the eco-hotel scene. Not that this stunning resort is showing its age—the Ventana is as fresh and up with the times as it was when it made its debut two decades ago. Set on the brow of a cha-parral-covered hill in the Santa Lucia Mountains, this modern, weathered-cedar inn is almost too serene and con-templative to be called decadent, yet too luxurious to be called anything else. The spacious 59 rooms, decorated in an upscale country style and divided among 12 low-rise buildings, look out over the plunging forested hillsides, wildflower-laced meadows, and roiling waters of the Big Sur coast. Several rooms have fireplaces, hot tubs, and wet bars, and breakfast is included. Three houses are also available to rent; the rooms in the Sycamore and Madrone houses have large private balconies and some of the best views of the ocean.

The other big draw is the Ventana Restaurant. Although critics have always been unanimous in praising its aesthet-ics, a revolving-door parade of chefs has kept them uncer-tain about the quality of the food since Bay Area superchef Jeremiah Tower did his star turn here years ago. Currently chef David Daniels is at the helm, serving artfully prepared creations such as potato-wrapped Sonoma quail with roasted-garlic mashed potatoes and Oregon morels. Or how about pan-roasted halibut cheeks with sweet corn pudding and red onion relish? Prices are steep, naturally, but the quality of the ingredients and preparation combined with the exceptional service and gorgeous atmosphere make the Ventana worth the splurge. *On Hwy 1, 28 miles south of Carmel, 2½ miles south of Pfeiffer–Big Sur State Park; (408)667-2331, (800)628-6500; Ventana, Big Sur, CA 93920; full bar; AE, DC, DIS, MC, V; checks OK; lunch, dinner every day; $$$&.*

DEETJEN'S BIG SUR INN AND RESTAURANT ☆

During the '30s and '40s, travelers making the long journey up or down the coast used to drop in and stay the night with Grandpa Deetjen, a Norwegian immigrant. No doubt weary of houseguests, he constructed a cluster of redwood buildings with 20 rooms to accommodate them. Grandpa's idea of comfort was a bit austere, but then again, he never expected to charge $70 to $150 per night. Located in a damp redwood canyon, most cabins are divided into two units, with dark-wood interiors, minimal lighting, and nonexistent insulation. Some have shared baths, and many of them are quite charming in a rustic sort of way. If you stay in one of the two-story units (some with fireplaces or wood stoves), be sure to request the quieter upstairs rooms. Grandpa's Room is particularly quaint and comfortable.

Deetjen's Bug Sur Inn Restaurant, which has garnered a loyal following, serves "Euro-California" cuisine that takes advantage of local produce and seafood. Meat eaters shouldn't pass up roasted New Zealand rack of lamb with a honey-mustard and pecan crust, while vegetarian folks will be pleased by the mix of spinach, mushrooms, feta cheese, and marinated tofu baked in flaky filo dough and served with a broccoli timbale and wild rice. *On Hwy 1, 3 miles south of Pfeiffer–Big Sur State Park; lodgings (408)667-2377, restaurant (408)667-2378; Hwy 1, Big Sur, CA 93920; beer and wine; MC, V; checks OK; breakfast, dinner every day; $$.*

RIPPLEWOOD RESORT ■ RIPPLEWOOD CAFE ☆

With its 16 spartan cabins clustered along a rugged section of Highway 1, Ripplewood Resort is the perfect place to go with a large group of friends. Try to book cabins 1 to 9, which are set on the river far below the highway. During the summer the popular units are booked four months in advance, so plan ahead. The adjoining Ripplewood Cafe is clean, cute, and perfectly good for breakfast or lunch. The muffins, sticky buns, and pies are house-made, and the cinnamon French toast is a big favorite. For lunch, try the marinated bean salad or the grilled Jack cheese sandwich slathered with green chiles. *On Hwy 1, about 1½ miles north of Pfeiffer–Big Sur State Park; (408)667-2242; Hwy 1, Big Sur, CA 93920; beer and wine; MC, V; no checks; breakfast, lunch every day; $$.*

BIG SUR CAMPGROUND AND CABINS

The 17 "cabins" here range from fully equipped mobile homes to wooden A-frames with sleeping lofts and kitchens. Several of the units sit along the Big Sur River, and each has a private bath and fireplace. In the summer, four tent cabins are also rented—with beds and bedding provided—or you can bring your sleeping bag and rough it at the 80 year-round campsites set in a large redwood grove. Guests often while away the day swimming or fishing in the river (steelhead season runs November 16 to February 28, on weekends, Wednesdays, and holidays only). Amenities include a store, laundry, playground, basketball courts, and innertube rentals. *On Hwy 1, about 3 miles south of Andrew Molera State Park; (408)667-2322; Hwy 1, Big Sur, CA 93920; MC, V; no checks; $.*

CARMEL

In the not-so-distant past, Carmel was regarded as a reclusive little seaside town with the sort of relaxed Mediterranean atmosphere that was conducive to such pursuits as photography, painting, and writing. Robert Louis Stevenson, Upton Sinclair, Ansel Adams—all found Carmel so peaceful and intellectually inspiring as to settle down here.

Not anymore. The charmingly ragtag bohemian village of yesteryear has long since given way to a cute but conservative tourist mecca filled with yogurt parlors, T-shirt stores, and chichi House and Garden marts offering $300 ceramic geese and other essentials. Traffic—both vehicular and pedestrian—can be maddeningly congested during the summer and on weekends, and prices in the shops, hotels, and restaurants tend to be gougingly high.

The funny thing is, no matter how crowded or expensive

Carmel gets, nobody seems to mind. Enamored of the village's eclectic dwellings, outrageous boutiques, quaint cafes, and silky white beaches, tourists arrive in droves during the summer to lighten their wallets and darken their complexions. In fact, most B&Bs are usually booked solid from May to October, so make your reservations far in advance and leave plenty of room on the credit cards—you'll need it.

ACTIVITIES

Shopping Nirvana. Carmel is a wee bit o' heaven for shoppers with hefty disposable incomes. Even if you can't afford a lizard-skin gym bag or a Waterford crystal bird bath, it's still fun—and free—to window-shop among Carmel's oh-so-chic boutiques. Some of the more interesting downtown spots are the Carmel Bay Company, purveyors of a large, classy collection of California-style gardening tools and household furnishings (on Ocean Avenue at Lincoln Street, Carmel; 408-624-3868); Dansk Designs, a housewares outlet store (on Ocean Avenue at San Carlos Street, Carmel; 408-625-1600); and the Secret Garden, which offers unique gardening gadgets (on Dolores Street, between 5th and 6th Avenues, Carmel; 408-625-1131). Just south of town are two luxe suburban malls also worth a stroll: the Barnyard (on Highway 1 at Carmel Valley Road; 408-624-8886) and the Crossroads (on Highway 1 at Rio Road; 408-625-4106).

Carmel Beaches. If your sprees have left you shopped out, visit one of the town's fabled beaches. Carmel Beach City Park, at the foot of Ocean Avenue, tends to be overcrowded in summer (even though its chilly aquamarine water is unsafe for swimming), but the satiny white sand and towering cypresses are worth the price of sunbathing among the hordes. Better yet, head a mile south on Scenic Drive (the street running alongside the beach) to spectacular Carmel River State Beach, where the locals go to hide from the tourists. The Carmel River enters the Pacific here, and the nearby bird sanctuary is often frequented by pelicans, hawks, sandpipers, and the occasional goose.

 Bookstore. The only thing better than a good bookstore is a good bookstore with a good cafe. Within the sea of Carmel's exorbitant boutiques and restaurants is the refreshingly unpretentious (and inexpensive) Thunderbird Bookshop and Cafe, located within the Barnyard shopping complex at Highway 1 and Carmel Valley Road. Peruse the largest book selection on the Central Coast, then sit your fanny at the adjacent cafe armed with a slice of quiche, a decaf latte, and your new read. Now *that's* vacationing. (Open daily 10am–8pm; 408-624-9414.)

Carmel Mission. At the south end of Carmel on the corner of Rio Road and Lasuen Drive is the restored Mission San Carlos Borromeo del Río Carmelo, better known as the Carmel Mission. Established in 1770, this was the headquarters of Father Junípero Serra's famous chain of California missions, as well as being his favorite (Serra is buried in front of the altar in the sanctuary). The vine-covered baroque church with its 11-bell Moorish tower is one of California's architectural treasures. The mission houses three extensive museums, and its surrounding 14 acres are planted with native flowers and trees. The cemetery has more than 3,000 graves of Native Americans who worked and lived in the mission; in place of a gravestone, many plots are marked by a solitary abalone shell; (408)624-3600.

Peace and Quiet. If the Carmel crowds are starting to drive you buggy, head to the intersection of Mountain View Avenue and Forest Road (off Ocean Avenue) and bask in the glorious silence of Mission Trails Park. Even on the busiest weekends, the north end of the park is usually deserted, allowing

To find the perfect picnic-basket ingredients for a day on the beach, go to the Mediterranean Market on Ocean Avenue at Mission Street, which stocks a large selection of meats, cheeses, and wines; (408)624-2022.

You can rent a mountain bike to explore Carmel for about $20 a day (cheaper than a parking ticket!) from Bay Bikes, on Lincoln Street between 5th and 6th Avenues; (408)625-2453.

those in the know a few hours' respite among the 35 shaded acres of tree-lined trails. Dogs are permitted, and plastic doo-doo bags are provided to keep things tidy.

Robinson Jeffers. Worth a gander is Tor House, the former home of poet Robinson Jeffers. Constructed over several years beginning in 1914, the rustic granite building looks as if it was transplanted from the British Isles (it's still occupied by one of the Jeffers clan). More intriguing, however, is the nearby four-story Hawk Tower, which Jeffers built for his wife, Una, with thousands of huge granite rocks he hauled up from the beach below his house. Guided tours of the house and tower are available for a fee on Friday and Saturday by reservation only. On 26304 Ocean View Avenue at Stewart Way, Carmel; no children under 12; (408)624-1813.

Theater. Carmel has an active theater scene, perhaps best represented by the Pacific Repertory Theatre company, which puts on an outdoor Shakespeare festival each summer and performs other classics such as *The Madness of George III* and *Death of a Salesman* in its indoor theater year-round. Tickets are reasonably priced; call (408)622-0700 or (408)622-0100 for details.

Johann's Bach in Town. The annual monthlong Carmel Bach Festival, now led by internationally famous conductor Bruno Weil, offers several concerts, recitals, lectures, and discussion groups—many of them free. In addition to Bach masterpieces, you'll hear scores by Vivaldi, Scarlatti, Beethoven, and Chopin. The classical-music celebration starts in mid-July; series tickets are sold starting in January, and single-event tickets (ranging from $10 to $30) go on sale in April. Call (800)513-BACH for a list of free events and additional festival facts.

RESTAURANTS

CALIFORNIA THAI RESTAURANT ☆☆☆

In a town groaning with chic little European restaurants, this relative newcomer provides a welcome change of culinary pace. Owners Pachara and Justin Hanley, who transplanted their restaurant from Santa Rosa, have created a spare, soothing, and sophisticated oasis. Everything from the high-backed chairs to the generous spacing between the tables speaks to customers' comfort, and you'd be hard pressed to find a staff (led by the charming Pachara) more dedicated to pleasing the patrons.

Distinctive appetizers include *miang kam* (fresh spinach leaves sprinkled with roasted coconut, fresh lime, onions, peanuts, dried shrimp, chiles, and ginger) and Bangkok Star (a series of delicate rice-flour cups filled with chicken, corn, sweet potatoes, and onions). A favorite entree is the grilled Chilean sea bass served with fresh mango-and-papaya chutney and topped with a mild green chile, garlic, and fresh lime sauce. Some interesting vegetarian and pasta selections also figure among the entrees, and by all means, if the incredible duck with mango-brandy sauce is offered as a special, order it. *At 4th Ave and San Carlos St, Carmel; (408)622-1160; beer and wine; AE, MC, V; local checks only; dinner every day; $$.*

CREME CARMEL RESTAURANT ☆☆☆

Located in a courtyard behind a liquor store, Crème Carmel is easy to miss. And that's a pity, because this intimate restaurant decorated with eclectic local art offers some of the most inventive food in town. Chef Kenn Leth Madsen and his wife, Elizabeth Stokkebye, who took ownership in January 1994, have retained many of the California-French dishes patrons have come to love. Depending on the season, these might include salmon with a basil-spinach sauce or a crisp breast of duck with a tamarind-ginger sauce. Appetizers range anywhere from Maui-onion-and-lobster pancakes to a prawn-and-goat-cheese tart with a jalapeño-shallot sauce. For dessert try the incredible bitter-sweet-chocolate soufflé spiked with whiskey and Cognac. *On San Carlos St between Ocean and 7th Aves, Carmel; (408)624-0444; beer and wine; AE, MC, V; dinner Mon–Sat; $$$.*

PRIMA 6TH AVENUE GRILL ☆☆☆

In late 1993, Prima became a noteworthy addition to Carmel's swelling ranks of stellar restaurants. Its repertoire of American regional dishes with Italian influences boasts remarkably well-balanced ingredients—spices and sauces are never allowed to overpower the taste of the meats, vegetables, or pastas. The wonderful breads that kick off the meal are from the in-house bakery downstairs; equally good are the salads, particularly the baby field greens with sliced pears and toasted walnuts. Main courses include grilled salmon in a Thai basil-curry sauce, and roasted duck in a mandarin-orange glaze with grilled shiitake mushrooms (yum!). Diet-busting desserts include a pear-cranberry crisp (with a dollop of heavy cream, naturally) and a rich mocha brownie with Belgian chocolate. The wine list is ample and thoughtfully selected, and, in keeping with the coffee-flavored decor, Prima offers a full selection of espresso drinks. Service is efficient and friendly, and there's a small patio for alfresco dining. *On 6th Ave at Mission St, Carmel; (408)624-6562; beer and wine; MC, V; checks OK; lunch, dinner every day; $$.&*

ANTON & MICHEL ☆☆

A longtime Carmel favorite, Anton & Michel reeks of elegance. The dining room—ensconced in peach walls, white wainscoting, and tall, slender pillars topped by elegant curlicued cornices—overlooks the Court of the Fountains with its Louis XV lions and verdigris garden pavilions. Despite the elaborate decor, the continental cuisine isn't very daring (though it's very well prepared). Standouts include the medallions of veal with a sautéed spinach and Madeira wine sauce, and the chicken Jerusalem in a wine-and-cream sauce, dotted with mushrooms and artichoke hearts. Anton & Michel also offers traditional French desserts such as crêpes Suzette and crème caramel. The extensive wine list has garnered an award from the *Wine Spectator*. *On Mission St between Ocean and 7th Aves, Carmel; (408)624-2406; full bar; AE, DC, DIS, MC, V; no checks; lunch, dinner every day; $$$.&*

CASANOVA RESTAURANT ☆☆

The former home of Charlie Chaplin's cook, this sunny cottage with a Mediterranean feel attracts happy throngs of locals and tourists alike. Casanova specializes in Italian and French country-style dishes; the pasta creations, such as linguine with seafood served in a big copper pot, are particularly fetching. Lunch on the big patio out back is informal and fun, with heaters keeping patrons warm on chilly afternoons. Inside, the cottage is a jumble of nooks and crannies decked out in rustic European decor. Casanova prides itself on its extensive and reasonably priced wine list, including the well-received Georgis merlot and cabernet, produced by one of the restaurant's owners. *On 5th Ave between San Carlos and Mission Sts, Carmel; (408)625-0501; beer and wine; MC, V; no checks; breakfast Sat, lunch Mon–Sat, dinner every day, brunch Sun; $$.*&

KATY'S PLACE ☆☆

When Katy's Place is closed for the day, there's no doubt about it: a big sign announces "Kitchen's closed—this chick's had it!" When it's open, however, Katy's has a reputation for serving the best breakfasts in town. The country kitchen–style restaurant specializes in comfort foods: big helpings and endless variations of pancakes, waffles, and eggs, including a dynamite eggs Benedict. On sunny mornings, request a table on the patio under the redwood trees. *On Mission St between 5th and 6th Aves, Carmel; (408)624-0199; beer and wine; no credit cards; local checks only; breakfast, lunch every day; $.*&

LA BOHEME ☆☆

La Bohème is very small, very cute, and—if you're lucky—very good. La Bohème's prix-fixe menu changes nightly, but the chef prints calendars listing the entrees for an entire month (knowledgeable patrons make it a point to pick up a schedule at the restaurant's doorstep as soon as they hit town). Recent offerings included Coquelet de la Prairie (Cornish game hen with pine-nut stuffing and wine sauce), Gigot d'Agneau au Porto (lamb in a mushroom port sauce), and Saumon d'Or (salmon with leeks and lemon-pepper butter). The soups, such as the salmon bisque, and the salads, with Carmel Valley organic greens, are universally wonderful. The entrees, alas, are less predictable, due to the varying quality of the meat preparation (though vegetarian dinners are available nightly). On the other hand, when everything works, La Bohème's cuisine ranks among the best in Carmel. At worst, you can console yourself with the rich but fluffy chocolate mousse or the crème brûlée. *On Dolores St at 7th Ave, Carmel; (408)624-7500; beer and wine; MC, V; no checks; dinner every day; closed most of December; $$.*

MONDO'S TRATTORIA ☆☆

Since he opened his doors in October 1993, Mondo has had a steady stream of customers pile into his humble restaurant with its cozy old-European-style setting (beamed faux-Tudor

As a "dine" of the times, Carmel's La Bohème restaurant now lists its monthly dinner schedule on the Internet at http://www.carmel net.com/laboheme

walls, tapestry-like upholstery, candles, etc., etc.). The first-rate pasta dishes include a veggie lasagne with spinach and mushrooms and a penne with calamari, prawns, and scallops in spicy tomato sauce. The *pollo arrosto* is redolent of fresh herbs, and the *bistecca Florentina* is *primo*. Nightly specials, seafood dishes, and delicately made pizzas round out the menu. *On Dolores St between Ocean and 7th Aves, Carmel; (408)624-8977; beer and wine; AE, DIS, MC, V; checks OK; lunch, dinner every day; $$.&*

SANS SOUCI ☆☆

True to its name, Sans Souci is determined that you'll never have to worry about the quality of its food or service. Despite the traditional white linens, silver, china, and crystal, this classic French restaurant isn't a bit stuffy. Owner John Williams' infectious sense of humor sets the tone of the place, and the servers are friendly and efficient. The changing menu offers a large selection of appetizers, including escargots in sorrel leaves baked in basil butter, and a lobster salad with fried onions and a light vinaigrette. Entrees on the seasonal menu might include duck with raspberry sauce, filet mignon with shallots in a red-wine sauce, or sole with capers, lemon, and parsley. *On Lincoln St between 5th and 6th Aves, Carmel; (408)624-6220; full bar; AE, MC, V; no checks; dinner Thurs–Tues; $$$.*

HOG'S BREATH INN ☆

If rowdy crowds and loud music are your idea of a good time, then join the dinnertime melee at Clint Eastwood's Hog's Breath Inn (look for the fire-breathing pig out front). You'll always find a horde of tourists and locals plowing their way through the standard pub grub, such as the juicy Dirty Harry Burger on a fresh-baked bun and the Sudden Impact Sandwich, a broiled Polish sausage with Jack cheese and jalapeño peppers on a French roll. Thanks to half a dozen heat lamps and fireplaces, you can eat outside on the brick patio—with its immense bucolic mural of Carmel Valley—in just about any weather, but first take a gander at the pseudo-rustic tavern complete with mounted hog's heads and split-wood furnishings. *On San Carlos St between 5th and 6th Aves, Carmel; (408)625-1044; full bar; AE, DC, MC, V; no checks; lunch, dinner every day, brunch Sun; $.*

PATISSERIE BOISSIERE ☆

After you've shopped 'till you dropped in Carmel, this is the place to go to rest those tootsies while you refuel with some of the most deliciously decadent desserts in town. For more than 30 years, *la pâtisserie* has turned out a tempting array of masterful cakes, tarts, mousses, and other delights, all displayed in big glass cases so you can visually caress each one before making your selection. *On Mission St between Ocean and 7th Aves, Carmel; (408)624-5008; beer and wine; AE, MC, V; no checks; breakfast Sat and Sun, lunch every day, dinner Wed–Sun; $$.*

RIO GRILL ☆

This noisy Southwestern-style grill is packed to the rooftop from opening to closing. Like so many big nouveau restaurants, the Rio Grill really shines with its side dishes. The salads, such as Chinese chicken with sliced ginger and whole almonds, are wonderfully fresh, and the polenta, seasoned with nutmeg and cayenne, draws raves. Unfortunately, the entrees are less interesting, with the exception of the tasty barbecued baby back ribs and the chicken with papaya and fermented black-bean salsa. Don't bother with the sandwiches (the eggplant version sometimes arrives cold and over-oiled). *At 101 Crossroads Blvd (in the Crossroads Shopping Center, at Hwy 1 and Rio Rd), Carmel, CA 93921; (408)625-5436; full bar; AE, MC, V; no checks; lunch, dinner every day; $$.&*

"Why do we come to Carmel every year? I don't know why. Honey? Why do we come to Carmel every year? We don't know why we come to Carmel every year. We just do."—Marin County residents Tami and Tim Riddle, when asked why they come to Carmel every year

LODGINGS

HIGHLANDS INN ■
PACIFIC'S EDGE RESTAURANT ☆☆☆

 Set high above the rocky coastline with breathtaking views of nearby Point Lobos, the Highlands Inn has long been regarded as one of Carmel's finest lodgings. In the main lodge, a skylit promenade leads to a series of glass-walled salons designed for soaking in the breathtaking view. Outside, flower-lined walkways connect the cottagelike collection of 142 rooms and suites. Though the inn's muted earth-tone decor is a tad sterile, the view from almost any room is so stunning you probably won't even notice. Most rooms have a fireplace and private deck, whereas suites

At no cost to you, the staff at Carmel's Tourist Information Center will help you find a place to stay in your price range— if one exists. They're located on San Carlos Street between 5th and 6th Avenues; (800)847-8066 or (408)624-1711.

come loaded with full parlor, kitchen, and two-person spa tub. Pacific's Edge, the inn's flagship restaurant, shares the same view as the promenade, and serves such inspired creations as honey-roasted duck with an apple-rosemary jus or grilled salmon wrapped in pancetta and topped with a tangy onion-rosemary sauce. *On Hwy 1, 4 miles south of Carmel; (408)624-3801, (800)538-9525; PO Box 1700, Carmel, CA 93921; full bar; AE, DC, DIS, MC, V; checks OK; breakfast, lunch, dinner every day, brunch Sun; $$$.*&

LA PLAYA HOTEL   ☆☆☆

 The top choice of Carmel's midtown lodgings, the venerable La Playa Hotel is a real charmer. Brick paths lit by faux gas lamps wind among lush gardens toward the hotel's 75 rooms, each appointed with handsome Spanish-style furnishings and views of the ocean, gardens, or village. The heated outdoor pool is an enticing alternative to Carmel Beach, a mere stroll away. Families may want to reserve one of the five Cottages-by-the-Sea, which are separate from the hotel and come with full kitchens, fireplaces, and private patios. The hotel's restaurant, the Terrace Grill, has a fine view of the gardens and serves such California fare as sole piccata, prime rib, eggplant ravioli, and roasted duck. *On Camino Real at 8th Ave, Carmel; (408)624-6476, (800)582-8900; PO Box 900, Carmel, CA 93921; full bar; AE, DC, MC, V; checks OK; breakfast, lunch, dinner every day, brunch Sun; $$$.* &

MISSION RANCH   ☆☆☆

 When Clint Eastwood was a young recruit stationed at Fort Ord 40 years ago, he happened to venture onto the Mission Ranch and it was love at first sight. Once a working dairy farm, the place was all set to be razed by developers a few decades later—until Eastwood rode to the rescue. He poured a ton of money into restoring the Victorian farmhouse, cottages, bunkhouse, and other buildings, determined to be true to the original spirit of the place. The result is wonderful: a peaceful, Western-style spread that offers everything a guest needs to feel comfortable without a single silly frill. The 31 rooms, distributed among a clutch of pretty, immaculately maintained buildings, tennis courts, exercise room, and putting green, are sparsely but tastefully appointed, with props from Eastwood's films scattered nonchalantly among the furnishings. Handmade quilts grace the custom-made country-style wooden beds, which are so large you literally have to climb into them, and each guest room has its own phone, TV, and bathroom. Rates include a generous continental breakfast, and the lodge's Restaurant at Mission Ranch serves good California-style fare for brunch, lunch, and dinner. The place's only shortcoming is that the scene in the piano bar can get a little rowdy, causing guests in nearby buildings to reach for their earplugs. Otherwise, stetsons off to Clint. *At the intersection of Rio Rd and Lasuen Dr; lodgings (408)624-6436, restaurant (408)625-9040; 26270 Dolores St, Carmel, CA 93923; AE, MC, V; checks OK, lunch Sat only, dinner every day, jazz buffet brunch Sun; $$$.&*

CYPRESS INN   ☆☆

Movie star and animal-rights activist Doris Day owns this pleasant Mediterranean-style inn in the center of town. Pets, naturally, are more than welcome; the hotel even provides dog beds for its four-footed guests upon request. While some admirers see the Cypress as "old Carmel," others just see it as old: the walls in the 33 guest rooms have been treated to a rather slapdash coat of bright peach paint, the beds can be rickety, the drains in the sink and tub are a bit sluggish, and the dark-wood furniture has seen better days. However, the hotel is redeemed by the staff, who, luckily for the guests, seem to think they're working in a much grander place—the service is uniformly professional and courteous. The rooms contain some thoughtful touches such as fresh fruit, packages of peanuts, bottles of spring water, shampoo and hand lotion, chocolates left on the pillow at night, and a decanter of sherry. Some have sitting rooms, wet bars, private verandahs, and ocean views. There's a spacious Spanish-style living room with a comforting fire, and a friendly bar that dishes out a rather meager continental breakfast in the morning, as well as libations of a more spirited kind at night. Posters of Doris Day movies add a touch of glamour and fun to the otherwise suburban decor. *On Lincoln St at 7th Ave, Carmel; (408)624-3871, (800)443-7443; PO Box Y, Carmel, CA 93921; full bar; AE, MC, V; checks OK; $$$.*

SAN ANTONIO HOUSE   ☆☆

Built in the late 1920s, this white-painted wood-shingled home with teal (*"not* green," groans the owner) trim has four cozy, wood-paneled rooms, each with a fireplace, private bath, refrigerator, and telephone. Two rooms, the Doll House and the Patio Suite, have separate sitting areas. In the morning, a tray of fruit, coffee cake, scones, and juice arrives at your door with the morning paper. After breakfast, stroll the lovely gardens with their interesting little nooks and arbors, or venture off to Carmel Beach just a block away. *On San Antonio St between Ocean and 7th Aves, Carmel; (408)624-4334; PO Box 3683, Carmel, CA 93921; MC, V; checks OK; $$$.*

THE STONEHOUSE INN ☆☆

This ivy-covered, hand-cut-stone house is one of those inns to which people come back again and again—and have since it opened in 1948. Six individually decorated rooms are named after artists or writers who have stayed here. The Jack London Room has gabled ceilings, a queen-size brass bed, and a ruffled day bed with a sea view. The Sinclair Lewis Room has a king-size bed, a writing desk, and a fine view of the ocean (though who knows what Lewis—that loather of the bourgeois—would think of the giant teddy bears). Only one of the rooms has a private bathroom, a definite drawback for some folks. Downstairs, you can lounge in the wing chairs before the fireplace and help yourself to wine and cheese in the late afternoon. Breakfast is included with the room. *On 8th Ave between Monte Verde and Casanova Sts, Carmel; (408)624-4569; PO Box 2517, Carmel, CA 93921; MC, V; checks OK; $$.*

THE GREEN LANTERN INN ☆

Built in 1925, the Green Lantern's cluster of rustic cottages is nestled among lush gardens just a few blocks above Ocean Beach. Renovated in 1993, the inn was treated to new wallpaper, carpets, and bathrooms, enhancing the old-Carmel charm of the place. Four of the 19 guest rooms have fireplaces, the staff is accommodating, and a continental breakfast is served in the morning—all for about half to two-thirds the price of very similar B&Bs. *On Casanova St at 7th Ave, Carmel; (408)624-4392; PO Box 1114, Carmel, CA 93921; AE, MC, V; no checks; $$.*

CARMEL RIVER INN

Families and couples on a limited budget favor the Carmel River Inn's 24 cottages and 19 motel units, which offer utilitarian but homey accommodations at reasonable prices. Though it's close to the highway, noise isn't a problem because the inn is set back along the river and surrounded by a natural buffer of trees. Children and adults alike enjoy the year-round heated pool, the rustic Sierra-cabin look, and the river location. Some of the cottages have kitchens, many have fireplaces and separate bedrooms, and all are far superior to the motel rooms. *Take Oliver Rd exit off Hwy 1 at the south end of Carmel River Bridge, Carmel; (408)624-1575; PO Box 221609, Carmel, CA 93922; MC, V; no checks; $$.*&

PEBBLE BEACH

How much is a room and a round of golf at Pebble Beach these days? Put it this way: if you have to ask, you can't afford it. If the 6,000 or so residents of this exclusive gated community had their way, Pebble Beach would probably be off-limits to mere commoners. Perhaps more of an indignity, though, is the $6.50 levy required to trespass on their gilded avenues and wallow in envy at how the ruling class recreates. If you have no strong desire to tour corporate-owned hideaways and redundant— albeit gorgeous—seascapes along 17-Mile Drive, save your lunch money: you're not missing anything that can't be seen elsewhere along the Monterey Coast.

ACTIVITIES

📷 **17-Mile Drive.** They say it's one of those things you must do at least once in your life—17-Mile Drive. Five entrances, manned by spiffy security guards adept at making change, lead into this fabled enclave that serves as home and playground of the absurdly wealthy. Though it can be whizzed through in about 30 minutes, two to three hours is about the average touring time. The $6.50 toll fee includes a map and guide, but all that's required to stay on course is to follow the dotted red line painted on the road. Aside from a few scenic overlooks, the third of the drive that passes through the Del Monte Forest is rather dull—a better bet is to double back along the coastal stretch. Among the 21 "points of interest," the most entertaining is Bird Rock, a small offshore isle covered with hundreds of seals and sea lions (bring binoculars). On your way out, splurge on an $8 margarita at The Inn at Spanish Bay's oceanside cocktail lounge (hey, who's gonna know?).

Any questions about 17-Mile Drive? Call Pebble Beach Security at (408)624-6669.

If paying $6.50 to tour 17-Mile Drive seems like highway robbery, drive the 5-mile coastline of Pacific Grove— along Sunset Drive and Ocean View Boulevard—3¹/2 times for free instead. You'll hardly tell the difference.

GOLF COUNTRY

The Monterey coast is golf country, hosting some of the most famous (and lucrative) tournaments in the world. While all of the following courses are open to the public, green fees of up to $245 tend to keep the oceanside clubs rather exclusive. Not to worry, though—drive a little ways inland and the fees slice rather nicely.

Pebble Beach Golf Links: 6,799 yards, 18 holes, driving range, green fee $245 (nonguests); (408)624-6611.

The Links at Spanish Bay: 6,820 yards, 18 holes, green fee $165 (nonguests); (408)624-6611.

Spyglass Golf Course: 6,859 yards, 18 holes, driving range, green fee $195 (nonguests); (408)624-6611.

Laguna Seca Golf Course: 5,711 yards, 18 holes, green fee $55; (408)373-3701.

Fort Ord Golf Courses: 6,982 and 6,396 yards, 18 holes each, driving range, green fees $25–$50; (408)899-2351 (some restrictions, call ahead).

Old Del Monte Golf Course: 6,007 yards, 18 holes, green fee $65 (includes cart); (408)373-2436.

Pacific Grove Municipal: 5,553 yards, 18 holes, driving range, green fee $28; (408)648-3175.

Poppy Hills Golf Course: 6,219 yards, 18 holes, green fee $105; (408)625-2035.

Rancho Cañada East & West: 6,113 yards, 18 holes, driving range, green fee $50–$65; (408)624-0111.

LODGINGS

THE INN AT SPANISH BAY   ☆☆☆

 Slightly less expensive than its world-famous sister resort at Pebble Beach, the ultraluxurious Inn at Spanish Bay still packs a wallop in the ol' pocketbook. Set along 236 acres of premium beachfront property off 17-Mile Drive, the 270-room inn comes with all the fancy bells and whistles, including access to the Pebble Beach, Spanish Bay, and Spyglass golf courses, as well as eight championship tennis courts, a fitness club, a swimming pool, and miles of hiking and equestrian trails. All of the luxuriously appointed rooms and suites have gas fireplaces, quilted down comforters, and elegant sitting areas with plush sofas. Most have private patios or balconies affording superb views of the rocky coast or cypress forest. Enjoy Euro-Asian cuisine at Roy's (yet another successful branch from Hawaiian restaurateur Roy Yamaguchi), or opt for a more formal affair at the well-regarded Bay Club, serving fashionable Northern Italian fare. Follow dinner with a sampling from the selection of single-malt scotches at Traps Bar or the Lobby Lounge, where Brazilian virtuoso percussionist Helcio Milito and pianist Weber Drummond perform Thursdays through Saturdays. *On 17-Mile Dr near the Pacific Grove entrance; (408)647-7500, (800)654-9300; 2700 17-Mile Dr, Pebble Beach, CA 93953; full bar; AE, DC, DIS, MC, V; checks OK; $$$.*&

Every evening as the sun sets, a lone bagpiper strolls the headlands between the ocean and the Inn at Spanish Bay while playing a farewell-the-day tune.

THE LODGE AT PEBBLE BEACH ☆☆☆

 Despite green fees that top the $200 mark, Pebble Beach remains the mecca of American golf courses: most avid golfers feel they have to play it at least once before retiring to that Big Clubhouse in the Sky. Until the rooms in the lodge were renovated a few years ago, the scattered cluster of accommodations surprised many guests with its rather run-down appearance; it was clear that golf and the spectacular natural setting, not the rooms, were Pebble Beach's principal allure. Now, however, the guest rooms have been tastefully revamped, swathed in soothing earth tones and outfitted with a sophisticated, modern decor. There are 161 suites and rooms, most with private balconies or patios, brick fireplaces, sitting areas, and magnificent views. All the usual upscale amenities are provided, from phones by the commode to honor-bar refrigerators, plush robes, and cable TVs (the whole effect is very East Coast country club). Four restaurants cater to guests, including Club XIX, which resembles a fancy French bistro, and the Cypress Room, whose menu offers six different preparation styles for the fish—everything from poached in champagne to seared in Cajun spices. *On 17-Mile Dr near the Carmel gate; (408)624-3811, (800)654-9300; 17-Mile Dr, Pebble Beach, CA 93953; full bar; AE, DC, DIS, MC, V; checks OK; $$$.*&

Though bicyclists can enter any gate into Pebble Beach for free, on weekends and holidays they may enter only through the Pacific Grove gate.

For good books
(particularly local
guidebooks), coffee,
and pastries, head
over to Pacific
Grove's most
cerebral hangout,
Bookworks.
(Open daily
8:30am–10pm;
667 Lighthouse
Avenue at
Park Street;
(408)372-2242.)

Asilomar translates
as "haven by
the sea."

PACIFIC GROVE

Established more than a century ago as a retreat for pious Methodists, this venerable Victorian seacoast village still retains much of its decorous old-town character, though it's loosened its collar a bit since the early days. Less tourist-oriented than Carmel and less commercial than Monterey, P.G. (as locals call it) is the place to settle down, buy a home, and raise 2.5 obedient children. There's no graffiti, no raucous revelers, and not an unleashed dog in sight. The area exudes peace and tranquility— a city of gorgeous vistas, impressive architecture, and even reasonably priced accommodations just a jog from the sea.

ACTIVITIES

 Coastal Trail. The best way to start your vacation in Pacific Grove is to stroll the 4 miles of trails that meander between Lover's Point Beach and Asilomar State Beach. Start at grassy Lover's Point (which, by the way, was named for lovers of Jesus Christ, not the more carnal kind), located off Ocean View Boulevard next to the Old Bath House Restaurant, and work your way west past the numerous white-sand beaches, tide pools, and rocky coves to Asilomar on the west side of Point Pinos. A second, shorter option is the mile-long Monterey Peninsula Recreation Trail, which parallels Ocean View Boulevard from Lover's Point to the Monterey Bay Aquarium. Be sure to keep an eye out for sea otters sleeping atop the kelp beds—there's tons of them here.

Lighthouse. At the tip of Point Pinos (Spanish for "Point of the Pines") stands the Cape Cod–style Point Pinos Lighthouse, the oldest continuously operating lighthouse on the West Coast: its 50,000-candlepower beacon has shone since February 1, 1855. This National Historic Landmark is open to the public on Thursdays and weekends, 1pm to 4pm, and admission is free. On Asilomar Boulevard at Lighthouse Avenue, Pacific Grove; (408)648-3116.

Butterflies. Pacific Grove bills itself as "Butterfly Town, U.S.A." in honor of the thousands of monarchs that migrate here from late October to mid-March. Two popular

MONARCH BUTTERFLIES

Are the only insects known to migrate annually • Travel up to 2,000 miles between ancestral wintering sites • Can fly 100 miles a day at altitudes up to 10,000 feet • Live only 6-9 months, so are guided on their annual migration purely by instinct • Congregate in groups of up to 50,000 in a single grove • Feed on milkweed, a poisonous plant that makes them inedible to birds

Punishment for "molesting or interfering in any way with the peaceful occupancy of the monarch butterfly" is a $1,000 fine or a six-month jail term.

places to view the butterflies are the Monarch Grove Sanctuary (at Lighthouse Avenue and Ridge Road) and George Washington Park (at Sinex Avenue and Alder Street). To learn more about the monarchs, visit the informal and kid-friendly Pacific Grove Museum of Natural History, which has a video and display on the butterfly's life cycle, as well as exhibits of other insects, local birds, mammals, and reptiles. Admission is free. At the intersection of Forest and Central Avenues, Pacific Grove; (408)648-3116.

Art Gallery. A perennial Best Art Gallery winner in the "Best of Monterey" survey by *Coast Weekly*, the nonprofit Pacific Grove Art Center has four galleries with rotating displays ranging from sculpture to photography to drawings and even children's artwork. Poetry readings, plays, workshops, and the occasional concert are also on the menu if you time it right. Open Tues–Sat, noon-5pm, Sun 1–4pm; 568 Lighthouse Avenue at Grand Avenue; (408)375-2208.

Factory Outlets. Who would have guessed you could *save* money shopping in Pacific Grove? Within the American Tin Cannery factory outlet center are dozens of high-quality clothing stores—Anne Klein, Bass, London Fog, Reebok, Big Dog—selling their wares for about half of what you'd normally pay. Particularly worth a look are the amazing deals at the Woolrich outlet, where most items are 50 percent off. At 125 Ocean View Boulevard, around the corner from the Monterey Bay Aquarium; (408)372-1442.

Every October, some of Pacific Grove's most beautiful and artfully restored buildings are opened to the public on the Victorian Home Tour. $10 per person; (408)373-3304.

Locals' consensus: First Awakenings, a small cafe within the Tin Cannery Outlet Center at 125 Ocean View Boulevard, serves the area's best breakfast.

RESTAURANTS

PASTA MIA ☆☆☆

A century-old Victorian provides a homey setting for Pasta Mia's good, hearty Italian fare. The soup and appetizers tend to be tried-and-true standards, such as minestrone, mozzarella fresca, and the antipasto misto, but the house-made pastas include some intriguing choices. There's black-and-white linguine with scallops, caviar, and cream, for instance, or half-moon pasta stuffed with pesto and dotted with chicken and sun-dried tomatoes. The lasagne is said to be made from a 600-year-old recipe. Second plates include a grilled veal chop with polenta and vegetables, and a breast of chicken with a garlic, wine, and rosemary sauce. Portions are generous in this popular and pleasantly informal restaurant. *Near 13th St; (408)375-7709; 481 Lighthouse Ave, Pacific Grove; beer and wine; AE, MC, V; no checks; dinner every day; $$.*

TASTE CAFE & BISTRO ☆☆☆

When it opened a few years ago, Taste Cafe quickly developed a loyal and enthusiastic word-of-mouth following that's the envy of several more established restaurants in town. You'll be hard-pressed to find higher-quality food for the same price anywhere else on the coast. Chef-owners Paulo Kautz and Sylvia Medina describe their preparations as rustic with French and Southern Italian accents, but that doesn't come close to describing the wonders coming out of their kitchen. The grilled salmon fillet, served on a bed of mashed potatoes, braised leeks, and chive beurre blanc, is utterly delectable. Be sure to save room for one of Sylvia's wonderful desserts: hearty bread pudding or wine-poached pears in raspberry sauce with crème Anglaise (seasonal). Regulars, wary of the usual wait for a table, elbow up to the wine and espresso bar to dine. *At Prescott Ave; (408)655-0324; 1199 Forest Ave, Pacific Grove, CA 93950; beer and wine; no credit cards; local checks only; dinner Tues–Sun; $$.&*

ALLEGRO GOURMET PIZZERIA ☆☆

With its merry festoons of garlic and red peppers, colorful Italian posters, and trilling Italian music, Allegro Pizzeria is the choice of locals in search of *la dolce vita* on the cheap.

The handmade pizzas, which come either whole or in generous slices, have crisp, flavorful crusts, just the right amount of cheese, and well-seasoned sauces. You can choose your own favorite toppings or pick one of Allegro's creative combinations such as the *quattro stagione* (salami, artichoke hearts, mushrooms, anchovies, roasted garlic, and capers) or the *del mare* (shrimp, scallops, garlic, and mozzarella). The caesar salad is a local favorite, but try the Caprese for a change (tomato slices, fresh mozzarella, fresh basil, and olive oil, sprinkled with mint and served on a bed of organic romaine). Much to the delight of Allegro's many fans, another branch just opened in Carmel. Take-out is available at both locations. *In the Forest Hills Shopping Center, near Prescott Ave; (408)373-5656; 1184-E Forest Ave, Pacific Grove; beer and wine; AE, DIS, MC, V; local checks only; lunch, dinner every day; $.& ■ At the Barnyard at Hwy 1 and Carmel Valley Rd; (408)626-5454; 3770 The Barnyard, Carmel; beer and wine; AE, DIS, MC, V; local checks only; lunch, dinner every day; $.&*

EL COCODRILO ROTISSERIE
AND SEAFOOD GRILL   ☆☆

Drawing on the sharp, exotic flavors of the Caribbean and Central and South America, Julio Ramirez' exciting, hybrid-Hispanic cuisine manages to cater to the tender sensibilities of *norteamericanos* without sacrificing authenticity. Dozens of crocodile chatchkas and Latin icons set an appropriate mood for fiery, flavorful, fish-focused meals. Appetizers include Jamaican curry crab cakes, Salvadoran *pupusas* (fat tortillas stuffed with two cheeses and served with black beans and salsa), and, somewhat ironically considering this place's affection for crocodiles, actual alligator nuggets with a passion-fruit dipping sauce. Grilled specialties include Red Snapper Mardi Gras and spit-roasted Yucatán chicken. El Cocodrilo's interesting selection of desserts includes *paletas tropicales*, those addictive frozen-fruit sweets so familiar to travelers in Mexico. *At Congress Ave; (408)655-3311; 701 Lighthouse Ave, Pacific Grove; beer and wine; AE, DIS, MC, V; no checks; dinner Wed–Mon; $$.&*

FANDANGO   ☆☆

A lively Spanish dance is the perfect name for this kick-up-your-heels restaurant specializing in Mediterranean country cuisine. It's a big, sprawling, colorful place with textured adobe walls and a lively crowd filling five separate dining rooms; the glass-domed terrace in the back with its stone fireplace and open mesquite grill is especially pleasant. Start with a few tapas—perhaps spicy sausage, roasted red peppers, or a potato-and-onion frittata. If you're feeling adventurous, order the Velouté Bongo Bongo, an exotic creamy soup with oysters, spinach, and Cognac. The flavorful Paella Fandango is served at your table in a huge skillet; the Cannelloni Niçoise is stuffed with spinach, ham, veal, and tomato; and the Couscous Algérois is a 130-year-old family recipe featuring lamb, vegetables, and North African spices. Fandango's wine list is one of the best in the area, featuring an impressive selection of French, California, Spanish, and Italian varietals. For dessert, try the profiteroles filled with chocolate ice cream and topped with hot fudge sauce. *One block East of Lighthouse Ave; (408)372-3456; 223 17th St, Pacific Grove; full bar; AE, DC, DIS, MC, V; no checks; lunch, dinner every day, brunch Sun; $$$.&*

THE FISHWIFE ☆☆

Locals swear by the fish dishes in this casual seaside restaurant bedecked with brightly colored cloth parrots and fish pillows, and the reasonable prices and separate kids' menu make Fishwife a good choice for folks with children in tow. The menu is Californian with a Caribbean accent, offering such dishes as sautéed halibut with nectarine salsa, prawns Belize, sautéed calamari, and grilled snapper with Cajun spices. The Boston clam chowder is justly famous, as is the Key lime pie. For those who eschew eating our finned friends, the Fishwife also serves a fair selection of standard pasta dishes. *At Asilomar Blvd, next to the Beachcomber motel; (408)375-7107; 1996 1/2 Sunset Dr, Pacific Grove; beer and wine; AE, DIS, MC, V; no checks; lunch, dinner Wed–Mon, brunch Sun; $$.*

THE OLD BATH HOUSE ☆☆

 This former (you guessed it) bath house at Lover's Point has a fine view of the rocky coast and a wonderful wood interior with a low, carved ceiling. Although many locals are quick to dismiss the Old Bath House as a pricey tourist restaurant (and it is indeed guilty on both counts), the continental cuisine is meticulously prepared, and it's an undeniably romantic spot for a special-occasion meal. Chef Jean

Hubert, formerly of Sans Souci in Carmel, offers a large, varied menu with savory selections such as an oven-roasted Jamaican duck confit with a mango-cayenne glaze, or rack of lamb with couscous in a garlic coriander sauce. Tempting desserts include hot pecan ice-cream fritters and amaretto tiramisu. The service is impeccable and the wine list extensive. *At Lover's Point Park; (408)375-5195; 620 Ocean View Blvd, Pacific Grove; full bar; AE, DC, DIS, MC, V; no checks; dinner every day; $$$.*

Having trouble finding a vacancy? Call Resort-II-Me, the Monterey Bay area's most popular reservation service, at (800)757-5646 for a free recommendation in any price range.

PEPPERS ☆☆

This Pacific Grove hot spot (pun intended) is famous for its house-made tamales, chiles rellenos, and fresh-Mex seafood. The delicately flavored seafood tacos with mahi-mahi, swordfish, or salmon, and the prawns Gonzalez (doused with tomatoes, chiles, cilantro, and lime juice) are also worth a try. The chips and salsa are dynamite, and there's a good selection of beers to cool your singed palate. Owners Scott and Linda Gonzalez are on hand to make sure everything runs smoothly; consequently, the service is always super-friendly even though the place is usually packed. *By Lighthouse Ave; (408)373-6892; 170 Forest Ave, Pacific Grove; beer and wine; AE, DC, DIS, MC, V; local checks only; lunch Mon, Wed–Sat, dinner Wed–Mon; $.*

LODGINGS

THE MARTINE INN ☆☆☆

 Perched like a vast pink wedding cake on a cliff above Monterey Bay, this villa with the Mediterranean exterior and Victorian interior is arguably Pacific Grove's most elegant bed and breakfast. Built in 1899 for James and Laura Parke (of Parke-Davis Pharmaceuticals), the inn has 19 spacious rooms, all with private baths and gloriously unfussy high-quality antiques (including interesting beadwork lamps). Most of the rooms have fireplaces and views of the water or of the garden courtyard with its delightful dragon fountain. If you feel like splurging, the Parke Room at the very top of the house is an outstanding choice. Originally the master bedroom, it has a magnificent picture window, a four-poster canopy bed, and a Victorian corner fireplace. No matter which room you choose, you'll find a

Does the Seven Gables Inn look strangely familiar to you, as if you've seen it somewhere before? Here's a hint: "The Seven Gables Inn gladly accepts Visa, but it doesn't take American Express."

silver basket of fruit and a rose waiting for you when you arrive, and a newspaper by your door in the morning. Spend the day lounging in one of the several intimate sitting rooms, common areas, or within the eight-person Jacuzzi in the old conservatory. Expect a well-prepared breakfast and afternoon wine and hors d'oeuvres. *4 blocks West of Cannery Row; 255 Ocean View Blvd, Pacific Grove, CA 93950; (408)373-3388; (800)852-5588; AE, MC, V; checks OK; $$$.&*

SEVEN GABLES INN ▪
GRAND VIEW INN ☆☆☆

 A cheerful yellow mansion built in 1886 and surrounded by elaborate gardens, the Seven Gables Inn commands a magnificent view of Monterey Bay. Chock-full of formal European antiques, Seven Gables will seem like paradise found to those who revel in things Victorian (those who prefer a more restrained, less fussy decor will fare better at the Grand View Inn next door). Once you're ensconced in one of the 14 rooms, which are divided among the main house, a guest house, and a smattering of cottages, the warm and welcoming Flatley family sees to your every comfort. The beautifully appointed rooms feature ocean views, private baths, and queen-size beds, and a pull-out-all-the-stops breakfast is served in the imposing dining room, as is afternoon tea.

Equally elegant yet far less endowed with Victorian-era bric-a-brac is the Flatleys' newest family member, the Grand View Inn. All 10 rooms within the 3-story mansion have marble bathrooms and queen beds and include the same elaborate breakfasts and afternoon tea settings as its next-door neighbor. Not all rooms overlook the bay, so be sure to request one that does. *At Fountain Ave; (408)372-4341; 555 Ocean View Blvd, Pacific Grove, CA 93950; MC, V; checks OK; $$$.&*

THE CENTRELLA INN ☆☆

Located smack in the center of town, the aptly named Centrella combines the down-home glow of an Old West boarding house with the comfort and attentive service of a modern hotel. A spacious 1889 Victorian, this old-timer offers 23 rooms, all with private baths. The upstairs rooms overlooking the garden are particularly attractive and comfortable, as are the two intimate attic suites with skylights, TVs, telephones, and fireplaces. Outside, a brick path meanders through an old-fashioned garden of gardenias and camellias, leading to five private—and well-appointed—cottages. You'll find crisp waffles hot from the antique waffle iron for breakfast, and complimentary beverages and dainty hors d'oeuvres in the evening. *At 17th St; (408)372-3372, (800)233-3372; 612 Central Ave, Pacific Grove, CA 93950; AE, MC, V; checks OK; $$$.*&

GATEHOUSE INN ☆☆

When State Senator Benjamin Langford built this ocean-view Victorian in 1884, Pacific Grove was less a town than a pious Methodist meeting ground, swathed in rules and regulations and separated from wicked, worldly Monterey by a white picket fence to keep the devil out. Decorated in refreshingly plain and simple Victoriana, the inn's nine individually decorated rooms have private baths and queen-size beds, with the exception of the Cannery Row Room, which features a king-size bed, gas-log stove, and claw-footed tub. The Langford Room ranks as the inn's largest and most luxurious, and includes an ocean-view sitting area and claw-footed bathtub that commands a stunning vista of the coast. Hors d'oeuvres, tea, and wine are served in the evening, but you can help yourself to cookies and beverages from the kitchen any time of day or night. *At 2nd St; (408)649-8436, (800)753-1881; 225 Central Ave, Pacific Grove, CA 93950; AE, MC, V; checks OK; $$$.*

LIGHTHOUSE LODGE AND SUITES ☆☆

Less than a block from the beach, the Lighthouse Lodge and Suites is really two entities with rather distinct personalities. The lodge, a Best Western property, consists of 68 motel-like rooms with access to a heated pool, spa, and sauna. Those seeking more luxurious accommodations should spring for one of the 31 newer suites down the road. The suites, all with beamed ceilings, plush carpeting, fireplaces, vast bathrooms with marble Jacuzzis, large-screen TVs, mini-kitchens, and king-size beds, glow in peacock hues of purple, green, and fuchsia. The overall effect is a bit nouveau riche, but riche all the same. After a made-to-order breakfast, take a morning stroll around the grounds, cleverly landscaped with native plants and fountains. *At Asilomar Blvd; (408)655-2111, (800)858-1249; 1150 and 1249 Lighthouse Ave, Pacific Grove, CA 93950; AE, DC, DIS, MC, V; no checks; $$ (lodge), $$$ (suites).*&

THE ASILOMAR CONFERENCE CENTER ☆

Many of the original buildings at Asilomar, located at the tip of the Monterey Peninsula on a wooded stretch of beach, were designed by famed Bay Area architect Julia Morgan. Donated to the YWCA by Phoebe Apperson Hearst and now owned by the State Division of Beaches and Parks, Asilomar feels a bit like a grown-up Girl Scout camp, albeit a little more luxurious. Its 105 acres of park-like grounds include a heated, Olympic-size swimming pool, wooded trails, and a fine stretch of beach where you can watch otters, seals, and, depending on the season, whales. There are 315 units in the complex; the older rooms, designed by Morgan, have hardwood floors, but are much smaller and more rustic than the newer suites, most of which have wall-to-wall carpeting and fireplaces. The apartment-style Guest Inn Cottage and Forest Lodge Suite can accommodate a large group or family. Breakfast is included in the price. *At Sinex Ave; (408)372-8016; 800 Asilomar Blvd, Pacific Grove, CA 93950; MC, V; checks OK; $$.*&

ROSEDALE INN ☆

While its name may conjure up images of pink petals and white lace, the Rosedale is more like an upscale motel (complete with a huge wooden bear welcoming guests). Despite a somewhat rustic appearance, each of the inn's 19 rooms is equipped with a wealth of electronic conveniences: multiple TV sets, a couple of phone lines, a Jacuzzi, a clock radio, a microwave and refrigerator, a VCR, and a hair dryer. Located across the road from the Asilomar Conference Center, the Rosedale is well suited for conference-goers, business travelers, and families. *At Sinex Ave; (408)655-1000, (800)822-5606; 775 Asilomar Blvd, Pacific Grove, CA 93950; AE, DC, DIS, MC, V; no checks; $$.*&

THE BEACHCOMBER

 This modern, comfortable nonsmoking motel offers 25 rooms in a variety of sizes, including a few with balconies overlooking Spanish Bay. When the weather heats up, you can jump into the swimming pool, which is sheltered from the sea breezes by a glass wall, or dive into the Pacific at Asilomar State Beach a mere three blocks away. Seafood fans will appreciate having the Fishwife Restaurant (see Restaurants, above) right next door. To sweeten the deal, innkeepers John and Diana keep a rack of bicycles to lend free of charge to guests who wish to explore 17-Mile Drive. *At Asilomar Blvd; (408)373-4769, (800)634-4769; 1996 Sunset Dr, Pacific Grove, CA 93950; AE, MC, V; no checks; $.&*

MONTEREY

If you're looking for the romantically gritty, working-class fishing village of John Steinbeck's *Cannery Row*, you won't find it here. Even though Monterey was the sardine capital of the Western Hemisphere during World War II, overfishing forced most of the canneries to close in the early '50s. Resigned to trawling for tourist dollars instead, the city converted its low-slung sardine factories along Cannery Row into a rather tacky array of boutiques, knickknack stores, yogurt shops, and—its only saving grace—the world-famous Monterey Bay Aquarium.

As you distance yourself from the Row, however, you'll soon see that Monterey also has its share of plusses that help even the score: dazzling seacoast vistas, stately Victorians, historic architecture, and a number of quality lodgings and restaurants. More important, Monterey is only minutes away from Pacific Grove, Carmel, Pebble Beach, and Big Sur, which makes it a great place to set up base while exploring the innumerable attractions lining the Monterey coast.

ACTIVITIES

Aquarium. Easily Monterey's top draw is the amazing Monterey Bay Aquarium, the most popular aquarium in the nation. Formerly a boarded-up old cannery until David and Lucile Packard (of Hewlett-Packard electronics) got things rolling with a $55 million donation, the 313,000-square-foot building features over a hundred galleries—including two of the world's largest indoor aquariums—with more than 120,000 specimens of animals, plants, and birds found in Monterey Bay. Two of the most popular exhibits are the bat-ray petting pool (not to worry, their stingers have been removed) and the two-story sea-otter tank, particularly when the sea otters get to scarf down a mixture of clams, rock cod, and shrimp at 10:30, 1:30, and 3:30 every day.

The aquarium's newest attraction is "The Outer Bay," a

"One of my favorite things to do on a weekend is drive to Monterey, ride a bike along the shore, and watch the sea otters play in the kelp. No matter how down I am, that always cheers me up."—Dyan Miller, Salinas resident

A good day in Monterey: Renting bicycles or in-line skates at Adventures by the Sea (299 Cannery Row; 408-372-1807) and biking or skating the 3^1/3-mile Monterey Bay Recreation Trail along the shore.

million-gallon, record-breaking exhibit that showcases aquatic life living in the outer reaches of Monterey Bay. Blue sharks, seven-foot-tall sunfish, green sea turtles, barracuda, stingrays, and schools of yellowfin tuna can be seen through the largest window on earth: an acrylic panel 15 feet high, 13 inches thick, and 54 feet long that weighs 78,000 pounds. Predictably, things get a little crowded on summer weekends, enough so that reservations are recommended in summer and on holidays. (Open daily 10am–6pm except Christmas; 886 Cannery Row, Monterey; call 408-648-4888 for general information, 800-756-3737 for tickets.)

Historical Walking Tour. To get the flavor of Monterey's heritage, follow the 2-mile Path of History, a walking tour of the town's most important historic sites and splendidly preserved old buildings—remember, this city was thriving under Spanish and Mexican flags when San Francisco was still a crude village. Free tour maps are available at various locations, including the Custom House, California's oldest public building (at the foot of Alvarado Street, near Fisherman's Wharf, Monterey; 408-649-7118) and Colton Hall, where the California state constitution was written and signed in 1849 (on Pacific Street between Madison and Jefferson Streets; 408-646-5640).

Maritime History. Nautical history buffs should visit the Maritime Museum of Monterey, which houses ship models, whaling relics, and the 2-story-high, 10,000-pound Fresnel lens, used for nearly 80 years at the Point Sur lighthouse to warn mariners away from the treacherous Big Sur coast (5 Custom House Plaza, in Stanton Center near Fisherman's Wharf; 408-373-2469).

Shopping Destinations. The landmark Fisherman's Wharf, the center of Monterey's cargo and whaling industry until the early 1900s, is awash today in mediocre (or worse) restaurants and equally tasteless souvenir shops. Serious shoppers will be better off strolling Alvarado Street, a pleasantly low-key, attractive downtown area with a much-less-touristy mix of art galleries, bookstores, and restaurants. Alvarado Street is also the site of the popular Old Monterey Farmer's Market and Marketplace, a good spot for free family entertainment and picnic-basket goodies. It's held Tuesdays year-round from 4pm to 7pm in winter and 4pm to 8pm in summer.

 Wynton Rome . . . For a toe-tappin' time in Monterey, visit on the third weekend in September, when top talents like Wynton Marsalis, Etta James, and Ornette Coleman strut their stuff at the Monterey Jazz Festival, one of the country's oldest (and best) continuous jazz celebrations. Tickets and hotel rooms sell out fast, so plan early (diehard jazz fans make reservations at least six months before showtime); (800)307-3378 or (408)373-3366.

Kayaking Monterey Bay. One of the most enjoyable ways to spend a sunny day on the Monterey Coast is by paddling a sea kayak among the thousands of seals, sea lions, sea otters, and shorebirds that live within the Monterey Bay National Marine Sanctuary. No kayaking experience is necessary—just follow behind the instructor for an interpretive tour of the bay. For reservations call Monterey Bay Kayaks at (408)373-KELP.

RESTAURANTS

FRESH CREAM ☆☆☆☆

Fresh Cream has long been regarded as the finest restaurant in Monterey, with a veritable mountain of rave reviews—proudly displayed on the lobby walls—to its credit. Specializing in French cuisine with hints of California, chef Gregory Lizza offers exquisitely prepared creations in a highly romantic setting overlooking Monterey Bay. Appetizers may include lobster ravioli with black and gold caviar, Maryland soft-shell crab in a garlic lemon butter, and a smooth-as-silk goose-liver pâté with capers and onions. Entrees range from pan–seared duck breast with cabernet cherry sauce to grilled Dover sole browned in butter and lemon (and boned at the table) to the definitive full rack of lamb Dijonnaise. For dessert try the Grand Marnier soufflé or the amazing *sac au chocolat*, a dark-chocolate sack filled with a creamy espresso milk shake. Service tends to be a bit on the formal side, and dinner for two isn't cheap, to be sure, but this is one restaurant that's worth the splurge. *Suite 100C at the North end of the Heritage Harbor complex across*

During the summer and fall, Monterey Whale Watch takes passengers on 6-hour whale-watching excursions departing from Fisherman's Wharf; (408)375-4658.

What better way to explore Monterey and nearby Pacific Grove than on a moped? Monterey Moped Adventures, located at 1250 Del Monte Avenue (at Sloat), can set you up for about $50 a day on a single- or double-seat scooter; (408)373-2696.

from Fisherman's Wharf; (408)375-9798; 99 Pacific St, Monterey; full bar; AE, MC, V; checks OK; dinner every day; $$$.&

CIBO RISTORANTE ITALIANO ☆☆☆

Terra-cotta walls, slick track lighting, and urban-rustic archways set the mood for Rosa Catalano's blend of Old and New World Italian food at this popular restaurant. A large selection of antipasti is ready to tempt diners, including the *carciofo alla Signora Catalano* (an artichoke filled with bread crumbs, pancetta, and cheeses) and the scrumptious prawns wrapped in pancetta with roasted red-pepper purée. Cibo's imaginative pastas include *ditaloni picchi pacchi* (an aromatic concoction of short pasta tubes, fresh tomato, basil, garlic, fried eggplant, and ricotta cheese) and *tagliatelle ciociara* (thin ribbons of porcini-mushroom pasta with sausage, mushrooms, parsley, peas, and saffron). The wine list features Italian and California varietals, and take-out is now available. Every night but Monday, live music—sometimes jazz, sometimes reggae or maybe salsa—lures patrons onto the dance floor. *At Del Monte Blvd; (408)649-8151; 301 Alvarado St, Monterey; full bar; AE, DC, MC, V; no checks; dinner every day; $$$.&*

TARPY'S ROADHOUSE ☆☆☆

When a restaurant that's located close to nowhere is consistently packed with locals, you know it must be good. On a lonely stretch of Highway 68 is Tarpy's Roadhouse, a sprawling ranch-style affair with an upscale Southwestern decor (and a decidedly whimsical approach to art) inside, and a broad, sunny patio out front. Lunch emphasizes well-prepared sandwiches and salads, but dinner is when Tarpy's really shines. Appetizers might include grilled polenta with wild mushrooms and Madeira, or fresh Puget Sound oysters with red-wine mignonette. Entrees run the gamut from bourbon-molasses pork chops to honey-mustard rabbit, sea scallops with saffron penne noodles, or a grilled vegetable plate with sweet-corn succotash. Desserts include a orange-ginger crème brûlée, a triple-layer chocolate cake, and olallieberry pie. The wine list is modest and skewed toward the expensive side, but thoughtfully selected. *At Hwy 68 and Canyon Del Rey, 1 mile East of the airport turnoff; (408)647-1444; 2999 Monterey-Salinas Hwy (Hwy 68), Monterey; full bar; AE, DIS, MC, V; local checks only; lunch, dinner every day, brunch Sun; $$$.&*

CAFE FINA ☆☆

 Most locals agree this is the only restaurant worth dining at on Fisherman's Wharf. And, indeed, Cafe Fina is a refreshing outpost of quality amid all the tourist-carnival trappings. Owner Dominic Mercurio offers mesquite-grilled chicken and beef, salads, and pizzas hot from the brick oven, but his specialties are the seafood and pasta dishes, including the flavorful Pasta Fina (linguine with baby shrimp, white wine, olives, clam juice, olive oil, tomatoes, and green onions) and a superb sand dab special. The food is delicious and carefully prepared, the atmosphere is casual and fun, and the view is a maritime fantasy filled with frolicking sea otters, seals, and sea lions (beg for a window seat). *Halfway down the wharf on the West side; (408)372-5200; 47 Fisherman's Wharf, Monterey; full bar; AE, DC, DIS, MC, V; no checks; lunch, dinner every day; $$.*

LODGINGS

OLD MONTEREY INN ☆☆☆

Even those who feel they've seen it all on the bed-and-breakfast circuit are likely to be awed by the elegantly appointed Old Monterey Inn. Nestled among giant oak trees and lush gardens, this Tudor-style country inn positively gleams with natural wood, skylights, and stained-glass windows. The 10 beautifully decorated guest rooms, each with private bath, are filled with lovely antiques and comfortable beds with plump down comforters and huge, fluffy pillows. Most of the rooms have fireplaces, and although none have TVs or telephones, TVs will be brought into a few of the cable-equipped rooms on request, and there are also cordless phones for guests' use. For the utmost privacy, ask for the lacy Garden Cottage, which has a private patio, skylights, and a fireplace-appointed sitting room. The deluxe Ashford Suite has a sitting area, a separate dressing room, a king-size bed, and a panoramic garden view. Another standout: the handsome Library guest room, with its book-lined walls, stone fireplace, and private sun deck. Breakfast—available in the dining room, the resplendent rose garden, or in the privacy of your room—might include baked apples, French toast, crêpes, cheese rolls, and such curiosities as coconut-lime muffins. Afternoon snacks and evening hors d'oeuvres assure that you'll never go hungry between meals. *Near Pacific St; (408)375-8284, (800)350-2344; 500 Martin St, Monterey, CA 93940; MC, V; checks OK; $$$.*

SPINDRIFT INN ☆☆☆

 With its soaring four-story atrium and rooftop garden, the Spindrift is an unexpected and elegant refuge amid the hurly-burly tourist world of Cannery Row. All 41 rooms have canopy feather beds with down comforters, fireplaces, hardwood floors, telephones, and marble-tiled bathrooms with tubs. You'll also discover terrycloth robes, cable TVs, and nightly turn-down service. The corner rooms, with their cushioned window seats and breathtaking ocean views, are the best in the house. In the morning, there'll be a newspaper, a dewy rose, and a delicious breakfast of fruit, orange juice, croissants, and sweet rolls waiting outside your door on a silver tray. Whether staying at the inn or just taking in the local sights, be sure to have lunch or dinner at Spadaro's Ristorante on the ground floor of the hotel. A beautifully designed, family-run restaurant with an amazing view of the bay, Spadaro's serves topnotch creative Italian food and fresh fish. *At Hawthorne St; lodgings (408)646-8900 or (800)841-1879, restaurant (408)372-8881; 652 Cannery Row, Monterey, CA 93940; full bar; AE, DC, DIS, MC, V; checks OK; lunch, dinner every day; $$$.*&

HOTEL PACIFIC ☆☆

 Like a Modigliani looming angular and bold in a gallery full of Fra Angelicos, this pseudo-modern, neo-hacienda hotel tries to look gracefully unobtrusive in the midst of Monterey's authentic old adobes. A sparkling fountain burbles beside the entrance; inside you'll find handwoven rugs, muted Southwestern colors, terra-cotta tile, and beamed ceilings soaring above rounded, adobe-style walls. Connected by tiled courtyards, arches, and flowered pathways, a scattering of low-rise buildings holds 105 junior suites, all with private patios or terraces, fireplaces, goosedown feather beds, three telephones, and two TVs (one is in the bathroom). Request one of the rooms on the fourth level with a panoramic view of the bay, or a room facing the inner courtyard with its large fountain. A continental breakfast is provided in the morning, and guests may indulge in afternoon tea. *Near Scott St and Del Monte Blvd;*

(408)373-5700, (800)554-5542; 300 Pacific St, Monterey, CA
93940; AE, DC, DIS, MC, V; checks OK; $$$.&

THE JABBERWOCK   ☆☆

 Set well back from the bustle of nearby Cannery Row, this 1911 former convent—run by the warm and witty Jim and Barbara Allen—is a modern, luxurious B&B that keeps from taking itself too seriously by throwing in a Lewis Carrollian twist. For example, whimsical breakfast dishes (written on a board in backwards mirror-writing) are called "razzleberry flabjous" and "snarkleberry flumptious," and each of the seven immaculate guest rooms have names like the Toves, the Brilling, and Tulgey Woods. Two favorites are the spacious and grand Borogrove Room, which boasts wraparound picture windows with views of the town, bay, and the inn's garden, and the Mome Rath Room, with its mahogany claw-footed bed big enough for any beast. The large, beautifully landscaped garden has a pond, a waterfall, a nifty sundial, and, certainly no surprise, a rabbit (who's very late). *At Hoffman Ave; (408)372-4777; 598 Laine St, Monterey, CA 93940; MC, V; checks OK; $$$.*

DEL MONTE BEACH INN

True to its name, this small, European-style hotel is right across the street from Del Monte Beach (and close to the majority of Monterey's other main attractions, including nearby Dennis the Menace Playground). Each of the 19 individually decorated rooms comes with period furniture, quilts, and fresh flowers hanging from boxes outside the window. An added bonus is the free buffet-style continental breakfast. Most rooms share a bath, and entertainment is limited to board games in the lounge, but quit your whining: with prices starting a $40 a night, you won't find a better deal in town. *At Park Ave; (408)649-4410; 1110 Del Monte Ave, Monterey, CA 93940; AE, DC, DIS, MC, V; checks OK; $.*

CASTROVILLE

Gilroy made history with garlic; Castroville chose the artichoke. The undisputed Artichoke Capital of the World, Castroville holds its Artichoke Festival on the third weekend in September. It's mostly small-town stuff: the crowning of the Artichoke Queen, a 10K run, artichoke cook-offs, and the Firefighters'

Pancake Breakfast; (408)633-2465. Also check out the humongous cement version of the thistlelike plant, otherwise known as the Giant Artichoke Restaurant—it's good for a chuckle, a silly photo, and a bowl of artichoke soup; 11261 Merritt Street; (408)633-3204.

RESTAURANTS

LA SCUOLA ☆☆☆

This *buonissimo* Italian restaurant on the main street of Castroville is a real find. Tucked away in a schoolhouse that's more than a century old, this elegant little place offers classic Italian staples such as veal Parmigiana, saltimbocca, and chicken cacciatore. A favorite dish is the chicken Firenze, a tender breast stuffed with prosciutto and fontina and topped with a light Marsala sauce with a hint of sage. The fettuccine with clams is also very good—the house-made pasta comes perfectly al dente and the fresh clams explode with flavor. The vegetable side dishes are cooked just enough to bring out their flavor and color, and the buttery, oven-roasted potatoes are delicately crisp on the outside and creamy-smooth within. The house wine, from the Moresco winery in Stockton, is also pretty good. *At Preston Rd, downtown; (408)633-3200; 10700 Merritt St, Castroville, CA 95012; beer and wine; AE, MC, V; no checks; lunch Tues–Fri; dinner Tues–Sat; $$.&*

THE
SANTA
CRUZ
COAST

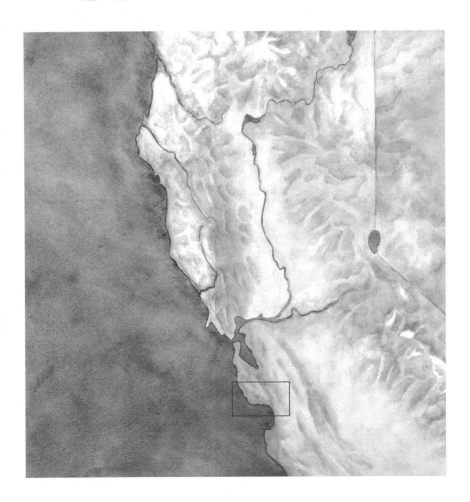

THE SANTA CRUZ COAST

Long regarded as a seaside nirvana for dope-smoking hippies and anyone else eschewing the conventional lifestyle, the Santa Cruz coast simply ain't what it used to be—spend a day on the boardwalk and you'll see more bike locks than dreadlocks. What it all comes down to, of course, is money. Tourism is the big draw here: some 3 million annual visitors help fill the county's coffers, which in turn are doing everything possible to make Santa Cruz a respectable, *safe* place to bring the family.

The result? A little of everything. Walk down gilded Pacific Avenue and you're bound to see the homeless mix it up with the alternative lifestylers within a sea of yuppie shops and shiny cafes. The cultural dichotomy is painfully manifest, but nobody seems to mind; rather, most locals are pleased with the turnout. As one resident put it, "Anything but Carmel."

APTOS

Other than a handful of B&Bs and a few state beaches and parks, Aptos has little in the way of tourist entertainment, leaving that messy business up to neighboring Capitola and Santa Cruz. The focus here is on quality lodgings in quiet surroundings. The only drawback is that the beaches are too far to walk to from town, but if you don't mind the short drive, Aptos is the ideal place for a peaceful vacation on the coast.

ACTIVITIES

Redwood Trails. The Forest of Nisene Marks State Park is one of the largest parks in central California and also one of the least known. Comprising mostly second-growth redwoods, the entire forest was clear-cut less than a century ago. Today, however, a solid canopy of trees shades the 2½-mile dirt road leading to the trailhead, where more than 30 miles of trails—ranging from cakewalks to lung-busters—disappear into the 10,000-acre forest. The most popular hiking trail is the Loma Prieta Grade, a 6-mile round-trip past the wooden remnants of a turn-of-the-century lumber camp. Mountain bikers and leashed dogs are also welcome. (At the end of Aptos Creek Road off Soquel Drive; free; open year-round.)

RESTAURANTS

CAFE SPARROW ☆☆☆

Chef/owner Bob Montagne had big plans when he bought this quaint French country restaurant in June 1989. Then along came the Loma Prieta quake, whose epicenter lay just a short distance away, and Montagne had little more than a pile of rubble on his hands. Fortunately, he and his wife didn't throw in the towel, and their remodeled restaurant is still one of the top places in Aptos. Two dining rooms, decorated with French printed fabric and country furniture, provide a romantic backdrop for Montagne's spirited cuisine. Lunch may include a baguette with shrimp bathed in lemon, fresh dill, and crème fraîche; or a bowl of creamed spinach with a vinaigrette salad and bread. Dinner, however, is when Montagne puts on the Ritz. Start with a pâté of fresh chicken livers seasoned with herbs and Cognac, then progress to such entrees as grilled chicken breast with pears topped with Brie, lamb chops in a rich red-wine and mint sauce, or pan-sautéed calamari steak with lemon, butter, and capers. Desserts are as decadent as you'd expect from a place that seems intent on spoiling its customers rotten. The wine list is far ranging and agreeably priced, and the service is amiable. *Near Trout Gulch Rd; (408)688-6238; 8042 Soquel Dr, Aptos; beer and wine; MC, V; checks OK; breakfast Sat, lunch Mon–Fri, dinner every day, brunch Sun; $$.*

The city of Aptos had the unenviable honor of being the epicenter of the 1989 Loma Prieta earthquake. A trail within the Forest of Nisene Marks leads to the exact point where the trouble began.

The Aptos Creek fire road within the Forest of Nisene Marks is regarded as one of the premier mountain bike trails along the Central Coast.

LODGINGS

MANGELS HOUSE ☆☆☆

This sprawling Italianate mansion, set on an imposing green lawn in the middle of a redwood forest, was built as a summer house for Spreckels sugar magnate Claus Mangels in 1886. British-born Jacqueline Fisher and her husband, Ron, who bought the place in 1979, have decorated the six guest rooms—all with private baths—in an artful yet whimsical way that enlivens the house's stately Victorian demeanor. One room sports a huge bed and chocolate-brown walls decorated with African masks, shields, and other souvenirs that sometimes come as a shock to guests expecting a more traditional approach to Victorian decor. Other rooms feature pastel stenciling that dances across the walls and dramatic modern vases atop antique marble sinks. Lavish breakfasts are served in the dining room, featuring such dishes as apple-puff pancakes, a spicy chili-cheese fluff, and homemade scones. *On the road into the Forest of Nisene Marks State Park; (408)688-7982; 570 Aptos Creek Rd, PO Box 302, Aptos, CA 95001; MC, V; checks OK; $$.*

APPLE LANE INN BED AND BREAKFAST ☆☆

Set back from the road in the middle of an orchard, the Apple Lane Inn (circa 1870) features five rooms decorated with handmade quilts, high-quality Persian rugs, claw-footed bathtubs, and maybe a few too many country-style knickknacks. Guests who aren't playing darts or croquet are cuddling in the white gazebo. In the parlor, stern-looking Victorian portraits watch over a player piano. Hosts Doug and Diana Groom serve a generous breakfast featuring old-fashioned delicacies such as Monte Cristo sandwiches. Coffee and sherry are available all day in the library. *Just west of Cabrillo College; (408)475-6868; 6265 Soquel Dr, Aptos, CA 95003; DIS, MC, V; checks OK; $$.*

BAYVIEW HOTEL BED AND BREAKFAST INN ☆

Built in 1878 on former Spanish land-grant property, Santa Cruz County's oldest hotel combines Old West ambience with up-to-date comfort. The steep staircase, book-lined parlor, and bustling cafe-bar downstairs recall Aptos' frontier past. Each of the 11 rather sparsely furnished rooms has its own bath and antique bed frame; two rooms have fireplaces. Within the hotel is the Veranda restaurant, though a better dining choice is Cafe Sparrow across the street (see Restaurants above). *At Trout Gulch Rd; hotel (408)688-8654, restaurant (408)685-1881; 8041 Soquel Dr, Aptos, CA 95003; AE, MC, V; checks OK; lunch Mon–Fri (seasonal), dinner every day, brunch Sun; $$$.*

CAPITOLA

Capitola's Mediterranean-style buildings, curved streets, white-sand beaches, outdoor cafes, and perpetually festive atmosphere seem more suitable for the French Riviera than Monterey Bay. The verdict? If you're staying on the coast for more than a day, a visit to this ultra-quaint hamlet is highly recommended. Park the car anywhere you can, feed the meter (bring quarters), spend an hour browsing the dozens of boutiques along the esplanade, then rest your bones at Zelda's sunny beachside patio with a pitcher of margaritas. That's the Capitola shuffle.

ACTIVITIES

 Ocean Fishing. Even if you don't know an outboard from a Ouija board, the friendly staff at Capitola Boat & Bait have faith that you'll bring their fishing boats back in one piece. From $49 to $59 buys you a four-person boat for the day, including an outboard motor, fuel, safety equipment, anchor, oars, seat cushions, and free maps of the hot fishing spots. Fishing gear can also be rented and one-day licenses purchased, so there's no excuse not to brave the open ocean just for the halibut. (Open daily sunrise to 4pm; closed Jan to mid-Feb. 1400 Wharf Road, at the end of Capitola Wharf; 408-462-2208.)

That ship-shaped dock east of Capitola City Beach is the Palo Alto, built during World War I as part of the "concrete fleet." After the war, she was towed to nearby Seacliff, blasted to the ocean floor, and used as a floating casino and dance hall. In 1965 the state purchased the $2 million ship for a buck and converted it into a fishing pier.

RESTAURANTS

GAYLE'S BAKERY & ROSTICCERIA ☆☆

Take a number and stand in line: it's worth the wait at this wildly popular place, which is packed with local folk on weekend mornings. A self-service bakery and deli with patio seating, Gayle's offers numerous imaginative sandwiches, pastas, casseroles, roasted meats, salads, cheeses, appetizers, breads, and desserts. The variety is staggering and the quality topnotch. There's a good selection of wines, beers, waters, and espresso drinks, too. Once you've fought your way to the counter, you'll have the makings of a first-class picnic to take to one of the nearby parks or beaches. *By Capitola Ave; (408)462-1200, (408)462-1127; 504 Bay Ave, Capitola; beer and wine; MC, V; checks OK; open 6:30am–8:30pm every day; $.&*

Founded in 1869 by lumber baron Frederick A. Hihn, Capitola is purportedly California's oldest seaside resort.

SHADOWBROOK RESTAURANT ☆☆

While locals are forever undecided about the quality of the food at Shadowbrook, they nevertheless insist that all Santa Cruz visitors dine here at least once. The menu features such items as seafood cakes with smoked salmon, prawns

In the summer, the mouth of Capitola's Soquel Creek is bulldozed with sand to create a small lagoon that attracts shorebirds and paddleboat vendors.

Capitola derives its name from an attempt in 1869 to locate the state's capitol here; the town lost its bid to Sacramento.

wrapped in applewood-smoked bacon, and lake trout grilled with fresh garden herbs. The thick-cut prime rib has long been Shadowbrook's most popular selection, the mud pie and the Bailey's cheesecake its most popular desserts. Guests arrive in style aboard the "hillavator," which ambles down terraced gardens to the multistoried, woodsy restaurant bedecked in white lights. The best tables are on the brickwork terraces, nestled romantically among rock gardens and rhododendrons. *Near the end of Capitola Rd; (408)475-1511; 1750 Wharf Rd, Capitola; full bar; AE, DC, DIS, MC, V; local checks only; dinner every day, brunch Sun; $$$.*

COUNTRY COURT TEA ROOM ☆

Local debutantes and gentlewomen have long flocked to Donna Des Jarlais' Tea Room, wandering past the topiary and friendly English bric-a-brac for an afternoon tea plate—a pot of tea accompanied by soup, salad, fresh fruit, delicate little sandwiches, and homemade cookies (how utterly civilized). The house blend of spiced tea is strong and excellent; coffees and wines are provided for heathens. Light suppers are also served four days a week, as well as a traditional high tea every Sunday from 4:30 to 5:30pm. *Between Bay Ave and Hwy 1; (408)462-2498; 911B Capitola Ave, Capitola; beer and wine; no credit cards; local checks only; breakfast Mon–Fri, lunch (including the tea plate) every day, supper Tues–Sat, brunch Sat and Sun; $.*

LODGINGS

THE INN AT DEPOT HILL ☆☆☆

Located in a turn-of-the-century train station, the Inn at Depot Hill's eight lavishly designed rooms seem to have sprung directly from the pages of *Architectural Digest*. The terra-cotta-walled Portofino Room, patterned after a coastal Italian villa, sports a stone cherub, ivy, frescoes, and a brick patio with private Jacuzzi. No less opulent is the Stratford-Upon-Avon, a faux English cottage with a cozy window seat. The Paris Room with its toile-covered walls dazzles in black and white, while the rather fussy Côte d'Azur boasts an ornate canopy bed with bronze vines climbing the four-posters. Every room has a fireplace, TV and VCR, stereo, and marble-appointed bathroom. In the morning, enjoy a buffet of pastries and quiche, as well as a hot dish such as French toast or a spinach omelet; evening wine and hors d'oeuvres are served in the downstairs parlor. *Near Park Ave, next to the railroad tracks; (408)462-3376, (800) 57-B-AND-B; 250 Monterey Ave, Capitola, CA 95010; AE, MC, V; checks OK; $$$.*♿

SANTA CRUZ

For nearly a century, Santa Cruz has been synonymous with "beach and boardwalk," as if this seaside city of 50,000 exists solely to sustain what is now the only major beachside amusement park left on the Pacific Coast. Considering that the annual number of boardwalk visitors is 62 times greater than the city's population, it's no surprise that Santa Cruz's other highlights are all but ignored by the hordes of thrill-seekers who head straight for the waterfront each year.

Not that the boardwalk (now a cement walk) isn't worthy of the limelight. Ranked among the top amusement parks in the nation, with a higher attendance than either Marine World–Africa USA or Paramount's Great America, the privately owned amusement park has cleaned up its once-tarnished act by pouring a pile of money into improvements and security; the boardwalk is truly safe and clean these days. Then, of course, there's the legendary Giant Dipper, considered by those-who-would-know to be the greatest roller coaster ever built, and the hand-carved horses of the Looff Carousel, the last bona fide brass ring merry-go-round in North America. These two rides alone are worth a walk down the boardwalk.

Yet even without its celebrated amusement park, Santa Cruz would still be one of California's top coastal destinations. Where else can you find a vibrant, cross-cultural (remember, this used to be the LSD capital of the world) college town perched on the edge of an immense bay teeming with marine life, ringed by miles of golden beaches, and backed by dense redwood forests? Remove those boardwalk blinders for a day and you'll find out that there's a whole lot more to Santa Cruz than boardwalk cotton candy and arcades.

Downtown Santa Cruz is silly with free parking: along Cedar, Pacific, and Front Streets there are 3 parking garages and 16 surface lots that offer 3 hours of emancipated parking.

Open:
Most weekends and
holidays Jan–Nov;
daily Memorial
Day through Labor
Day (call ahead in
bad weather).

Closed:
December 1–29.

Hours:
Open at 11am in
summer, noon in
winter. Closing
hours vary.

Admission:
Free.

Information:
(408)426-7433.

Location:
400 Beach Street,
at the south end of
Front Street.

GETTING THERE

The most scenic route to Santa Cruz is along Highway 1 from San Francisco, which, aside from the "you fall, you die" stretch called Devil's Slide, cruises at a steady 50mph along the coast. Faster but far less romantic is Route 17, which is accessed near San Jose from I-280, I-880, or Highway 101 and literally ends at the foot of the boardwalk. The exception to this rule is on weekend mornings, when Route 17 tends to logjam with Bay Area beachgoers while Highway 1 remains relatively uncrowded.

ACTIVITIES

Power Shopping. When it comes to shopping, Santa Cruz doesn't fool around. Walk down Pacific Avenue and *hay caramba!* More than 250 shops and restaurants are crammed into Santa Cruz's 29-block business district, which has recovered rather nicely from the 1989 Loma Prieta earthquake (the epicenter was only 10 miles away). As you make your way down the mall, look for the Octagon Building, an ornate, eight-sided Victorian brick edifice built in 1882 that has survived numerous quakes. Previously serving as the city's Hall of Records, it's now part of the McPherson Center for Art and History, which showcases 10,000 years of the area's past as well as contemporary art of the Pacific Rim. (Open Tues–Sun, 11am–4pm; 705 Front Street at Cooper Street; 408-454-0697.)

Sea Kayaking. The best ride on the boardwalk isn't the Giant Dipper roller coaster, it's paddling a sea kayak around the Santa Cruz coast. Vision Quest Kayaking, located on the northeast end of the Santa Cruz Wharf, rents single-, double-, and triple-seater kayaks for exploring the nearby cliffs and kelp beds where a multitude of sea otters, seals, sea lions, and other marine animals congregate. No experience is necessary, and all ages are welcome. Guided tours are also available; (408)425-8445.

Redwoods State Park. The perfect antidote to an overdose of sun and sand is a walk through the redwoods at Henry Cowell Redwoods State Park. Only a few miles from downtown Santa Cruz on Highway 9 (from Mission

Street, turn north on River Street/Highway 9 and continue north), the 1,800-acre park has 20 miles of trails through thick, cool forests and golden meadows. Top pick for a leisurely walk is the ¾-mile Redwood Grove Trail, a wide and flat loop around an ancient stand of giant redwoods. On summer weekends at 2pm, docent-led tours of the Grove Trail start from the Nature Center, but call ahead first; (408)335-7077 or (408)335-4598. (Secret tip: About 1½ miles south of the main entrance on Highway 9 is the Ox Road Parking Lot. Park here—for free!—then take the short trail down to the locals' favorite swimming hole, the Garden of Eden.)

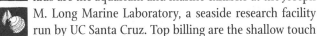 **Aquarium.** Mildly entertaining for adults but a blast for kids are the aquarium and marine exhibits at the Joseph M. Long Marine Laboratory, a seaside research facility run by UC Santa Cruz. Top billing are the shallow touch tanks that allow visitors to handle—and learn about—sea stars, anemones, sea cucumbers, and other slimy sea creatures. Behind the gift shop are the humbling skeletal remains of an 86-foot blue whale. (Open Tues–Sun, 1–4pm; $2 for adults, kids 16 and under free. From Highway 1 in west Santa Cruz, turn south on Swift Street and right on Delaware Avenue to end; 408-459-4308.)

 Music & Dancing. One good thing about a college town—it knows how to party. The Cruz's coolest blues are at Moe's Alley, featuring live music (and dancing) nightly (1535 Commercial Way, 408-479-1854). For traditional and modern jazz, it's the Kuumbwa Jazz Center, a nonprofit (and nonsmoking) landmark that's been around for the past two decades (320 Cedar Street, 408-427-2227). Local rock, reggae, blues, and world-beat bands mix it up at the Catalyst, which occasionally pulls in some big names, too (1011 Pacific Avenue, 408-423-1336). Even bluegrass, Hawaiian, and folk music find a venue at cavernous Palookaville dance club, which also has its share of rock and reggae (1133 Pacific Avenue, 408-454-0600).

 Bike Rental. Santa Cruz is a bicycler's heaven. The pedal-friendly downtown area is flat and wide (ditto the wharf and boardwalk), and the shoreline bike path along West Cliff Drive is sensational. If you can't bring your own wheels, the Bicycle Rental Center rents touring, tandem, and mountain bikes at hourly, daily, and weekly rates, and even throws in free

"Most students have mixed feelings about all the tourists. We rely on them to make a living, but we would rather they all spent their vacations elsewhere."
—Charmaine Hughes, UC Santa Cruz student and part-time waitress

Take the Beach Boys' advice— don't be afraid to try the greatest sport around. Learn to catch a wave at Club Ed Surf School, open year round in front of the Dream Inn just west of the Santa Cruz Wharf; (408)459-9283.

For organically grown produce, flowers, herbs, and other non-corporate-made goodies, shop at Santa Cruz's Farmers Market, held Wednesdays from 2:30pm to 6:30pm on Lincoln Street between Pacific Avenue and Cedar Street.

A GOOD DAY IN SANTA CRUZ

9–10am:	Breakfast at Dale's Diner in Felton.
10am–noon:	Walk through Henry Cowell Redwoods State Park.
Noon–1:30pm:	Lunch at Ristorante Avanti.
1:30–3:30pm:	Shop along Pacific Avenue.
3:30–5pm:	Sea kayaking from the wharf.
5–6:30pm:	A sunset walk along West Cliff Drive.
6:30–8pm:	Dinner at O'mei Restaurant.
8–10pm:	Browse the boardwalk.
10–11:30pm:	Decaf mocha and a good read at Bookshop Santa Cruz.

Santa Cruz's best hangout is Bookshop Santa Cruz, which has an enormous and diverse inventory (including a particularly good children's section) as well as the two other key elements to a good bookstore: plenty of places to sit, and a good cafe. (At 1520 Pacific Avenue; 408-423-0900.)

helmets and locks (415 Pacific Avenue, at Pacific and Front Streets; 408-426-8687).

 Surfing Museum. Within the small brick lighthouse building off West Cliff Drive is the Santa Cruz Surfing Museum. Photographs, videos, antique surfboards, and piles of other memorabilia depict the history and evolution of surfing around the world. After the tour, walk to the point's edge and watch the sea lions waddle around Seal Rock. (Open every day but Tuesday, noon–4pm; 408-429-3429.) Between the lighthouse and the boardwalk is that famous strip of the sea known as Steamers Lane, the summa cum laude California surfing spot (savvy surfers say this is the place—not Southern California—to catch the best breaks in the state).

 Beach & Butterflies. At the north end of West Cliff Drive is Natural Bridges State Beach, named after the three water-sculpted, bridgelike rock formations along its seawall (the last of which caved in during the quake of 1989). Popular with surfers, windsurfers, tide pool trekkers, and sunbathers, the beach does a brisk winter business as well: between October and March up to 200,000 monarch butterflies roost and mate in the nearby eucalyptus grove. Skip the $6 parking fee at the West Cliff Drive entrance and walk in from Delaware Avenue (just east of the entrance off Swanton Boulevard) for free; (408)423-4609.

On the Wharf. If you had to pay just to drive down the famous Santa Cruz Wharf, you'd probably feel ripped off. Fortunately, you don't: the first 20 minutes of parking are free, which is plenty of time to rubberneck the touristy shops, fish markets, and seafood restaurants that line the side of this venerable octogenarian; (408)429-3477. Dining tip: Within the wharf's sea of pricey establishments is the Riva Fish House, a surprisingly inexpensive restaurant with good food and a superb view (Building 31, Municipal Wharf; 408-429-1223).

On Friday summer nights, don't miss the boardwalk's free concerts, featuring the likes of The Shirelles, Chubby Checker, and Sha Na Na; (408)423-5590.

Coastal Walk. Santa Cruz's real premier attraction isn't the beach or boardwalk; it's the 2-mile walking-biking-jogging path along West Cliff Drive. Proof positive is that locals don't go anywhere near the boardwalk, but you can see them in droves exercising up and down the 2 miles of paved coastal trail from the wharf to Natural Bridges State Park. The best time to visit is at sunset, when the alternative-lifestylers gather near the lighthouse to bang their drums and flail around.

On the south end of West Cliff Drive is Lighthouse Field State Beach, the birthplace of American surfing and one of the few beaches in town where doggies are allowed.

Localmotion. Locomotive buffs, kids, and closet tree-huggers should hop aboard the historic Roaring Camp train for a 6-mile, 1¼-hour round-trip excursion up the steepest narrow-gauge grades in North America. The steam-powered locomotive winds s-l-o-w-l-y through dense, cool redwood groves to the summit of Bear Mountain and back. A second train outfit, called Big Trees Railroad, offers an 8-mile ride through mountain tunnels and along ridges (with spectacular views of the San Lorenzo River) before stopping at the Santa Cruz Beach Boardwalk. Both trains are located on Graham Hill Road off Highway 17 in Felton (follow the signs), though the Big Trees Railroad can also be boarded at the east end of the boardwalk. Call for specific departure times. (Roaring Camp: Wednesdays–Sundays in winter, daily in summer; 408-335-4484. Big Trees: weekends and holidays, May–October, with daily runs in summer; 408-335-4400.)

Boardwalk Bargains. Save a bundle at the boardwalk by visiting on "1907 Nights." Every summer after 5pm on Monday and Tuesday, the Santa Cruz Beach Boardwalk celebrates the year it opened by reducing its prices to 50 cents a ride (it's normally $1.50 to $3.00), and two bits buys a hot dog, soft drink, cotton candy, or a red candy apple. At the end of summer the boardwalk also hosts "1907 Week," when you can get the same evening deals Monday through Friday before Labor Day; (408)423-5590.

RESTAURANTS

CAFE BITTERSWEET ☆☆☆

This sleek restaurant and wine bar has been embraced by Santa Cruz foodies since it opened its doors in 1992. A judicious use of wood, expansive floral displays, and huge, whimsical wreaths add to the sophisticated design of the dining room, a perfect setting for chef Thomas Vinolus' eclectic creations. The seasonal menu features everything from a robust version of moussaka to a winter risotto with roasted vegetables, grilled wild mushrooms, and white-truffle oil. Start with the grilled shrimp or the varied antipasto sampler, and for a main course order the garlic chicken with a Madeira-and-roasted-garlic jus, or the amazing fresh salmon fillet with a fresh herb crust. The wine list is extensive and varied, with some interesting if pricey older vintages among its treasures. *Near King St on the west side of town; (408)423-9999; 2332 Mission St, Santa Cruz; beer and wine; MC, V; local checks only; dinner Tues–Sun; $$$.*

O'MEI RESTAURANT ☆☆☆

Named after a mountain in the Sichuan province of China and pronounced oh-*may*, this acclaimed Chinese restaurant is a wondrous little paradox tucked into a drab Santa Cruz mini-mall. Owner-chef Roger Grigsby is not Chinese, nor are any of his cooks, but his food caters less to American sensibilities than do most Chinese restaurants. O'mei is, in fact, a veritable Asian adventure in California-land, pushing the envelope of Pacific Rim cuisine. While you may order predictable Northern Chinese offerings such as Mongolian beef and mu shu pork, those with adventurous palates should sample the date-and-sweet-potato chicken or sliced rock cod in black bean–sweet pepper sauce. A unique touch is the array of exotic "little-dish appetizers" (such as sesame-cilantro-eggplant salad and pan-roasted peppers with feta cheese) that are presented dim-sum style shortly after you're seated. *Near King St on the west side of town; (408)425-8458;*

2316 Mission St, Santa Cruz; beer and wine; AE, MC, V; no checks; lunch Mon–Fri, dinner every day; $$. &

CASABLANCA RESTAURANT ☆☆

 There's nothing very Moroccan about this boardwalk bastion of California cuisine, except, perhaps, the palpable air of romance. Soft music fills the candle-lit dining room, and stars wink on the water outside the many windows (don't fight the urge to hold hands across the table). The food can be a bit too subtle at times—such as the spiritless gazpacho—but chef Scott Cater's creations most often triumph. For an appetizer, try the meltingly soft, fire-roasted Anaheim chile stuffed with feta cheese. When it comes to ever-changing entrees, expect the unexpected: sole in macadamia-nut batter or fresh ahi in an avocado-tomatillo sauce. The book-length wine list offers local and international selections. *On the Santa Cruz waterfront; (408)426-9063; 101 Main St, Santa Cruz; full bar; AE, DC, MC, V; dinner every day, brunch Sun; $$$.*

EL PALOMAR ☆☆

Santa Cruz is gordo with good Mexican restaurants, but none compare to El Palomar, located within a former '30s hotel off Pacific Avenue. Peruse the imaginative, extensive menu while sipping an Ultimate Margarita and munching on delicate tortilla chips still warm from the oven. El Palomar is known for its seafood dishes, which are topped with exotic sauces, but the local favorites are the award-winning Burrito de Camarones (with sautéed prawns) and Jose's Special Appetizer (combo of charbroiled snapper, steak, and prawns with handmade corn tortillas). *Inside the Pacific Garden Mall near Soquel Ave; (408)425-7575; 1336 Pacific Ave, Santa Cruz; full bar; AE, DIS, MC, V; local checks only; lunch, dinner every day, brunch Sun; $$.*&

INDIA JOZE RESTAURANT ☆☆

A cross-cultural wonder, India Joze has been wowing adventurous Santa Cruz diners for years. The portions served here are enormous, and each dish is . . . well . . . *different*. You'll find steaming, sunset-colored bowls of thick lentil dahl, platters of chicken dressed with a ginger-basil-tamarind glaze, and even a perky Berber Burger (half a pound of spiced lamb with a garlic-walnut sauce and wonderful

Live Balinese music played on actual Balinese instruments can be heard on Saturdays between 3–5pm at India Joze Restaurant.

A consistent winner for Santa Cruz's "Best Breakfast" is Dale's Diner, a funky old restaurant in the mountain town of Felton that's renowned for its burly pancakes. (6560 Highway 9, 6 miles north of Santa Cruz; 408-335-2000.)

cassava chips). Even normally understated items such as hash browns arrive at your table crowned with artichokes, peppers, and sour cream. The house blend of *chai* (spiced tea) is sweet, dense, and intense. Eclectic decor—Chinese lanterns, hanging woks, sitar music—accompanies the equally cosmopolitan entrees. On sunny afternoons, request a table on the shaded garden patio. *At Union St; (408)427-3554; 1001 Center St, Santa Cruz; beer and wine; DIS, MC, V; local checks only; lunch Mon–Sat, dinner every day, brunch Sun; $$.*

RISTORANTE AVANTI ☆☆

In keeping with the Santa Cruz lifestyle, this local favorite for Italian food prides itself on serving "the healthiest meal possible" (think organic veggies and free-range chicken and veal). The modern, casual decor provides an amiable setting for aromatic, well-prepared seasonal dishes such as sweet squash ravioli with sage butter, lasagne primavera, muffalata sandwiches, and house-made Italian sausages with onions and peppers. Many of the classic Italian offerings, such as chicken cacciatore and linguine carbonara, are rendered with a delicate touch. Considering the quality of the ingredients and the modest prices, Ristorante Avanti is a terrific bargain that makes you forgive its shopping-strip location. *Near Bay St; (408)427-0135; 1711 Mission St, Santa Cruz; beer and wine; AE, MC, V; local checks only; breakfast, lunch, dinner every day; $$.&*

PONTIAC GRILL ☆

Most everyone in town agrees that the Pontiac Grill is the best place to take the kids. The servers are decked out in pleated skirts and sweater vests, and each of the streamlined booths has a working mini-jukebox. The menu dishes up relentless automobile puns: appetizers are called "first gear," side orders are "spare parts," drinks are "heaters and coolants," drumettes with barbecue sauce are "chicken pistons." Of course, children love the french fries, onion rings, burgers, milk shakes, and the opportunity to color in the Pontiacs on the place mats. *At Cathcart St; (408)427-2290; 429 Front St, Santa Cruz; beer and wine; MC, V; no checks; breakfast Sat and Sun, lunch, dinner every day; $.*

LODGINGS

In 1993, state legislators passed a bill giving Santa Cruz exclusive rights to the name "Surf City."

THE BABBLING BROOK INN ☆☆☆

The Babbling Brook Inn, Santa Cruz's oldest B&B, is still one of the best on the coast. Secluded in a fantastical garden with waterfalls, wishing wells, gazebos, and, of course, a babbling brook, the inn offers 12 rooms named after French impressionists. The mauve-and-blue Van Gogh Room has a private deck, fireplace, beamed ceiling, and whirlpool tub for two. Peach and ivory predominate in the Cézanne Room with its generous bath and canopy bed, while the blue-and-white Monet Room comes with a corner fireplace, canopy bed, private deck, and Jacuzzi tub for two. In the morning innkeeper Helen King lays out a delectable spread of fruit compote, pastries, French toast, fresh-squeezed orange juice, coffee, and more (she'll even whip up dishes for guests with special diets). Breakfast in the luxurious dining room, on the flowery patio, or in your suite. *Near California St; (408)427-2437, (800)866-1131; 1025 Laurel St, Santa Cruz, CA 95060; AE, DIS, MC, V; checks OK; $$$.*&

THE DARLING HOUSE ☆☆☆

There are probably no better ocean views (and no softer carpeting) in all of Santa Cruz than those you'll find at the Darling House, a Spanish Revival mansion built as a summer home for a Colorado cattle baron in 1910. From its postcard-perfect location in a quiet residential neighborhood, you can see endless miles of gray-blue sea, the glittering boardwalk, and the lights of faraway towns. The Pacific Ocean Room, decorated like a sea captain's quarters, has an extraordinary view of the bay and boardwalk, a tiled fireplace, and the requisite telescope. Across the hall, the Chinese Room features brightly colored lanterns and an exotic canopied Chinese wedding bed. Owners Darrell and Karen Darling have outfitted all seven rooms with museum-quality antiques, but, alas, only two rooms have private baths. Fluffy white robes in every closet keep you warm between trips to the backyard hot tub. Karen's breakfasts include fresh fruit, oven-fresh breads and pastries, and homemade granola made with walnuts from the Darlings' own farm. *On W Cliff Dr between the wharf and the lighthouse; (408)458-1958; 314 W Cliff Dr, Santa Cruz, CA 95060; AE, DIS, MC, V; checks OK; $$$.*

EDGEWATER BEACH MOTEL ☆

So old-fashioned it's retro-contemporary, the Edgewater hasn't changed many of its furnishings since the late sixties—even the brochures (check out the beehive hairdos) are from 1966. The odd part is, everything is still miraculously new-looking, as if you've stumbled upon the set for *The Brady Bunch on Vacation*. The list of amenities runs long: all rooms—including the family suites with kitchens, nonsmoking rooms, and rooms with fireplaces—have refrigerators, cable TV, phones, free coffee, and even access to a heated pool, sun deck, and a barbecue picnic area; most have microwaves. Parking is free, and the boardwalk is only a block away. Be sure to ask about the mini-vacation packages, which are a real deal. *Off the ocean end of Front St; (408)423-0440; 525 Second St, Santa Cruz, CA 95060; AE, DC, DIS, MC, V; checks OK in advance; $$.*

THE CARMELITA COTTAGES

From the street you'd never guess that this gaggle of whitewashed Victorian cottages is a hostel. Located a mere two blocks from the boardwalk in a quiet residential neighborhood, the Carmelita Cottages consist of simple dormitory-style cabins with three to five small beds per room (avoid the creaky bunk beds). All paths lead to the main house, which has a communal kitchen and comfy common rooms. Prices range from $12 to $14 per person (less than what you'd pay for parking at the boardwalk, which is free at the hostel), $30 for couples' rooms, and a bit more for family rooms. A morning chore is appreciated, lock-out is 10am to 5pm, and curfew is at 11pm (though no one seems to remember any of this). Reservations are a must during the summer, as are earplugs. *Off Beach St, 2 blocks north of the wharf; (408)423-8304; 321 Main St, PO Box 1241, Santa Cruz, CA 95061; checks OK via mailed reservation; $.&*

DAVENPORT

About 10 miles north of Santa Cruz on Highway 1 is the former whaling and lumber-shipping town of Davenport, which now serves mainly as a snack stop for road-weary travelers. At the Whale City Bakery, Bar & Grill you can get an ample slice of hot apple or pecan pie for the road, but a better plan is to take your fixin's across the highway for an impromptu picnic underneath the cliff-side grove of cypress trees (490 Highway 1, 408-423-9803).

ACTIVITIES

Nude Beach. Those who don't know any better pay a whopping $7 to lie in the buff at Red and White Beach, located 4 miles south of Davenport. Obviously they don't know about the secret gold-sand beach exactly 1 mile south of Davenport. Park at the dirt pull-off on your right, climb over the railroad levee, and there she is: one of the most beautiful and secluded nude beaches in California.

THE
SAN
FRANCISCO
COAST

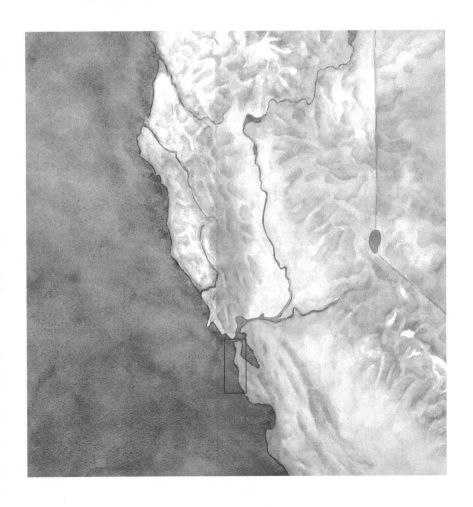

THE SAN FRANCISCO COAST

A south-to-north sweep of the San Mateo County coastline, beginning at the Año Nuevo State Reserve and ending at the Golden Gate Bridge in San Francisco.

It's sort of a mixed blessing, the almost ceaseless barrage of chilly winds and frigid, dangerous waters that predominate along the San Francisco coast. Too cold and cruel for profitable development—aside from a few sheltered coves such as Half Moon Bay—the stretch of shore between the Golden Gate and Santa Cruz has, for the most part, been left undisturbed and open to the public. While this is a boon for nature lovers, those in search of the perfect tan will probably be disappointed—sunshine tends to be an afternoon event. Be sure to dress warm, pack your hiking boots, and dig around the closet for those binoculars, 'cause it's time to get next to nature.

PESCADERO

Were it not for the near-mythical status of Duarte's Tavern, Pescadero would probably enjoy the sane, simple small-town life in relative obscurity. Instead, you can pretty much count on the town's population tripling on weekends as everyone piles into the bar and restaurant to see what all the hubbub is about. Whether it's worth the visit depends mostly on your interest in seeking out Duarte's holy recipe for artichoke soup.

ACTIVITIES

Farmers Market. A few miles east of Duarte's Tavern on Pescadero Road is Phipps Ranch, a sort of Knott's Berry Farm in miniature. Kids can ride ponies for only $2.50 while Mom and Dad load up on the huge assortment of fresh, organically grown fruits and vegetables (including an amazing selection of dried beans) or browse the nursery and gardens. In the early summer, pick your own olallieberries and boysenberries in the adjacent fields. (Open daily, 10am–7pm, winter 10am–6pm; pony rides 10am–4pm, summer only; 2700 Pescadero Rd; 415-879-0787.)

General Store. About 7 miles north of Pescadero on Highway 1 is the turnoff to Highway 84 and the legendary San Gregorio General Store. Since 1889, this funky old place has been providing the nearby ranching and farming community a bewildering assortment of "shoat rings, hardware, tack, bullshit, lanterns," and just about everything else a country boy needs to survive. It's truly worth a gander, particularly on Saturday and Sunday afternoons when the Irish R&B or Bulgarian bluegrass bands are in full swing. (Open daily, 9am–6pm; located 1 mile up Highway 84 from the Highway 1 intersection; 415-726-0565.)

In the late 1800s, the clipper ship Carrier Pigeon crashed onto the rocks off Pigeon Point near Pescadero, spilling its load of white paint. Villagers, making the best of a bad situation, whitewashed their entire town.

 Nature Reserve. At the turnoff to Pescadero is one of the few remaining natural marshes left on the central California coast, the Pescadero Marsh Natural Preserve. The 600 acres of wetlands—part of the Pacific flyway—are a refuge for more than 160 bird species, including great blue herons that nest in the northern row of eucalyptus trees. Passing through the marsh is the mile-long Sequoia Audubon Trail, accessible from the parking lot at Pescadero State Beach on Highway 1 (the trail starts below the Pescadero Creek Bridge). Docent-led tours take place every Saturday at 10:30am and every Sunday at 1pm, weather permitting; (415)879-0832.

Seaside Sex Show. You're not the only one having fun in the sun: About 10 miles south of Pescadero along Highway 1, you'll come upon Año Nuevo State Reserve, a unique and fascinating breeding ground for northern elephant seals. A close encounter with a 2½-ton male elephant seal waving his humongous schnoz is an unforgettable event. Even more memorable is the sight of two males fighting and snorting (they can be heard for miles) over a harem of females. The mating season starts in December and continues through March. Reservations are required for the 2½-hour naturalist-led tours (held rain or shine December 15 to March 31). Tickets are quite cheap, but they sell out fast, so plan about two months ahead; (800)444-7275.

RESTAURANTS

DUARTE'S TAVERN ☆☆

Duarte's (pronounced "DOO-*Arts*") is a rustic gem, still owned and operated by the family that built it in 1894. Back then it was the place to buy a 10-cent shot of whiskey on the stagecoach ride from San Francisco to Santa Cruz.

When Duarte's Tavern caught fire in 1927, local fire fighters examined their priorities and sacrificed the restaurant to save the bar.

Nowadays Duarte's is half bar, half restaurant, but it's still set in an Old West–style wood-and-stucco building near Pescadero's general store. The bar is dark and loud, filled with locals drinking beer, smoking, and spinning tales (hunting license fees are posted twice lest we forget). The unassuming wood-paneled restaurant next door serves steak, prime rib, and plenty of fresh coastal fare such as red snapper, halibut, sole, sand dabs, and salmon in season. Most of the fruits and vegetables come from the Duartes' own gardens behind the restaurant (be sure to go take a peek after lunch). It's sort of a county misdemeanor if you don't start dinner with a bowl of cream-of-artichoke soup and finish with a slice of fresh fruit pie. Reservations are recommended for dinner. *At Pescadero Rd; (415)879-0464; 202 Stage Rd, Pescadero, CA 94060; full bar; AE, MC, V; local checks only; breakfast, lunch, dinner every day; $$.*

The Pigeon Point Lighthouse, one of the most commonly photographed lighthouses in the United States, offers self-guided tours from 8am till sunset.

LODGINGS

PIGEON POINT HOSTEL

 Located halfway between San Francisco and Santa Cruz at the base of one of the tallest lighthouses on the Pacific Coast, Pigeon Point Hostel has a 270-degree view of the ocean that can't be matched anywhere in the region. The hostel's four buildings were originally home to the Coast Guard lighthouse staff until high-tech lighthouse electronics gave them the boot. The 52 bunks are separated into his and hers, but for an extra $10 per night you can make your own foghorn noises in one of the couples-only rooms. The facilities are clean and comfortable, and the price—$14— can't be beat. The hot tub overlooking the ocean is well worth the $3-per-half-hour fee (guests only). Reservations are strongly recommended, although some bunk beds are held for walk-ins starting at 4:30pm. *On Hwy 1 south of the Pescadero turnoff; (415)879-0633; 210 Pigeon Point Rd, Pescadero, CA 94060; MC, V; checks OK; $.&*

HALF MOON BAY

Most Bay Area families know Half Moon Bay as the pumpkin capital of the West, where thousands of pilgrims make their annual journey in search of the ultimate Halloween jack-o'-lantern. Since 1970 the Half Moon Bay Art & Pumpkin Festival has featured all manner of squash cuisine and crafts, as well as the Giant Pumpkin weigh-in contest, won recently by an 875-pound monster. A Great Pumpkin Parade, pumpkin-carving competitions, pie-eating contests, and piles of great food pretty much assure a good time for all; for more information call the Pumpkin Hotline at (415)726-9652.

Pumpkins aside, Half Moon Bay is a jewel of a town, saved from mediocrity by diverting its historic Main Street well away from the fast-food chains and gas stations of Highway 1. The locals are disarmingly friendly, actually bestowing greetings as you walk along the rows of small shops and restaurants. Then, of course, there are the 4 miles of golden crescent-shaped beach, one of the prettiest in all of California; bustling Pillar Point Harbor, launching point for whale-watching and deep-sea-fishing trips; and myriad hiking and biking trails along the coast and into the redwood forests. Combine this with an array of commendable accommodations and restaurants and you have the perfect ingredients for a peaceful weekend getaway.

ACTIVITIES

 Fishing & Whale Watching. It's hard not to like a big ol' fishing harbor. The pungent aroma of the sea, the rows of

In the past dozen
years, the 180 (give
or take) boats of
Pillar Point Harbor
have pulled in
nearly 10 million
pounds of seafood,
sold mostly in the
Bay Area.

rusty trawlers, and the salty men and women tending to endless chores evoke a sort of Hemingwayish sense of romance. Pillar Point Harbor, 4 miles north of Half Moon Bay off Highway 1, is just that sort of big ol' fishing harbor. Visitors are encouraged to walk along the pier and even partake in a fishing trip. Captain John's Fishing Trips (415-726-2913; 800-391-8787) and Huck Finn Sportfishing (415-726-7133; 800-572-2934) each charge around $50, including rod and reel, for a day's outing—a small price to pay for 60 pounds of fresh salmon. Between January and March, whale-watching trips also depart daily.

 Biking. The best way to explore the small, flat town of Half Moon Bay and its beaches is on a mountain bike. Lucky for you, they're available for rent at the Bicyclery at 432 Main Street in Half Moon Bay. Prices range from $6 an hour to $24 all day. Helmets—also for rent—are required; (415)726-6000. Be sure to ask one of the staffers about the best biking trails in the area, particularly the wonderful beach trail from Kelly Avenue to Pillar Point Harbor.

Farmers Market. If you like vegetables, you'll love the Andreotti Family Farm. Every Friday, Saturday, and Sunday one of the family members slides open the old barn door at 10am sharp to reveal a cornucopia of just-picked artichokes, peas, brussels sprouts, beans, strawberries, and just about whatever else is growing in their adjacent fields. The Andreotti enterprise has been in operation since 1926, so it's a sure bet they know their veggies. The barn is located at 227 Kelly Avenue, halfway between Highway 1 and the beach in Half Moon Bay; (415)726-9461 or 726-9151. (Open till 5pm year-round.)

Serious green
thumbs know
that Half Moon
Bay Nursery,
located on Highway
92 3 miles east
the Highway 1
intersection, has
one of the finest
selections of indoor
and outdoor plants
in California. (Open
daily, 9am–5pm;
11691 San Mateo
Rd; 415-726-5392.)

Maverick Beach. If the name sounds familiar, that's because this local Half Moon Bay surf spot made national headlines as the site where famed Hawaiian surfer Mark Foo was drowned in 1995 after being thrown from his board by a 20-foot wave. On calmer days, though, secluded Maverick Beach is still a good place to escape the weekend crowds because, although everyone's heard about the beach, few know where it is and you won't find it on any map. Here's the dope: From Capistrano Road at Pillar Point Harbor, turn left on Prospect Way, left on Broadway, right on Princeton, then right on Westpoint to the West Shoreline Access parking lot (on your left). Park here, then continue up Westpoint on foot toward the Pillar Point Satellite Tracking Station. Take about 77 steps, and on your right will be a trailhead leading to legendary Maverick Beach a short distance away.

 Wine-Tasting. Wine-tasting in Half Moon Bay? Wine not? While the actual Obester Winery is located up north in the Anderson Valley, its satellite Wine-Tasting & Sales Room is only a few miles from Half Moon Bay up Highway 92. It's a pleasant drive—passing numerous fields of flowers, Christmas tree farms, and pumpkin patches—to this wood shack filled with award-winning grape juice. Behind the tasting room is a small picnic area that's perfect for an afternoon lunch break. (Open daily, 10am–5pm; 12341 San Mateo Rd; 415-726-9463.)

 Kayaking. If you're one of those Type A people who can't just lie on the beach and relax, California Canoe & Kayak has the answer. For $80 they'll take you out on the bay for a 7-hour lesson in the fundamentals of sea kayaking and even "surf-zone" kayaking. Sure, it's expensive, but the rewards are priceless. Classes are from 9am to 4pm Saturdays and Sundays, May through October (call for winter schedule); rentals and retail sales are also available. CCK is located on Pillar Point Harbor at the Half Moon Bay Yacht Club; (415)728-1803.

Redwood Forest. The best place to hike and mountain-bike around Half Moon Bay is Purisima Creek Redwoods, a little-known sanctuary frequented mostly by locals. Located on the western slopes of the Santa Cruz Mountains, the preserve is filled with fern-lined creek banks, lush redwood forests, and fields of wildflowers and berries that are accessible to hikers, mountain bikers, and equestrians along miles of trails. From the Highway 1/Highway 92 intersection in Half Moon Bay, drive 1 mile south on Highway 1 to Higgins Purisima Creek Road and turn left, then continue 4½ miles to a small gravel parking lot—that's the trailhead; (415)691-1200.

Skip the $5 state beach parking fee at Half Moon Bay by parking along Medio Ave off Highway 1, or at Surfer's Beach, the first dirt parking lot south of Pillar Point Harbor.

"I love everything about Half Moon Bay: the fog, the rolling hills, the cows . . . even the coyotes, except for when they eat my cats."—Half Moon Bay resident Marta Drury

The Flying Fish Grill
at the corner of
Main Street and
Highway 92 in Half
Moon Bay makes a
mean fish taco—
with fresh avocado
and jack cheese
wrapped in a soft
corn tortilla—for
less than $2.50.
(Open Wed–Sun,
11am–7pm;
415-712-1125.)

RESTAURANTS

PASTA MOON ☆☆☆

This inventive nouveau-Italian restaurant—widely considered the best in Half Moon Bay—follows three time-honored rules of Mediterranean cooking: use only the freshest ingredients, make everything from scratch, and don't forget the garlic. Despite her fondness for the stinking rose, chef Sean Lynd's wonderfully creative pastas and main entrees are remarkably well balanced. The fresh pasta, which is always flavorful and perfectly cooked, might include capellini *con pesce fresco* (ahi tuna sautéed in olive oil with anchovies, garlic, capers, kalamata olives, and lemon juice). Another favorite is the medallions of pork tenderloin with a sweet-and-sour cherry sauce. If you still have room, the tiramisu, with its layers of Marsala-and-espresso-soaked ladyfingers and creamy mascarpone, is wonderful. *In the Tin Palace, north end of Main St; (415)726-5125; 315 Main St, Half Moon Bay; $$; beer and wine; AE, DIS, MC, V; local checks only; lunch, dinner every day; $.*

MEZZA LUNA ☆☆

Don't be fooled by the cheesy red-and-green cinder-block exterior: while Mezza Luna lacks the romantic ambience of Pasta Moon (see above), it more than makes up for it with the gaggle of suave, sexy Italian waiters (you'd swear the accents are fake) and painfully authentic *secondi Italiano*. Be sure to start with the *antipasto della casa*, a platter of marinated grilled vegetables doused with the perfect blend of extra-virgin olive oil and red wine vinegar. For dinner the *penne del pastore*—perfectly cooked tube pasta quenched with a tangy tomato sauce, fresh eggplant, and topped with aged ricotta cheese—is strongly recommended. Even the dipping sauce for the warm focaccia bread is fantastic (be sure to ask for the recipe). Though the wine list and decor could use a little work, the Italian cuisine at Mezza Luna is as *bene* as it gets. *On Hwy 1 next to the Ramada Inn on the north end of the bay; (415)712-9223; 3048 N Cabrillo Hwy, Half Moon Bay; DIS, MC, V; local checks only; lunch Mon–Sat, dinner every day; $$.⅙*

2 FOOLS CAFE AND MARKET   ☆ ☆

2 Fools prides itself on serving "clean meals," a rather silly euphemism for dishes made with organic produce and hormone-free meats. No matter: breakfast waffles are still light and crunchy, lunch salads and sandwiches are always fresh and flavorful, and dinner entrees run the gamut from buttermilk-roasted free-range chicken to organic meat loaf with shiitake mushroom gravy. All the items on the menu may be ordered to go, and an array of wines, teas, olives, jellies, and other treats made from organically grown goods are available for purchase. *On Main St near the center of town; (415)712-1222; 408 Main St, Half Moon Bay; beer and wine; MC, V; local checks only; breakfast Sat and Sun, lunch every day, dinner Tues–Sat; $$.*&

A lunchtime hot spot in Half Moon Bay is the tiny Garden Deli Cafe, a hole-in-the-wall lunch counter that cranks out huge, topnotch sandwiches on thick house-made bread. (At 356 Main Street; 415-726-3425.)

BARBARA'S FISH TRAP   ☆

 To get any closer to the ocean than Barbara's Fish Trap, you'd have to get your feet wet. Situated on stilts above the beach, Barbara's has indoor and outdoor dining with panoramic views of Half Moon Bay. The decor is classic fish 'n' chips (complete with checkered plastic tablecloths, fishnets on the ceilings, and a wooden fisherman by the door), but the food is a cut above. Barbara's offers a selection of deep-fried seafood as well as broiled items such as tangy Cajun-spiced snapper. The garlic prawns and steamed mussels are also quite good, as is the ever-important beer selection. *4 miles north of Half Moon Bay on Hwy 1, west on Capistrano Rd to Pillar Point Harbor; (415)728-7049; 281 Capistrano Rd, Princeton; beer and wine; no credit cards; checks OK; lunch, dinner every day; $$.*

SAN BENITO HOUSE   ☆

In happier times, the San Benito House—a pastel blue Victorian on Half Moon Bay's Main Street—enjoyed a solid reputation for consistently good, imaginative cooking under the direction of chef Carol Mickelsen. Nowadays, she makes infrequent visits to the kitchen and alas, it shows. The food is not always up to past standards, even though the menu still announces scads of mouth-watering choices such as mesquite grilled scallops with crayfish sauce served over wilted chard, or braised leg of lamb with caponata demiglace baked under pastry. Desserts, fortunately, are still magnificent. If you don't mind swooning in public, try the *Gioia Mía*, a chocolate tart in a pecan crust with strawberry sauce. Skip brunch. *On Main St near the center of town; (415)726-3425; 356 Main St, Half Moon Bay; full bar; AE, DC, MC, V; no checks; lunch (in the cafe only) every day, dinner (in the main restaurant only) Thurs–Sun, brunch Sun; $$.*

LODGINGS

CYPRESS INN ON MIRAMAR BEACH ☆☆☆

 With Miramar Beach literally 10 steps away, Cypress Inn is *the* place to commune with the ocean along the Peninsula coast. From each of the 12 rooms you not only see the ocean, you hear it, smell it, even feel it when the fine mist drifts in with the morning fog. The artistic, modern building—set at the end of a residential block—has beamed ceilings, skylights, terra-cotta tiles, colorful folk art, and warm, rustic furniture made of pine, heavy wicker, and leather: sort of a Santa-Fe-meets-California effect. Each room has a feather bed, private balcony, gas fireplace, private bath, and an unobstructed ocean view. Proprietors Dan Floyd and Suzie Lankes, who also own the stylish Inn at Depot Hill down in Capitola, recently added a conference room and four guest rooms with such amenities as built-in stereo systems and hidden TVs. (The older rooms don't come with televisions, but the obliging innkeepers will put one in your room if you ask.) An above-average breakfast, afternoon wine and hors d'oeuvres, and tender ministrations of the in-house masseuse (upon request) sweeten the deal. *3 miles north of the junction of Hwys 92 and 1, west on Medio to the end; (415)726-6002, (800)83-BEACH; 407 Mirada Rd, Half Moon Bay, CA 94019; AE, MC, V; checks OK; $$$.*&

MILL ROSE INN ☆☆

One of the oldest bed and breakfasts on the Peninsula coast, the Mill Rose Inn fancies itself an old-fashioned English country house, with its extravagant garden and flower boxes at the windows, plus the requisite lace curtains, antique beds, and nightstands. Romantics may love it here, but the inn's profusion of fabric flowers and slightly garish wallpapers (think William Morris on LSD) take it over the top for many folks; frankly, the overall effect is more Harlequin romance than authentic British country manor. The six spacious rooms are chock-full of creature comforts such as private entrances and baths, king- or queen-size feather beds, fireplaces (with the exception of the baroque Rose Room), televisions with cable and VCRs, well-stocked refrigerators, and access to a Jacuzzi that's tucked inside a frosted-glass gazebo (quite enjoyable on a chilly coastal evening). In the morning you'll find a newspaper outside your door and breakfast in the dining room or bedroom. *1 block west of Main St; (415)726-9794; 615 Mill St, Half Moon Bay, CA 94019; AE, DIS, MC, V; checks OK; $$$.*

PILLAR POINT INN ☆☆

 Considering the location—across from Pillar Point Harbor with its thriving fishing fleet and busy pier—this modern inn is surprisingly quiet. Cheerily reminiscent of Cape Cod, the Pillar Point Inn's 11 sunny, smallish rooms have private baths, gas fireplaces, feather beds, and televisions with VCRs. Some have private steam baths, and all but one have harbor views. Breakfast, served in the common room (or, if you prefer, taken to your room), includes coffee, juice, hot muffins, granola, and a hot dish such as waffles, scrambled eggs, or crêpes. Afternoon tea is set up by the fire in the living room or outside on the sun deck. *4 miles north of Half Moon Bay on Hwy 1, west on Capistrano Rd; (415)728-7377; 380 Capistrano Rd, Princeton, (PO Box 388, El Granada, CA 94018); AE, MC, V; checks OK; $$$.* ♿

OLD THYME INN ☆

A comfortable and informal B&B, this 1899 Victorian sits on the quieter, southern end of Half Moon Bay's Main Street. Floral wallpapers and bedspreads, period antiques, and lots of teddy bears grace the seven cozy guest rooms, each named after one of the fragrant herbs in the inn's garden. The Thyme Room has a double whirlpool tub, a fireplace, and a queen-size canopy bed. Behind the main house is a spacious detached unit, the Garden Suite, with a queen-size four-poster canopy bed, a fireplace, a double whirlpool tub under a skylight, a TV with VCR, and a refrigerator stocked with complimentary beverages. Hosts George and Marcia Dempsey are eager to please and knowledgeable about the area's attractions and restaurants. A full breakfast, served in the parlor, includes such items as Swedish egg cake, quiche, cinnamon-raisin scones, and seasonal fruit;

refreshments are also provided in the evening. *On Main St near Filbert St; (415)726-1616; 779 Main St, Half Moon Bay, CA 94019; MC, V (to hold reservations only); checks OK; $$.*

THE ZABALLA HOUSE ☆

This pale-blue Victorian, the oldest building in town, is set back from the busy street and surrounded on three sides by a colorful flower and herb garden. Homey, pretty, and unpretentious, the nine guest rooms are decorated with understated wallpaper and country furniture. Some have fireplaces, vaulted ceilings, or Jacuzzi tubs. None have telephones, but, in a bow to pressure from guests, three rooms now have TVs. Wine, hors d'oeuvres, and cookies are served in the late afternoon and evening by the fireplace in the wood-paneled living room. Come morning, guests are treated to a lavish all-you-can-eat buffet breakfast. The staff is friendly, and the prices are reasonable for this area. *North end of town on Main St; (415)726-9123; 324 Main St, Half Moon Bay, CA 94019; AE, DIS, MC, V; local checks only; $$.*

MONTARA/ MOSS BEACH

Don't take it personally if you've never heard of Montara or Moss Beach; these two neighboring towns between Pacifica and Half Moon Bay have had a long history of being discreet. During the Prohibition years, bootleggers stored their illegal wares along the hollowed-out seacliffs below and depleted them at the Moss Beach Distillery above. Today, despite the excellent selection of beaches and tide pools in the area, Montara and Moss Beach are anything but tourist towns—for shopping, dining, and such, a short drive down to Half Moon Bay is a requisite.

ACTIVITIES

 Marine Reserve. At high tide, one wonders what all the excitement is about, but come back to the James V. Fitzgerald Marine Reserve at minus low tides and wow! Thirty-five acres of tidal reef house more than 200 species of marine animals—sea anemones, urchins, snails, hermit and rock crabs, starfish, sponges—making it one of the most diverse tidal basins on the West Coast (and one of the safest, thanks to a wave-buffer-ing rock terrace 50 yards from the beach). It's okay to touch the marine life as long as you don't pick it up, but nothing—not even a rock—is available as a souvenir. Call the reserve before coming to find out about the tide and the docent-led tour schedules (tours are usually on Saturdays). No dogs are allowed, and rubber-soled shoes are recommended. Located at the west end of California Avenue off Highway 1 in Moss Beach; (415)728-3584.

 Nude Beach. Here's something you don't see often—a clothing-optional beach run by the government. Gray Whale Cove State Beach, a glorious little gold-sand beach hidden between two enormous bluffs, is located on the southern slope of Devil's Slide, 1½ miles north of the Chart House (heading south, look for the first dirt parking lot on your left). It's open 9am to sunset, costs $5 (kids free), and no cameras or binoculars permitted; (415)728-5336. Warning: Be very careful when crossing the highway on foot, as cars come screaming around the corner.

 Hiking/Biking Trail. Across from Whale Cove State Beach is McNee Ranch State Park, virtually unknown and recognizable only by the rusty yellow gate blocking the trailhead. The first part of the 3¾-mile hiking/biking trail to the top of Montara Mountain is a real lung-buster, but the reward—unsurpassed views of the entire Bay Area and beyond—makes it worth the effort; (415)726-8820.

 State Beach. About a mile south of Gray Whale Cove is Montara State Beach, a ½-mile-long cove with silky-soft sand that's superior even to Half Moon Bay's. Since this is the first free public beach that's worth a hoot heading south from San Francisco, it's often packed on summer weekends. Dogs are allowed on a leash. If the parking lot is full at the north end of the beach, try parking next to the Chart House Restaurant at the opposite end; (415)726-8820.

One of most serene, pleasant walks in the Moss Beach area is along the bluffs above the Fitzgerald Marine Preserve, which loops through a grove of century-old, wind-sculpted Monterey cypress. From the preserve's main entrance off California Avenue, walk toward the beach and you'll see the trailhead on your left.

RESTAURANTS

THE FOGLIFTER ☆☆

Don't let the Foglifter's ramshackle front patio and weather-beaten facade fool you—they're probably ruses to scare away the tourists. This tiny restaurant, awash in muted pink, sea-green, and beige prints, is a real locals' favorite, serving satisfying seafood and Italian dishes in a homey atmosphere. If the light-as-a-feather crêpe filled with scallops is listed among the appetizers, grab it—*mama mía*, that's good eating. Portions are generous, so you might not have room for dessert (which is okay, since the selections tend to be a bit heavy, with the exception of a wondrous Key lime pie). Sunday brunch features such items as seafood crêpes and the Foglifter Special—scrambled eggs mixed with onions, spinach, and ground beef. On a clear day, the view of the Pacific right across the road is an added bonus. *Hwy 1 at 8th St; (415)728-7905; 8455 Cabrillo Hwy, Montara; beer and wine; no credit cards; local checks only; dinner Tues–Sun, brunch Sun; $$.*

MOSS BEACH DISTILLERY

 For almost a century, ever since its Prohibition bootlegging days, this old stucco distillery on a cliff above Moss Beach has been a local hangout. In the '20s, silent-film stars and San Francisco politicos frequented the distillery for drinks and the bordello next door for other pastimes. Things are considerably tamer these days, although the distillery has been spicing things up lately by sponsoring rather pricey séance dinners to rouse the spirits of its resident ghost, "The Blue Lady," and her ephemeral friends. The food here is not the best on the coast—your standard overpriced seafood-and-steak fare—but it's competently prepared. Most folks come for the oysters, the pleasingly rowdy bar scene, and the fine views of the sunset. *West on Cypress Ave off Hwy 1, right on Marine Blvd, which turns into Beach St; (415)728-5595; Beach St at Ocean St, Moss Beach; full bar; AE, DC, DIS, MC, V; no checks; lunch Mon–Sat, dinner Mon–Sun, brunch Sun; $$.&*

LODGINGS

SEAL COVE INN ☆☆☆

Karen Herbert (of *Country Inns* guidebook fame) knows what makes a superior bed and breakfast, and she didn't miss a trick when she and her husband, Rick, set up their own in June of '91. The result is a gracious, sophisticated

B&B that somehow manages to harmoniously blend California, New England, and European influences in a spectacular seacoast setting. The large, vaguely English-style country manor has 10 bedrooms that look out over a colorful half-acre wildflower garden dotted with birdhouses. All the rooms have wood-burning fireplaces, fresh flowers, antique furnishings, original watercolors, grandfather clocks, hidden televisions with VCRs, and refrigerators stocked with free beverages. In the morning you'll find coffee and a newspaper outside your door; later the Herberts serve breakfast. Brandy and sherry are always available in the living room next to the fire, and at night a plate of chocolates appears beside your turned-down bed. *6 miles north of Half Moon Bay on Hwy 1, turn west on Cypress Ave; (415)728-4114; 221 Cypress Ave, Moss Beach, CA 94038; DIS, MC, V; checks OK; $$$.*&

POINT MONTARA LIGHTHOUSE HOSTEL

 Sorta funny that the only two secluded oceanfront accommodations on the entire San Francisco Peninsula are hostels, but why should the rich get all the perks? Ten to fifteen dollars buys anyone a bunk for the night at the Point Montara Lighthouse Hostel, perched right on the edge of a cliff next to a functioning lighthouse. Family and couples' rooms are available by reservation, and guests even have access to an outdoor redwood hot tub ($5 per half hour). Hot showers, modern kitchens, a cozy common room, and laundry facilities make this a real deal. *Off Hwy 1 between Montara and Moss Beach; (415)728-7177; 16th St, Hwy 1, Montara, CA 94037; MC, V; no checks; $.*&

OCEAN BEACH

When San Francisco citizens and surfers say they're going to "the beach," they're talking about Ocean Beach, which stretches for 3 straight miles from Cliff House to Fort Funston. Alas, because of the consistently chilly west winds and dangerous riptides, most beachgoers are forced to bundle up as they walk along the shoreline or ride bicycles atop the esplanade—a remnant of the early days when the beach, the Cliff House, and Playland-on-the-Beach (now a condominium complex) were all part of the city's fabled seaside resort. If the weatherman mentions a heat wave, though, you can be sure parking will be scarce along the Great Highway as the locals take advantage of a rare thing (and so should you).

ACTIVITIES

 Fort Funston. It's a sure bet most San Franciscans have never heard of Fort Funston and even fewer have been there, which, considering all the park has to offer, is their loss. Located at the south end of Ocean Beach (off Skyline Boulevard), Fort Funston has a little something to entertain everyone. Kids and equestrians? How about horse and pony rides? Dog owners? On the weekend it looks like a leash-free kennel show. Fort Funston is even one of the nation's premier hang-gliding spots: a wheelchair-accessible viewing deck has been built on the bluff so that spectators can watch the pilots run off the edge (always a nerve-rattling thrill). Combine all this with miles of easy walking trails along the dunes and down to the nearly-deserted beach and it becomes a mystery why Fort Funston is still so little-known.

 Horseback Riding. Adjacent to Fort Funston is Mar Vista Stable, a junky little boarding stable that offers guided horse rides down to and along the beach for $20 an hour. Pony rides for seven-year-olds and up are also available. The stable is located just south of the Fort along Skyline Boulevard (look for the sign on the west side of the road); (415)991-4224.

THE PRESIDIO

For more than 200 years the Presidio served as San Francisco's principal military outpost, originally commandeered for its strategic importance and later retained for its private golf course. Though the Army still occupies a few officers' homes and barracks, the majority of the 1,480-acre installation has been turned over to the Golden Gate National Recreation Area (GGNRA) and is open to visitors as part of the largest urban park in the world. Think of it as a playground for all ages, a verdant oasis-by-the-bay filled with forts, beaches, and trails that are tempting enough to lure San Francisco's joggers, bicyclists, and wind surfers out of their apartments and into the fog.

GETTING THERE

Navigating your way into, through, and out of the Presidio is almost comical. Even locals get temporarily turned around as they attempt to negotiate the maze of winding roads, dead ends, and maddening loops, so don't even attempt the journey without a map. The smartest approach is to head due west on Geary Boulevard to the end, stop by the GGNRA visitors center at the Cliff House Restaurant and gift shop, and plunk down $2.50 for "The Official Map & Guide to the Presidio." (Open daily 10am–3pm; 415-556-0865.)

Story has it a lone World War II gunner spotted a tall, thin, black shape off the waters of the bay and was convinced it was a submarine periscope. After he fired the only "shot in anger" of San Francisco's entire military arsenal, the cormorant flew away.

Museum. If there was ever a museum that was truly "fun for all ages," it's the Musée Mécanique, a glorious old trove of antique mechanical amusement machines that actually work (providing you have a pocket full of quarters). Watch the children cower in fear as Laughing "Fat Lady" Sal—of San Francisco's Playland-at-the-Beach fame—gives her infamous cackle of a greeting, or see what Grandmother the Fortune Teller has to say about your future. Most older kids congregate around the far-less-imaginative video games in back. Behind the arcade museum is Camera Obscura, a replica of Leonardo da Vinci's invention that reflects and magnifies an image of nearby Seal Rocks and Ocean Beach on a giant parabolic mirror. Both are located directly below the Cliff House Restaurant at 1090 Point Lobos Avenue; (415)386-1170.

War Memorial. Of all the war memorials within the Presidio, the most poignant is the tribute to the men of the USS *San Francisco*. Sections of the actual bridge of the warship—riddled with enormous holes from enemy gunfire—flank a series of bronze plaques depicting the sad, heroic story of the 107 men lost in one of the fiercest close-quarter battles in naval history. (At the end of El Camino del Mar, one block up from the Cliff House.)

Why blow a fortune on a mediocre lunch or dinner at the Cliff House Restaurant when you can enjoy the same magnificent ocean view from the fireside cocktail lounge at Phineas T. Barnacle (or PTB as they call it) next door? A small, inexpensive, buffet-style deli takes care of the appetite, while the full bar helps recharge your batteries.

GOLDEN GATE BRIDGE BY THE NUMBERS

Total length: 8,981 feet
Span: 6,450 feet
Cost: $35 million
Completion date: May 28, 1937
Date paid in full: July, 1971
Engineer: Joseph B. Strauss
Road height: 260 feet
Tower height: 746 feet
Swing span: 27 feet
Deepest foundation: 110 feet under water
Cable thickness: 36 ½ inches
Cable length: 7,650 feet
Steel used: 83,000 pounds
Concrete used: 389,000 cubic yards
Miles of wire cable: 80,000
Gallons of paint annually: 10,000
Color: international orange
Rise, in cold weather: 5 feet
Drop, in hot weather: 10 feet
Traffic: 3 million vehicles per month
Toll: $3 (southbound only)

 Historical Site. The Cliff House's glory days may be gone for good, but business is still booming thanks to the busloads of tourists who pass through daily to see the adjacent Sutro Bath ruins, San Francisco's version of the Acropolis. All that remains of the illustrious 3-acre spa is its ugly concrete foundation, but that's apparently good enough for the tour companies. Time better spent is at the Sutro Bath photo exhibit at the visitors center below the Cliff House Restaurant, followed by a short walk to the charming—and practically deserted—Sutro Park across the street: the 200-degree view of the coast from atop the castle-like garden wall is outstanding.

Secret Overlook. Here's a little-known spot to escape the crowds, explore the rusty gun batteries, and revel in an amazing bay view: From Lincoln Road at the northwest end of the Presidio, turn west on Langdon Court, swing left around the cinder block building, and there it is—the Fort Scott overlook, home of one the best views on the California coast and the perfect launching point for the magnificent 1½-mile Coastal Trail, which curves along the Presidio's bluffs.

 Presidio Tours. To inquire about a wide array of free guided tours of Presidio highlights—everything from bike rides to pier crabbing and cemetery walks—call (415)556-0865. The top tour pick is Fort Point, where park rangers clad in authentic Civil War garb play soldier, loading and firing a smoothbore cannon from within the pre–Civil War brick fortress (open Wednesday–Sunday, 10am–5pm). After the tour, take a bayside walk along the Golden Gate Promenade, the most popular and scenic jogging route in the city. The 4-mile path, which starts (or ends) at Fort Point, leads past the windsurfers off Crissy Field, around the Yacht Harbor, and along the Marina Green toward Fort Mason and Aquatic Park.

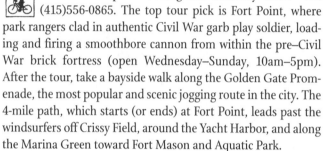 *A Walk on the Windy Side.* There are certain things everyone should do at least once in their life, and one of those is to walk across the world-famous Golden Gate Bridge. Simply driving across won't work; to feel the bridge swaying under your feet as you peer 260 feet down to certain death—now that's living. It's a 1¼ mile stroll across and takes about an hour round-trip. Pedestrians and bicyclists must use the path on the east side of the bridge, which is open daily from 5am to 9pm (bicyclists have to use the west side on weekends). Free parking is available at both ends of the bridge, but the lots are usually full on summer weekends. Dress warmly or you'll be sorry.

China Beach, at the end of Seacliff Avenue off El Camino del Mar in the well-to-do neighborhood of Seacliff, is the only safe swimming beach in San Francisco (that is, when the water's warm enough) aside from Aquatic Park on the bay. Great for kids.

THE
MARIN
COAST

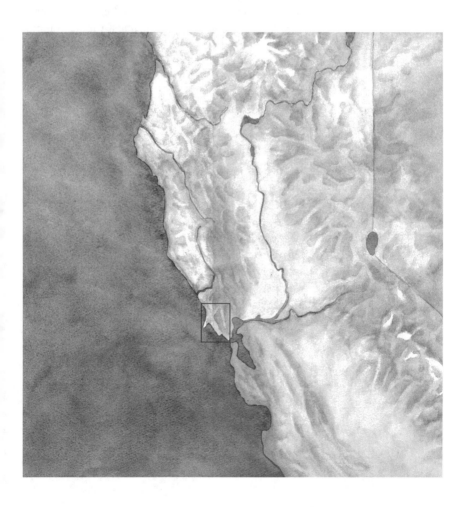

THE MARIN COAST

A south-to-north sweep of the Marin County coastline, beginning at the Marin Headlands and ending at Dillon Beach just north of Point Reyes.

When you consider that the San Francisco Bay Area has more people than the entire state of Oregon, and that Marin County has the highest per capita income in the nation, you would expect its coastline to be lined with gated communities and fancy resorts. Truth is, you won't find even a Motel 6 along the entire Marin coast, due partly to public pressure but mostly to the inaccessibly rugged, heavily forested terrain (it may *look* like a 15-minute drive from San Francisco on the map, but 90 minutes later you'll probably still be negotiating hairpin curves down the side of Mount Tamalpais). The only downside to the Marin coast's underdevelopment is the scarcity of affordable lodgings; expensive B&Bs reign supreme, which is fine if you don't mind blowing $125 a night for a bed and bagel. Otherwise, the Marin coast is just short of Eden, a veritable organic playground for city-weary nine-to-fivers in search of a patch of green or square of sand to call their own for a day.

THE MARIN HEADLANDS

On a sunny San Francisco day, there's no better place to spend time outdoors than the Marin headlands. For more than a century following the Civil War, this vast expanse of grass-covered hills and rocky shore was off-limits to the public, appropriated by the U.S. Army as a strategic base for defending the Bay against invaders. Remnants of obsolete and untested defenses—dozens of thick concrete bunkers and batteries recessed into the bluffs—now serve as playground and picnic sites for the millions of tourists who visit each year.

While there's a wealth of scheduled activities offered daily within the 15-square-mile Golden Gate National Recreation Area—birding clinics, bunker tours, wildflower hunts, geology hikes—most visitors are satisfied with poking their heads into a bunker or two, snapping a photo of the city, and driving home. For a more thorough approach, buy the handy $1.50 "Marin Headlands Map and Guide to Sites, Trails and Wildlife," at the headlands' Information Center at Fort Barry (follow the signs), and plan your day from there. Free hiking, mountain biking, and pets-permitted trail maps are available, too. (Open daily 9:30am–4:30pm; 415-331-1540. Dress warm.)

GETTING THERE

To reach the Marin headlands, head north across the Golden Gate Bridge, take the Alexander Avenue exit, and make your first left onto cliff-hugging Conzelman Road, which climbs high above the Bay—with magnificent views of the bridge and city—before ending at Point Bonita 5 miles west. Easy, huh? Getting back to the city, though, is a little trickier because of the one-way roads. Heading east on Bunker Road, either turn right on McCullough Road to get back to Conzelman Road, or continue on Bunker Road through the tunnel and back onto Highway 101. For a spectacular scenic route out of the headlands, turn left immediately after exiting the tunnel. The road will take you through East Fort Baker, past the pier, underneath the Golden Gate Bridge, and back on Highway 101 toward San Francisco.

Call (415)331-1540 for a current schedule of the free ranger-led walks through the Marin headlands; topics range from bird-watching to wildflowers and war relics. Then again, why walk? Tennessee Valley Miwok Stables offers interpretive guided horseback rides to nearby Muir Beach and various headland highlights; (415)383-8040.

ACTIVITIES

Mammal Center. A popular attraction at the Marin headlands is the Marine Mammal Center, a volunteer-run hospital for injured and abandoned mammals-of-the-sea. It's virtually impossible not to melt at the sight of the cute little baby seals as they lie in their caged pens (the center's staff, being no dummies, take donations right on the spot). Signs list each animal's adopted name, species, stranding site, and injury—the latter of which is usually human-caused. (Open daily 10am–4:30pm. Located at the east end of Fort Cronkhite near Rodeo Lagoon; 415-289-SEAL.)

Lighthouse. Closed to the public for the last three years due to storm damage, the precariously perched 1877 Point Bonita lighthouse is once again thrilling those tourists who are brave enough to traverse the long, dark tunnel and seven small footbridges leading to the beacon (the story goes that, because the cliffs along the passageway are so steep, one 19th century lighthouse keeper rigged ropes around his children to prevent them from slipping into the raging water below). The reward for such bravery is, among other things, a rare and sensational view of the entrance to the bay. Call for specific tour times, and be sure to inquire about the full-moon tours, which take place once a month by reservation only; 415-331-1540.

 As the World Terns. To witness the teeming sea and bird life—puffins, albatrosses, terns, whales, dolphins, seals, sea lions, and more—that congregates on and around the distant Farallon Islands, call the nonprofit Oceanic Society Expeditions at (415)474-3385 and reserve a space on its 63-foot boat. The exceptional tour, which lasts eight or nine hours, departs from the Fort Mason area in San Francisco's Marina district at 8:30am on Saturdays, Sundays, and occasional Fridays.

 Bird-watching. Within the Marin headlands is Hawk Hill, one of the most remarkable avian sites in the western United States and the biggest hawk lookout in western North America. Record count in 1992 was more than 20,000 birds, including 21 species of hawks. The best time to visit is during September and October, when thousands of birds of prey soar over the hill each day. (Located above Battery 129, where Conzelman Road becomes one-way.)

LODGINGS

MARIN HEADLANDS HOSTEL

Formerly known as the Golden Gate Hostel, the Marin Headlands Hostel is the only public lodging on the headlands. The converted army hospital—shaded under a canopy of eucalyptus trees—holds 66 bunks, a huge clean-up-your-own-mess kitchen, and large common room with TV, VCR, and other distractions. In 1995, the hostel acquired the adjacent commander's home, a plush 37-bed spread with Oriental carpets, two kitchens, and four carved-oak fireplaces (obviously, this is the place you want to request first). Bunks are a mere $11 a night, and hostel-association membership is not required. BYO food because there are no restaurants or stores within the headlands. *200 yards southeast of the visitors center; (415)331-2777, (800)444-6111; Fort Barry, Bldg 941, Sausalito, CA 94965; DIS, MC, V; no checks.*&

MUIR WOODS/ MUIR BEACH

"This is the best tree-lover's monument that could possibly be found in all the forests of the world."
—John Muir on Muir Woods

When you stand in the middle of Muir Woods, surrounded by a canopy of ancient redwoods towering hundreds of feet skyward, it's hard to fathom that San Francisco is less than 6 miles away. It's like walking into a den of wooden giants: tourists speak in hushed tones as they crane their necks in disbelief, snapping photographs that don't begin to capture the immensity of these living titans.

Although Muir Woods can get absurdly crowded on summer weekends, you can usually circumvent the masses by hiking up the Ocean View Trail and returning via Fern Creek Trail. Admission is free, but a donation box is prominently displayed to stroke your conscience. Picnicking is not allowed, but there is a snack bar and gift shop at the entrance. It's typically a cool, damp environment, so dress appropriately. (Open 8am–sunset. Located at the end of Muir Woods Road off the Panoramic Highway; from Highway 101 in Sausalito, take the Stinson Beach/ Highway 1 exit and head west; 415-388-2595.)

The average age of Muir Woods' redwoods ranges from 400 to 800 years old, though one old-timer is believed to have been around for 12 centuries.

ACTIVITIES

Beach. Three miles west of Muir Woods, along Highway 1, is a small crescent-shaped cove called Muir Beach. Strewn with bits of driftwood and numerous tide pools, Muir Beach is a more sedate alternative to the beer-'n'-bikini crowds at the ever-popular Stinson Beach up north. If all you're looking for is a sandy, quiet place for some R&R, you may want to park the car right here and skip the trip to Stinson altogether (swimming, however, isn't allowed at Muir Beach because of the strong rip currents).

RESTAURANTS

THE PELICAN INN   ☆ ☆

One of the better ways to spend a Sunday afternoon in the Bay Area is to take a leisurely drive to this homey little English pub, grab a table at the glassed-in patio or by the fireplace, and gorge yourself proper on a steaming shepherd's pie. Rack of lamb, prime rib, and a few meatless dishes are also on the menu, and in the bar you'll find a goodly number of British, Irish, and Scottish beers on tap. After lunch, burn a few calories with a stroll down Muir Beach. *Off Hwy 1 at the entrance to Muir Beach; (415)383-6000; 10 Pacific Way, Muir Beach; beer and wine; MC, V; no checks; breakfast (guests only) every day, lunch, dinner Tues–Sun (and Mon if it's a holiday); $$.*

LODGINGS

THE PELICAN INN ☆☆

Romantic intentions of a homesick expatriate led to the creation of this 16th-century English Tudor country inn, and by God if it isn't filled with convivial dart-playing chaps chugging pints of bitter as lovebirds snuggle in front of the hearth's glowing fire. The inn, named after Sir Francis Drake's ship the *Pelican*, has seven small yet cozy rooms that are decked with canopy beds, lead-glass windows, heavy brocade curtains, and English antiques (the top pick is room 3 with its authentic Half-Tester bed). There's also a "snug" (i.e., common room) for lounging by the fire or playing the piano. In the morning, guests are treated to an authentic English breakfast of bangers and eggs, toast and marmalade, and—but of course—tea. *Off Hwy 1 at the entrance to Muir Beach; (415)383-6000; 10 Pacific Way, Muir Beach, CA 94965; beer and wine; MC, V; no checks; $$.*

GREEN GULCH FARM ZEN CENTER

When was the last time your bodhisattva spirit—the spirit of kindness—had a vacation? Green Gulch Farm, a Soto Zen practice center hidden in a lush, verdant valley near Muir Beach, offers fantastically priced "guest practice retreats" for those interested in learning the art of Zen meditation. If you participate in the retreat, there's a minimum three-night stay (Sunday through Thursday only), and you are expected to attend *early*-morning meditations (read: 5am), then work until noon, usually in the organic gardens. After that, you're on your own to wander down to Muir Beach, hike through Muir Woods or on the trails surrounding Green Gulch, participate in classes on Buddhism, or do whatever else your karma desires. Rates are an enlightening $30 per person per day ($50 for double occupancy), *including* three squares a day. You may also stay here on a nightly basis without participating in any of the center's programs, but it will cost about twice as much. *Off Hwy 1, a few miles west of the Muir Woods turnoff; (415)383-3134; 1601 Hwy 1, Sausalito, CA 94965; no credit cards; checks OK; $.&*

STINSON BEACH

On those treasured weekend days when the fog has lifted and the sun is scorching the Northern California coast, blurry-eyed Bay Area residents grab their morning paper and beach chairs, pile into their cars, and scramble to the sandy shores of Stinson Beach—the North Coast's nice-try answer to the fabled beaches of Southern California.

Stinson Beach is one of Northern California's most popular beaches, a 3½-mile stretch of beige sand that offers enough elbow room for everyone to spread out beach blankets, picnic baskets, and toys. Although swimming is allowed and lifeguards are on hand from May to mid-September, notices about riptides (not to mention the sea's toe-numbing temperatures and the threat of sharks) tend to discourage folks from venturing too far into the water. Joined at the hip with *la playa* is the town of Stinson Beach, which does a brisk summer business serving lunch alfresco at the numerous cafes.

"Responsible woman seeks peace and tranquillity at Stinson. Looking for a small cottage or special place to call home. Will pay up to $900 a month."—From the message board at Stinson Beach Books.

ACTIVITIES

The Merchant of Venice Beach. Ol' Billy would have been proud to see the turnout at Stinson Beach's *Shakespeare at the Beach*, which is packed to the partitions every weekend with sold-out crowds. The new 125-seat outdoor theater is a real charmer, encircled on all sides by 20-foot walls with grass for flooring and plastic lawn chairs for seats. The elevated stage, though, is the real thing, complete with faux balconies, arched entrances, and a raked stage. The theater is located next to the Stinson Beach Post Office at Highway 1 and Calle del Mar. Show times are Friday at 7pm and Saturday and Sunday at 6pm, May through October, and tickets ($15 for adults, $12 for kids under 18) are available in advance by calling (415)868-9500. Dress warmly, bring a blanket, and hiss only when appropriate.

"Nine hundred dollars sounds about right, though I remember when you could rent a place around here for fifty bucks a month."—Stinson Beach Fire Chief and longtime resident Kendrick Rand, when asked about escalating property values.

So, you remembered the beach chair but forgot your sloppy romance novel. Stinson Beach Books, located on the main strip in the center of town, can supply your literary fix. Good selection of children's books and toys, too; (415)868-0700.

For recorded weather and surf conditions at Stinson Beach call (415)868-1922.

GETTING THERE

Stinson Beach is located right off Highway 1 at the base of Mount Tamalpais in Marin County, 10 miles from San Francisco as the crow flies but a winding 20 miles as the wheel turns. To reach the beach from the Bay Area, take the Stinson Beach/Highway 1 exit off Highway 101 just north of Sausalito and follow Highway 1 all the way to the shore. A few miles before you reach the ocean, there's a fork in the road (the Muir Woods turnoff) that allows wimpy drivers to avoid the thrilling cliff-side drive along Highway 1 by taking an inland detour along Panoramic Highway, which isn't as scenic as its name suggests but dumps you right into town.

Kayaking. Scott Tye, a kayak instructor for Off the Beach Boats in downtown Stinson Beach, offers two-hour lessons on the basics of sea kayaking. Rentals are surprisingly cheap ($25 for 4 hours), and they even rent a kayak that can hold an entire nuclear family. Call (415)868-9445 or drop by the shop at 15 Calle del Mar next to the Stinson Beach post office.

Wildlife Sanctuary. A short drive north of Stinson Beach on Highway 1 leads to Bolinas Lagoon, a placid saltwater expanse that serves as refuge for numerous shorebirds and harbor seals hauled-out on the sandbars. Across from the lagoon is the Audubon Canyon Ranch's Bolinas Lagoon Preserve, a 1,014-acre wildlife sanctuary that supports a major heronry of great blue herons. This is the premier spot along the Pacific Coast to watch the immense, graceful seabirds as they court, mate, and rear their young, all accomplished on the tops of towering redwoods. Admission is free, though donations are requested. (Open mid-March to mid-July on Saturday, Sunday, and holidays, 10am–4pm, and by appointment for groups. 4900 Highway 1, Stinson Beach; 415-868-9244.)

RESTAURANTS

THE PARKSIDE CAFE ☆

During the day this popular neighborhood cafe bustles with locals and Bay Area beachgoers who stop for an inexpensive breakfast or lunch before shoving off to Stinson Beach around the corner. Morning favorites are the omelets, blueberry pancakes, and the not-to-be-missed raisin-walnut bread. For lunch there are basics like burgers, grilled sandwiches, and soups, as well as a few daily specials. Once the beach crowd departs, chef Candido Di Terlizzi starts preparing the evening menu, which includes a wide variety of Italian dishes ranging from lamb chops and veal scallops to mussel linguine, seafood pizza, and baked eggplant. On sunny days dine alfresco on the brick patio; otherwise, cozy up to the fire. For a quick bite to go, the cafe's snack bar sells great burgers, fries, and shakes daily March through September, and on weekends October through February. *Off Calle del Mar in downtown Stinson Beach; (415)868-1272; 43 Arenal Ave, Stinson Beach; beer and wine; MC, V; local checks only; breakfast, lunch every day, dinner Thurs–Mon; $.*

LODGINGS

CASA DEL MAR ☆☆☆

 After stints as a lawyer and fisherman, proprietor Rick Klein jumped headfirst into the B&B business by designing, building, and running the Casa del Mar, a beautiful Mediterranean-style haven that overlooks Stinson Beach. Each of the six sun-drenched rooms has large windows (with views of Mount Tamalpais, the ocean, or the spectacular terraced garden), French doors that open onto a private balcony, and a private bath. The spartan but comfortable furnishings include a few cushy chairs and a platform bed topped with a down comforter and piles of pillows. Fresh flowers and whimsical artwork by local artists brighten the rooms while the sound of the ocean provides the ambience. Breakfast features an ever-changing array of wonders such as black-bean, scallion, and ginger-root pancakes or three-egg omelets with fresh sugar peas. *Heading north into Stinson Beach, turn right at the fire station; (415)868-2124, (800)552-2124; 37 Belvedere Ave, PO Box 238, Stinson Beach, CA 94970; AE, MC, V; checks OK if mailed 2 weeks in advance; $$$.*

STINSON BEACH MOTEL ☆

If you can't afford the Casa del Mar, try this place. The Stinson Beach Motel has six small rooms in a cute little garden setting, each individually decorated with aging yet homelike

About a mile south of Stinson Beach off Highway 1 is Red Rock Beach, one of the few nude beaches on the Marin coast. It's easy to miss since you can't see it from the road: park at the first dirt pull-off on your right after leaving Stinson Beach and look for a steep trail leading down to the beach.

"Just call me Dino," an immediately likable Stinson Beach local, offers guaranteed-you'll-get-up surfing lessons for one to three persons. The price—$100 for two hours including board and wet suit—weeds out the weenies; (415)868-1607.

furnishings and private baths. Prices range from about $60 for a studio to less than $90 for a small apartment that sleeps up to four (a steal, given the prime location in downtown Stinson Beach). Try to reserve room 7, which is separated from the rest and offers the most privacy. *At the south end of town near the fire station; (415)868-1712; 3416 Hwy 1, PO Box 64, Stinson Beach, CA 94970; MC, V; checks OK; $$.*

STEEP RAVINE ENVIRONMENTAL CABINS

 How much would you expect to pay for a night in a romantic oceanside cabin with its own small, secluded beach? $200? $300? Try 30 bucks. Once the private getaway of powerful Bay Area politicians (who lost their long-term leases in a battle with the state, poor dears), this cluster of small cabins is now available to those lucky enough to snag a reservation and who don't mind bringing their own sleeping bag and pad. Platform beds, running water, woodburning stoves, and outhouses are provided, but there is no electricity, and firewood costs an extra $4. Each cabin sleeps up to five, and whether you plan to go solo or bring four friends, the low per-night rate stays the same (though only one car per cabin is allowed). *Off Hwy 1, a mile south of Stinson Beach (look for a paved turnout and a brown metal sign); reservations required (taken up to 8 weeks in advance); call Destinet at (800)444-7275; V, MC; checks OK; $.*

BOLINAS

A sort of retirement community for aging rock stars, spent novelists, and former hippies, Bolinas is one of the most reclusive towns in Northern California. Residents regularly take down highway signs pointing the way to their rural enclave, an act that, ironically, has created more publicity for Bolinas than any road sign ever did. As a tourist, you don't have to worry about being chased out of town by a band of machete-wielding Bolinistas, but don't expect anyone to roll out the welcome mat, either. The trick is to not *look* like a tourist, but more like a Bay Arean who's only here to buy some peaches at the People's Store.

ACTIVITIES

 Organic Market. There couldn't be a better antithesis to the corporate supermarket mentality than the Bolinas People's Store, a town landmark that's famous for its locally grown organic produce (don't confuse it with the much larger general store down the street). It's a little hard to find, hidden at the end of a gravel driveway next to the Bolinas Bakery, but it's worth searching out just to see (and taste) the difference between Safeway and the Bolinas way. (Open 8:30am–6:30pm daily; 415-868-1433).

Tidepooling, Bird-watching, & Hiking. Three side trips near Bolinas offer some adventurous exercise. Just before entering downtown Bolinas, turn right (or west) on Mesa Road, left on Overlook Road, and right on Elm Road and you'll dead-end at the Duxbury Reef Nature Reserve, a rocky outcropping with numerous tide pools harboring a healthy population of starfish, sea anemones, snails, sea urchins, and other creatures that kids go gaga over. If you continue west on Mesa Road, you'll reach the Point Reyes Bird Observatory, where ornithologists keep an eye on more than 400 feathered species. Admission to the visitors center and nature trail is free, and visitors are welcome to observe the tricky process of catching and banding the birds. (Open daily 7am–5pm. Banding occurs daily 7:30am–noon; 415-868-0655.) At the very end of Mesa Road is the Palomarin Trailhead, a popular hiking trail that leads into the south entrance of Point Reyes National Seashore. The 6-mile round-trip trek—one of Point Reyes' prettiest hikes—passes several small lakes and meadows before it reaches Alamere Falls, a freshwater stream that cascades down a 40-foot bluff onto Wildcat Beach.

LODGINGS

THOMAS' WHITE HOUSE INN ☆☆

 This inn is Bolinas personified—charming, offbeat (e.g., the bathroom doubles as an aviary), and surrounded by incredible vistas. From the immense and beautifully landscaped front lawn—worth the room rate alone just to lounge on—

The Bolinas Bay Bakery & Cafe in downtown Bolinas is renowned for its cinnamon buns made with organic flour.

Smiley's Schooner Saloon in Bolinas has live music— anything from jazz to country, blues, or rock— every Friday and Saturday night, but be prepared to shell out $7 for the cover charge.

you get a sweeping view of the Bay Area coastline from Marin to Half Moon Bay. There are only two guest rooms, both located upstairs and decked out with cathedral ceilings and window seats that are ideal for gazing out at the sea. The larger room has a more rustic feel with old pine furnishings and an antique steam trunk, while the smaller room is done in softer tones with lace and white wicker. In the morning owner Jackie Thomas serves a simple continental breakfast. *Call for directions; (415)868-0279; 118 Kale Rd, PO Box 132, Bolinas, CA 94924; no credit cards; checks OK; $$.*

POINT REYES

Think of Point Reyes as Mother Nature's version of Disneyland, a sort of outdoor-lover's playground with one doozy of a sandbox. Hiking, biking, swimming, sailing, windsurfing, sunbathing, camping, fishing, horseback riding, bird-watching, kayaking: all are fair game at this 71,000-acre sanctuary of forested hills, deep-green pastures, and undisturbed beaches. Point Reyes is hardly a secret anymore—millions of visitors arrive each year—but the land is so vast and varied that finding your own space is never a problem (like the old saying goes, if you want to be alone, walk up).

There are four towns in and around the Point Reyes National Seashore boundary—Olema, Point Reyes Station, Inverness Park, and Inverness—but they are all so close together that it really doesn't matter where you stay, because you'll always be within a stone's throw of the park. While the selections of lodging in Point Reyes is excellent, it's also expensive, with most rooms averaging $100 per night. Be sure to make your reservation far in advance during the summer and holidays, and dress warm: Point Reyes gets darn chilly at night.

The Point Reyes Bird Observatory is one of the few full-time ornithological research stations in the United States.

ACTIVITIES

Point Reyes Station is also known as "Mootown," due to its noontime cow siren.

Lighthouse. On the westernmost tip of Point Reyes at the end of Sir Francis Drake Highway is the Point Reyes Lighthouse, the park's most popular attraction. Even if you loathe lighthouse tours, go anyway: the drive alone is worth the trip, a 45-minute scenic excursion through windswept meadows

For recorded
information on
daily weather
and special
activities at Point
Reyes National
Seashore, call
(415)663-9029.

GETTING THERE

Point Reyes is only 30 miles northwest of San Francisco, but it takes at least 90 minutes to reach by car (it's all the small towns, not the topography, that slows you down). The easiest route is via Sir Francis Drake Boulevard from Highway 101 south of San Rafael; it takes its bloody time getting to Point Reyes, but does so without any detours. A much longer but more scenic route: take the Stinson Beach/Highway 1 exit off Highway 101 just south of Sausalito and follow Highway 1 north. As soon as you arrive at Point Reyes, stop at the Bear Valley Visitors Center on Bear Valley Road (look for the small sign posted just north of Olema on Highway 1) and pick up a free Point Reyes trail map. (Open weekdays 9am–5pm and weekends 8am–5pm; 415-663-1092.)

Winds at the Point Reyes Lighthouse have reached up to 133mph, the highest wind speed recorded on the Pacific coast.

and working dairy ranches (watch out for cows on the road). When the fog burns off, the lighthouse and the headlands provide a fantastic lookout point for spying gray whales and thousands of common mures that inundate the rocks below. Visitors have free access to the lighthouse via a thigh-burning 308-step staircase. (Open 10am–4:30pm, Thursday–Monday, weather permitting; 415-669-1534.)

Drakes Estero, the large saltwater lagoon within the Point Reyes peninsula, produces nearly 20 percent of California's commercial oyster yield.

Oyster Farm. That mighty pungent aroma you smell on the way to the Point Reyes Lighthouse is probably emanating from Johnson's Oyster Farm. It may not look like much— a cluster of trailer homes, shacks, and oyster tanks surrounded by huge piles of oyster shells—but that certainly doesn't detract from the taste of fresh-out-of-the-water oysters dipped in Johnson's special sauce. Eat 'em on the spot, or buy a bag for the road; either way, you're not likely to find California oysters as fresh or as cheap anywhere else. (Open 8am–4pm daily except Monday; located off Sir Francis Drake Boulevard about 6 miles west of Inverness; 415-669-1149.)

Kayaking Tomales Bay. If the best things in life are free, then the next-to-best things must be in the $45 range, which is about how much money you'll need to rent a sea kayak from the friendly folks at Tomales Bay Kayaking. Don't worry, the kayaks are very stable and there are no waves to contend with

A great way to
spend an
afternoon in
Point Reyes is
browsing through
the boutiques,
galleries,
bookstores,
bakeries, antique
stores, and
saloons along
the main strip
in Point Reyes
Station.

POINT REYES TOP PICKS

**Limantour Beach for bird-watching, swimming, and
  dog-walking.**

Kehoe Beach during spring wildflower blooms.

**Bear Valley Trail for an easy, beautiful walk through the
  woods to the beach.**

**Hearts Desire Beach at Tomales Bay for kids, warmer water,
  and the safest swimming ($3 fee).**

Palomarin Trailhead for prettiest hike.

McClures Beach for tidepooling and solitude.

Stewart Trail for serious mountain biking.

Estero Trail for casual mountain biking.

**Drakes Beach for swimming, beach fires, and lunch at the
  small cafe.**

*Every third
Saturday in July,
Native American
basket makers,
wood- and stone-
carvers, singers,
and dancers
convene at Point
Reyes for an
annual public
celebration at Kule
Loklo, an authentic
reconstruction of
a village of the
indigenous Miwak
Indian tribe.*

because you'll be paddling through placid Tomales Bay, a haven
for migrating birds and marine mammals. Rental prices start at
about $45 for a half-day ($65 for a double-hulled kayak), and you
can sign up for a guided day trip, a sunset cruise, or a romantic
full-moon outing. Instruction, clinics, and boat delivery are
available, and all ages and levels are welcome. The launching
point is located on Highway 1 at the Marshall Boatworks in
Marshall, 8 miles north of Point Reyes Station. (Open
Friday–Sunday, 9am–6pm, and by appointment. For more information, call 415-663-1743.)

Mountain Biking. As most ardent Bay Area mountain
bikers know, Point Reyes National Seashore has some of
the finest mountain-bike trails in the region—narrow dirt paths
winding through densely forested knolls and ending with spectacular ocean views. A trail map is a must (available for free at the
Bear Valley Visitors Center) since many of the park trails are off-
limits to bikes. If you didn't bring your own rig, you can rent a
mountain bike at Bear Valley Inn and Rental Shop, located at the
intersection of Bear Valley Road and Highway 1 in Olema;
(415)663-1958.

RESTAURANTS

MANKA'S INVERNESS LODGE ☆☆☆

Half the fun of dining at Manka's is waiting for your table. Sit in the lobby's plush high-backed chairs, warm your toes by the small wood-burning fireplace, and watch in fascination as one of the cooks kneels beside you to grill the house-made wild boar sausages over the fire: it's like being in a freaking Jack London novel. To complement the hunting lodge illusion, Manka's serves "unusual game, local line-caught fish, oysters pulled from the bay, and bounteous greens from down the road and over the hill." Appetizers range from grilled California quail with wild mushroom sauce to fire-roasted figs with black pepper syrup. And the entrees? How about pan-seared elk tenderloin, black buck antelope chops with sweet corn salsa, and wild Canadian pheasant with mashed potatoes? The divine desserts—such as the cinnamon-croissant pudding with warm caramel sauce—are made from scratch, and the wine list is longer than the drive to get here. *On Argyle St off Sir Francis Drake Blvd, 3 blocks north of downtown Inverness; (415)669-1034, (800)58-LODGE; PO Box 1110, Inverness; beer and wine; MC, V; checks OK; dinner Thurs–Mon, brunch Sun; $$$.*

THE STATION HOUSE CAFE ☆☆

For more than two decades the Station House has been a favorite stop for West Marin residents and San Francisco day trippers. The menu changes weekly, but you can count on chef Denis Bold to work daily wonders with local produce, seafood, and organic beef from Niman-Schell Farms. Though most tables have a view of the open kitchen, the best seats are outside in the shaded garden area, particularly for breakfast. On summer days barbecued oysters are often served on the patio. *In the center of town; (415)663-1515; 11180 Main St, Point Reyes Station; full bar; DIS, MC, V; local checks only; breakfast, lunch, dinner every day; $$.*&

POINT REYES ROADHOUSE & OYSTER BAR ☆

Good for a lunch break is Point Reyes Station's latest roadside attraction, the Roadhouse & Oyster Bar. First choose from a wide selection of microbrews on tap or local wines by the glass, then order one of the daily lunch specials such as

Short on lunch money? The Gray Whale cafe in downtown Inverness serves all kind of salads, sandwiches, pastas, and pizzas for only $6. (Open daily; 415-669-1244.)

If you're having trouble finding a vacancy in Point Reyes, call the West Marin Network at (415)663-9543 for information on available lodgings.

POINT REYES ABLAZE

In the early afternoon of October 3, 1995, an unattended and illegal campfire sparked a blaze that destroyed 12,000 acres within the Point Reyes National Seashore. The numbers are staggering: $40 million in damage, including 45 homes destroyed; 2,164 firefighters recruited (some from as far as Oregon) at a cost of $4 million; and 75 percent of hiking trails ruined. The good news is that about 80 percent of the park was left untouched, and that most of the burn area will shortly be covered with a profusion of wildflowers. Rangers predict that there will be no loss in visitor traffic, and are making the best of the situation by turning the burned portion of the park into a classroom on forest regeneration.

barbecued short ribs or beef stroganoff. Regular menu items like burgers, salads, sandwiches, and barbecued oysters are also safe bets. Top things off with a chocolate malt and you'll be ready to roll. *On Hwy 1 at the south end of town; (415)663-1277; Hwy 1, Point Reyes Station; beer and wine; AE, MC, V; no checks; lunch, dinner every day (call in winter); $.&*

TAQUERIA LA QUINTA ☆

Mexican folk music fills the air and bright colors abound at this exuberant restaurant, where nothing on the menu costs more than *seis dólares*. La Quinta (Spanish for "the country house") offers a large selection of Mexican-American standards, as well as vegetarian dishes and weekend seafood specials. The service is fast, the food is fresh, the salsa is *muy caliente*. *At 3rd and Main Sts; (415)663-8868; 11285 Hwy 1, Point Reyes Station; beer only; no credit cards; checks OK; lunch, dinner Wed–Mon; $.*

VLADIMIR'S CZECH RESTAURANT ☆

The first thing you're likely to notice when you walk into the dark, wood-paneled dining room is an old guy neatly dressed in traditional Czech attire. This is Vladimir Nevl, who since 1960 has been entertaining guests with his war stories as they boldly sample the chicken paprikash, Moravian cabbage roll, beef tongue, klobasa, and Hungarian goulash—all of which come with dumplings. On weekends the place tends to feel like a tourist trap and the service can be lackadaisical, but hey, when you gotta have beef tongue, you gotta have it. *In downtown Inverness; (415)669-1021; 12785 Sir Francis Drake Blvd, Inverness; full bar; no credit cards; checks OK; lunch Wed–Sun, dinner Tues–Sun; $$.*&

LODGINGS

MANKA'S INVERNESS LODGE ☆☆☆☆

What a difference a Grade makes. For years Manka's was a mediocre Czech restaurant, but when Margaret Grade and family took over in 1989, things changed. This former hunting and fishing lodge soon became one of the most romantic places to stay in California, as well a wonderful place to eat (see Restaurants, above). The four guest rooms upstairs look as though they came out of a Hans Christian Andersen fairy tale—small and cozy, with tree-limb bedsteads, down comforters, high ceilings, and old-fashioned bathrooms; rooms 1 and 2 extend out to large private decks overlooking Tomales Bay, perfect for a sunrise breakfast. Manka's also offers four handsome rooms in its Redwood Annex, and two spacious one-bedroom cabins with living rooms and kitchenettes. For the ultimate romantic—or family—retreat, reserve Chicken Ranch, a private 19th-century hunting cabin protected by the wary eye of Duke, Manka's "guard" pony. Friendly, refreshingly unpretentious, and surprisingly affordable (special midweek rates start at about $65), Manka's Inverness Lodge is *the* idyllic weekend getaway. *On Argyle St (off Sir Francis Drake Blvd, 3 blocks north of downtown Inverness); (415)669-1034, (800)58-LODGE; PO Box 1110, Inverness, CA 94937; AE, MC, V; checks OK; $$$.*

BLACKTHORNE INN ☆☆☆

With its four levels, five rooms, multiple decks, spiral staircase, skybridge, and fire pole, the Blackthorne Inn is more like a tree house for grown-ups than a B&B. The octagonal Eagle's Nest, perched on the top level, has its own sun deck and a 360-degree view of the forest (the bath, however, is located across the skybridge—something of a nuisance on blustery nights); the spacious Forest View and Hideaway rooms, which share a bath, have sitting areas facing the woods; and the outdoor treetop-level hot tub offers a great view of the stars. A country buffet breakfast is included,

Before Manka's owner Margaret Grade came to Point Reyes, she was a neuropsychologist specializing in AIDS-related brain research at UC San Francisco. She happened upon Manka's while looking for a second home and couldn't resist the place when she discovered it was for sale.

Inverness' Czech-heavy population stems from a 1930s shipwreck in San Francisco Bay—several of the Czech deckhands jumped ship and settled here.

served on the upper deck when the sun's out. *Off Sir Francis Drake Blvd, ¼ mile up Vallejo Ave; (415)663-8621; 266 Vallejo Ave, PO Box 712, Inverness Park, CA 94937; MC, V; checks OK; $$$.*

DANCING COYOTE BEACH ☆☆☆

The local Miwok Indians called falling stars "dancing coyotes"—something to ponder as you stare at the heavens through the skylit sleeping lofts of this bayside bed and breakfast. Hidden in a pine-covered cove and within easy walking distance of downtown Inverness, each of the four adjoining natural-wood cottages is painted in pale Southwestern pastels and equipped with simple furniture, private decks, fireplaces, and full kitchens. The Beach Cottage, with its small upper deck overlooking Tomales Bay, should be your first choice; Acacia Cottage, which gets a fair amount of traffic noise, should be your last. The private lawn, beach, and sun deck are perfect spots for settling down with a good book. *Just north of downtown Inverness; (415)669-7200; 12794 Sir Francis Drake Blvd, PO Box 98, Inverness, CA 94937; no credit cards; checks OK; $$.*

HOLLY TREE INN ☆☆☆

Hidden in a 19-acre valley with a meandering creek and wooded hillsides is the blissfully quiet Holly Tree Inn. The family-owned B&B has four cozy guest rooms, each with a private bath (one with a fireplace) and decorated with Laura Ashley prints and country antiques. The large, airy living room has a fireplace and comfortable chairs where guests converse over a bottle of wine. If privacy is what you're after, tucked in a far corner of the estate is the Cottage-in-the-Woods, a two-room honeymooners' hideaway with a small fireplace, a king-size bed, and an old-fashioned bathtub from which you can gaze upon the garden. Families should inquire about the separate Sea Star Cottage—built on stilts over Tomales Bay—and Vision Cottage. In the morning enjoy a bountiful country breakfast. *Off Bear Valley Rd; (415)663-1554; 3 Silverhills Rd, PO Box 642, Point Reyes Station, CA 94956; AE, MC, V; checks OK; $$$.*

TEN INVERNESS WAY ☆☆☆

Follow the curving flagstone stairway through the garden and under the wisteria-laced entryway to this three-story Inverness bed and breakfast. Inside you'll find a fir-paneled living room with inviting couches facing a huge stone fireplace, and five warm, comfortable guest rooms equipped with plush chairs, hooked rugs, patchwork quilts, and private baths. The best room is the Garden Suite: separated from the others by an entire floor, it has its own sitting room, kitchen, and private patio. Innkeeper Mary Davies' banana-buttermilk-buckwheat pancakes, chicken-apple sausages, and fresh fruit will fortify you for a long day of hiking in the hills. When you return, soak your sore muscles in the garden hot tub. *Off Sir Francis Drake Blvd in Inverness; (415)669-1648; 10 Inverness Way, PO Box 63, Inverness, CA 94937; MC, V; checks OK; $$$.*

The block-long town of Olema marks the epicenter of the 1906 earthquake that devastated San Francisco.

POINT REYES SEASHORE LODGE ☆☆

For folks who want the beauty of the countryside combined with the creature comforts of the city, this is the place. Built in 1988, the three-story cedar inn has 21 guest rooms, most of which offer a fireplace, telephone, down comforter, whirlpool bath, and a view of the exquisite garden. If price is no object, opt for one of the two-story suites with a sleeping loft, refrigerator, and the perk of having breakfast delivered to your room. One note of caution: the lodge is located on Highway 1, next to a restaurant that does a brisk (read noisy) business. For peace and quiet, ask for a room in the north wing, or reserve the Casa Olema Retreat, a detached cottage that sleeps up to six and has a hot tub with room for eight. A continental breakfast, included in the nightly rate, is served in the lodge's common room. *At Sir Francis Drake Blvd and Hwy 1; (415)663-9000, (800)404-LODG; 10021 Hwy 1, PO Box 39, Olema, CA 94950; AE, DIS, MC, V; checks OK; $$$.&*

"Over six million people a year come to Point Reyes National Seashore. Only four million go to Yosemite. Believe that, eh?"—Mike Nelson, owner, Olema Ranch Restaurant

BEAR VALLEY INN ☆

Ron and JoAnne Nowell's pleasant (and reasonably priced) bed and breakfast is an ideal base for exploring Point Reyes. The two-story Victorian, built in 1899, has three guest rooms—the Rose Room is the quietest—and a shared bath. After breakfast, ask Ron for tips on where to bicycle in the area (he also runs the mountain-bike rental shop next door). When you return from your day of exploring, plop yourself into one of the overstuffed chairs and relax in front of the old wood stove. *At the intersection of Hwy 1 and Bear Valley Rd; (415)663-1777; 88 Bear Valley Rd, Olema, CA 94950; AE, MC, V; checks OK; $$.*

HIGH HOUSE ■ HELEN'S HOUSE ☆

Just above Tomales Bay State Park in a remote wooded area is one of the most . . . *unusual* lodgings along the coast: High House. Resting on steel stilts at a height normally reserved for the birds, this glass-walled '60s-era studio—perched among the pines of Point Reyes—is a one-of-a-kind retreat best suited for couples who don't suffer from acrophobia or vertigo. Below the High House is Helen's House, a homey two-bedroom cottage that sleeps up to six. While it lacks the exhilarating ambience of High House, it features a comfortable living room with a large stone fireplace and an expansive view of the woods and bay. *Off Sir Francis Drake Blvd, north of Inverness; (707)431-2331; 1208 Pierce Point Rd, Inverness, CA 94937 (PO Box 2003 Healdsburg, CA 95448); no credit cards; checks OK; $$.*

KNOB HILL ☆

Built atop a small bluff that overlooks Point Reyes Mesa is horse trainer Janet Schlitt's stable-side cottage. Perfect for couples and horse owners, it comes with a stereo, woodburning stove, and private deck. A continental breakfast is served in the morning, and the trailhead to Tomales Bay is right down the street. There's also a second room attached to Janet's house that is quite small yet comes with a private bath, entrance, and garden area for only $50 to $60 a night. Riding lessons are also available. *From Highway 1 north of Point Reyes Station turn west on Viento Way; (415)663-1784; 40 Knob Hill Rd, PO Box 1108, Point Reyes Station, CA 94956; no credit cards; checks OK; $$.*

POINT REYES HOSTEL

Slightly singed by the '95 wildfire, this popular hostel—isolated deep inside Point Reyes National Seashore—has 45 dormitory-style accommodations, including one room that's reserved for families. There are also two common rooms, each warmed by wood-burning stoves during chilly nights, as well as a fully equipped kitchen, barbecue, and patio. If you don't mind sharing your sleeping quarters with strangers, this is a $10-per-person deal that can't be beat. Reservations (and earplugs) are strongly recommended. Reception hours are 7:30–9:30am and 4:30–9:30pm daily. *Off Limantour Rd; (415)663-8811; PO Box 247, Point Reyes Station, CA 94956; no credit cards; no checks; $.&*

TOMALES

Most people don't even know the town of Tomales exists, which is just fine with the handful of people who live here. Comprising not much more than a general store, two churches, and a superb little bakery, the tiny ranching community looks pretty much the same it did a hundred years ago, which gives you an idea of the pace around here. It's in a prime location, though—only 30 minutes' drive from Point Reyes National Seashore, yet far enough away to avoid the traffic and commotion.

In 1927, 20-by-100-foot lots along Tomales Bay were offered for $69.50 to each new subscriber of the San Francisco Bulletin.

ACTIVITES

Coastal Drive. One of the most scenic drives on the Marin coast is along Dillon Beach Road from Tomales. The 4-mile drive passes through windswept meadows with wonderful vistas of Tomales Bay, Point Reyes, and the Pacific before ending at the privately owned Dillon Beach campground. For a proper grand finale to the drive, turn right on Oceana Drive in Dillon Beach and continue to a vacant cul-de-sac. On a clear day you can see all the way to Bodega Bay.

If you're cruising along Highway 1 toward Tomales and happen to see a guy sweating over a huge metal grill in front of Tony's Seafood Restaurant, pull over—barbecued oysters don't get any better.

Oyster Farm. Since 1909, the Tomales Bay Oyster Company has been selling its wares right off the shore at 15479 Highway 1 just south of Marshall. Sizes range from bite-size cocktails to big ol' hunkin' cowboys and are sold by the dozen or in sacks of 100, should you be feeling randy enough. Those in the know bring their own knife, lemons, cocktail sauce, and even bags of charcoal for the nearby barbecue pits. (Open daily 9am–5pm; 415-663-1242.)

LODGINGS

TOMALES COUNTRY INN   ☆☆

Owned for years by artist Byron Randall, this turn-of-the-century redwood house used to be an inexpensive, funky, serve-yourself kind of place, where the keys to the building were left outside and you could help yourself to the kitchen. The inn's ownership changed hands in 1989, when San Francisco's KQED public-broadcasting manager Jo Anne Wallace and NPR reporter John McChesney bought the place, spiffed it up, and renamed it Tomales Country Inn. While the B&B retains some of its past eccentricity by preserving much of the former owner's artwork (Randall, by the way, lives in a neighboring cottage), the serve-yourself days are over. Now innkeeper Laura Hoffman is there to greet you, show you to your room, and serve fresh-baked breads, fruit, granola, juices, and strong coffee in the morning. Of the inn's five guest rooms, the best are the two large first-floor units with private baths, and the romantic attic garret on the third floor (although you have to share the second-floor bathroom). You'll often find brainy and interesting fellow guests here, the sort you're likely to enjoy chatting with over breakfast or beside the fireplace. *From Hwy 1 in central Tomales head west on Dillon Beach Rd and turn left on Valley St; (707)878-2041; 25 Valley St, PO Box 376, Tomales, CA 94971; no credit cards; checks OK; $$.*

U.S. HOTEL ☆

With nothing more to go by than a photograph of the original inn—which burned down in 1920—the owners of the U.S. Hotel built it from the ground up in 1989. The result? This place is so evocative of a bygone era that you could film a Western here and never need a set decorator. The pleasingly plain interiors are a welcome alternative to the typical lace-and-patchwork B&B decor: each of the immaculate rooms has high ceilings, a private bath, and simple yet attractive faux-antique furnishings. While the staff could be a bit more accommodating, the reasonable room rates—which include a self-serve continental breakfast—more than compensate. *In the center of Tomales; (707)878-2742; 26985 Hwy 1, Tomales, CA 94971; MC, V; no checks; $$.*

THE
SONOMA
COAST

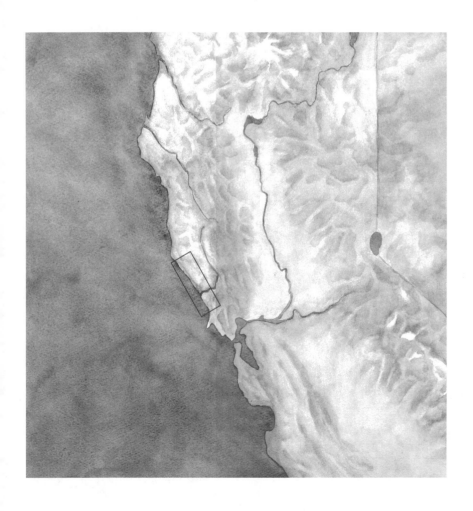

THE SONOMA COAST

A south-to-north sweep of the Sonoma County coastline, beginning at Bodega Bay and ending at Gualala.

Mention Sonoma and everyone's immediate association is "wine country." What few Californians seem to know, however, is that Sonoma County gerrymanders a hefty chunk of the coast as well—more than 50 miles of mostly undeveloped shoreline from Bodega Bay to Gualala. And judging from the mostly vacant state parks and beaches, even fewer Californians seem to know what a good thing they're missing as they migrate lemming-like to Mendocino or Carmel. The Sonoma coast isn't for everyone, though; there's little in the way of shopping, sightseeing, and such. It's more of a place where inlanders return annually to bury themselves in a book, wiggle their toes in the sand, and forget about work for a while.

BODEGA BAY

When it comes to a selection of fancy restaurants, accommodations, and boutiques, Bodega Bay has a long way to go. As it

GETTING THERE

No matter which direction you're coming from, getting to Bodega Bay is a rather long haul; there are no fast, direct routes leading to this oceanside town. If you're approaching from the San Francisco area, the fastest (and most scenic) route is via Petaluma. From Highway 101, take the East Washington Street/Central Petaluma exit and turn west toward the town. After a straight shot though the center of Petaluma, you'll spend about 45 minutes on a pleasant drive through the rolling green hills before reaching the bay. Note: Don't make the common mistake of taking the Bodega turnoff onto Bodega Highway. Bodega and Bodega Bay are two different towns.

As you roll into Bodega Bay, keep an eye out for the Bodega Bay Area Chamber of Commerce, located in the center of the town at 850 Highway 1. Load up on free maps, guides, and brochures, including the "Bodega Bay Area Map & Guide," which gives the exact locations of all the town's attractions; (707)875-3422.

stands, there is only one three-star lodge and restaurant, and the town's most venerable store sells taffy and kites. Which is odd, considering Bodega Bay is only a few hours' drive from the Bay Area—a good *two to three* hours closer than Mendocino—and has all the beautiful scenery and golden beaches you could possibly hope for. Even 15 minutes of international fame as the setting for Alfred Hitchcock's *The Birds* hasn't changed things much. Spend a few hours meandering through town and it becomes apparent that Bodega Bay is, for the most part, still just a working-class fishing town—the sort of place where most people start their day before dawn mending nets, rigging fishing poles, and talking shop. But if all you want to do this weekend is breathe in some salty air and couldn't care less about Gucci boutiques and dancing till dawn, come to Bodega Bay—ain't much here, which is precisely the point.

ACTIVITIES

Walking Trails. Bodega Head, the small peninsula that shelters Bodega Bay, has two superb walking trails that follow the ocean. The first, a 4-mile round-trip trail, starts from the Head's west parking lot, leads past the Bodega Bay Marine Laboratory, and ends at the sand dunes of Salmon Creek Beach. An easier, 1½-mile round-trip walk begins in the east parking lot and encircles the edge of Bodega Head, branching off for an optional side trip to the tip of the point for a spectacular 360-degree view. From December through April, Bodega Head also doubles as one of the premier whale-watching points along the California coast. (From downtown Bodega Bay, turn west on Eastshore Road, then turn right at the stop sign onto Bay Flat Road and follow it to the end.)

Gone Fishing. A great way to spend a lazy afternoon in Bodega Bay is at the docks, watching the rusty fishing boats unload their catches. Tides Wharf, located at 835 Highway 1 in Bodega Bay, has the most active dock scene, including a viewing room near the processing plant that allows you to witness the fish's ultimate fate—a swift and merciless gutting by deft hands, followed by a quick burial in ice. Just outside, sea lions linger by the dock hoping for a handout; (707)875-3652.

Fun of a Beach. Linking Bodega Bay and the nearby town of Jenner are the Sonoma Coast State Beaches, 16 miles of pristine sand and gravel beaches, tide pools, rocky bluffs, hiking trails, and one heck of a gorgeous drive along Highway 1. While all the beaches are pretty much the same—divine—the safest for kids is Doran Park Beach, located just south of Bodega Bay. When the water's rough everywhere else, Doran is still calm enough for swimming, clamming, and crabbing (an added bonus: the adjacent Doran mud flats, a favorite haunt of egrets, big-billed pelicans, and other seabirds). Tide pool trekkers will want to head to the north end of Salmon Creek Beach (off Bean Avenue, 2 miles north of town), or Shell Beach, a small low-tide treasure trove 10 miles north of Bodega Bay near Jenner. If all you want to do is get horizontal in the sand, deciding which of the 14 beaches along Highway 1 looks the best will drive you nuts; just pick one and park.

Hitchcock's Bodega. Worth half an hour of any Hitchcock fan's day is a quick trip to the town of Bodega, located a few miles southeast of Bodega Bay off Highway 1. The attraction is a bird's-eye view of the hauntingly familiar Potter School House and St. Teresa's Church, both immortalized in Hitchcock's *The Birds*, which was filmed here in 1961. The two or three boutiques in downtown Bodega manage to entice a few visitors to park and browse, but most people seem content with a little rubbernecking and finger-pointing as they flip U-turns through the tiny town.

 Fishy-Suave. If you've never been ocean fishing, be forewarned that it is an extremely complicated four-step process: (1) get on the fishing boat; (2) grab a pre-rigged fishing pole; (3) lower your line in the water when everyone else does; and (4) reel in the fish. Everything else, from taking the fish off the hook to cleaning it, is taken care of by the friendly deckhands, which makes deep-sea fishing pretty much idiot proof. On the fish-and-crab combination trips (even more fun than the regular fishing trips), you get to keep your catch as well as a few of the enormous Dungeness crabs caught in the traps set out on the way to the fishing grounds. Both the fishing and fish-crab combo trips cost approximately $45 to $55 per person (rod-and-reel rental is an additional $7.50), and almost everyone takes home a gunnysack full of seafood. For information and reservations, call the Bodega Bay Sportfishing Center at (707)875-3344.

 Clamming. How often do you have a legitimate, legal excuse to get down and dirty on a public beach? Well, as long as you're on the hunt for a sack of fresh clams, you can do it year-round at Bodega Bay. The only skill required is digging, the only equipment is a shovel and a sturdy bag. The rest is childishly straightforward: find a good spot (hint: try the western side of Bodega Bay); wait for low tide; search the sand closest to the water for a small, bubbling siphon hole; then dig like heck with whatever's handy (a narrow clammer's shovel works best). What you'll discover is a long "neck" leading to a horseneck clam, the most abundant type of clam in Bodega Bay. A fishing license is required for anyone over 16 (one-day licenses are available at most sporting-goods stores and bait shops).

 Whalewatching. Sure, spotting gray whales from shore is exciting, but nothing compares to getting within *listening* distance of the 40-ton cetaceans, so close you can actually hear the blast of the blowholes. From late December through April several of Bodega Bay's fishing charters offer whale-watching trips, one of the best being on Captain George's 55-foot *Challenger* (707-875-2474). The typical charge is about $16 per person and trips last about three hours (or seemingly forever if you get seasick, so bring Dramamine).

 Fisherman's Festival. For a festive time in Bodega Bay, visit in April, when as many as 25,000 partiers tip their shucks and bottles at the annual Fisherman's Festival, a two-day orgy of lamb and oyster barbecues, Sonoma County wine tastings, craft fairs, pony rides, bathtub races, parades, kite-flying contests, live music, and dancing. The festival highlight is the Blessing of the Fleet, a colorful, jubilant boat parade in which clergymen stand on a vessel and bless the fishing fleet as it floats by. For more information, call the Bodega Bay Chamber of Commerce at (707)875-3422.

The only golf game in town—open to the public every day of the year—is the Bodega Harbor Golf Links, a championship 18-hole Scottish-style course designed by Robert Trent Jones Jr. and situated near the Bodega Bay Lodge. Call (707)875-3538 for starting times.

RESTAURANTS

THE DUCK CLUB   ☆☆☆

 Bodega Bay sure took its sweet time coaxing a four-star chef to the coast, but now that Jeff Reilly (formerly the executive chef at Lafayette Park) is in town, gastronomes up and down the coast are coming to the Bodega Bay Lodge to sample his wares. "Sonoma County Cuisine" best describes Reilly's penchant for local yields, with creations such as roasted Petaluma duck with Valencia orange sauce or a Sonoma farm-fresh asparagus strudel bathed in a mild curry sauce. *Le poisson de jour*, of course, comes straight from the docks down the street. Large windows overlooking the bay beg for window seating, so be sure to request that when making the required reservations. *At the south end of Bodega Bay; (707)875-3525; 103 Hwy 1, Bodega Bay; AE, DC, DIS, MC, V; no checks; breakfast, dinner every day; $$$.&*

LUCAS WHARF RESTAURANT AND BAR ■
LUCAS WHARF DELI   ☆

 Few tourists come to Bodega Bay for the food, as you'll soon discover if you spend more than a day here. There are only two seafood restaurants in town, Tides Wharf and Lucas Wharf, and both do little to excite the palate. Yes, the fish is fresh off the boats, but the preparations are basic and uninspired. The petrale sole *doré* is served with lemon butter. The red snapper filet is served with lemon butter. And the grilled ling cod? You guessed it: lemon butter. Folks must think the Lucas Wharf Restaurant whips up some pretty darn good lemon butter, though, because the place is always packed (as is the Tides Wharf, which is slightly more expensive and significantly less appealing). Your best bet is to skip both restaurants and go next door to Lucas Wharf Deli, pick up a $5 pint of crab cioppino or big ol' basket of fresh fish 'n' chips and make a picnic of it on the dock. *At the south end of Bodega Bay; 595 Hwy 1, Bodega Bay; Restaurant: (707)875-3522; full bar; DIS, MC, V; checks OK; lunch, dinner every day; $$.& Deli: (707)875-3562; beer and wine; DIS, MC, V; checks OK; lunch, early dinner every day; $.&*

BREAKERS CAFE   ☆

If you're not exactly crazy about lemon-buttered seafood
and can't afford the Duck Club, Bodega Bay's Breakers Cafe
is the answer. For breakfast, park your fanny among the
numerous plants in the sun-filled dining room and feast on
the yummy Belgian waffles topped with hot spiced peaches
and whipped cream. Lunch is mostly sandwiches, burgers,
and house-made soups, and dinner items range from fresh
seafood to chicken, pasta, and low-fat vegetarian dishes. *In
the Pelican Plaza at the north end of Bodega Bay; (707)875-
2513); 1400 Hwy 1, Bodega Bay; beer and wine; MC, V; local
checks only; breakfast, lunch, dinner every day.*&

LODGINGS

BODEGA BAY LODGE   ☆☆☆

 Granted, the competition isn't very fierce, but it's safe to say
that the Bodega Bay Lodge is the Sonoma coast's finest
accommodation. It's the view that clinches it: all 78
rooms—recently remodeled in handsome hues of cardinal
and forest green with wood-burning fireplaces and stocked
mini-bars—have private balconies with a wonderful
panorama of Bodega Bay and the bird-filled wetlands.
Should you ever leave your balcony, a short walk through
the elaborate flower gardens leads to an outdoor fieldstone
spa and heated pool overlooking the bay. A fitness center,
sauna, and complimentary morning newspaper are also
part of the package, as is free use of the lodge's bicycles. More
proof of Bodega Bay Lodge's top standing is its recent opening of the Duck Club Restaurant (see Restaurants above),
easily the Sonoma coast's best. *At the south end of Bodega
Bay; (707)875-3525, (800)368-2468; 103 Highway 1, Bodega
Bay, CA 94923; AE, DC, DIS, MC, V; checks OK; $$$.*&

INN AT THE TIDES   ☆☆

In Bodega Bay, the architectural style of most structures is
nouveau Californian—wood-shingled boxes with lots of
glass—and the Inn at the Tides is no exception. Perched on
a hillside overlooking Bodega Bay, it includes 86 units, all
with bay views, spacious interiors, and contemporary (albeit

dated contemporary) decor, and all with the usual amenities of an expensive resort: terrycloth robes, cable TV, refrigerators, fresh flowers, continental breakfasts, and access to the indoor/outdoor pool, sauna, and Jacuzzis. A few of the rooms have king-size beds and fireplaces. The inn's Bay View Restaurant serves expensive though unimpressive California cuisine. *Across from the Tides Wharf; (707)875-2751, (800)-541-7788; 800 Hwy 1, PO Box 640, Bodega Bay, CA 94923; full bar; AE, MC, V; checks OK; dinner Wed–Sun; $$$.&*

BODEGA HARBOR INN ☆

A homey old-timer in a town of mostly modern accommodations, the Bodega Harbor Inn consists of four clapboard buildings (with a total of 14 guest rooms) set on a large lawn overlooking the harbor. The rooms are small but tidy, with private baths, cable TV, double beds, and access to a private yard where you can kick back in the lawn chairs. If you're willing to shell out about $10 more, ask for room 12 or 14 and you'll get a partial ocean view and a small deck. The inn also rents seven houses and cottages, including the three-bedroom, two-bath Spyglass home that's located on the Bodega Harbor Golf Links and overlooks the ocean. *Off Hwy 1 at the north end of town; (707)875-3594; 1345 Bodega Ave, PO Box 161, Bodega Bay, CA 94923; MC, V; checks OK; $$.&*

JENNER

As you head north from Jenner on Highway 1, keep an eye open for the new wheelchair-accessible Sonoma Coast State Beach Vista Trail, a paved 1-mile loop trail on a bluff overlooking the ocean. On a clear day you can see all the way to Point Reyes.

About 16 miles north of Bodega Bay on Highway 1 is what seems to be every Northern Californian's "secret" getaway spot: Jenner. Built on a bluff rising from the mouth of the Russian River, the tiny seaside town consists of little more than a gas station, three restaurants, two inns, and a deli, which means the only thing to do in town is eat, sleep, and lie on the beach—not a bad vacation plan. Perhaps Jenner's best attraction, however, is its location: two hours closer than Mendocino to the Bay Area, yet with the same spectacular coastal scenery and a far better selection of beaches.

ACTIVITIES

 Seal Watching. One of the major highlights of the Jenner area is beautiful Goat Rock Beach, a popular breeding ground for harbor seals. Pupping season begins in March and lasts until June, and orange-vested volunteers are usually on

GETTING THERE

The most direct route to Jenner is via Highway 116, from the 116 turnoff on Highway 101 between Petaluma and Santa Rosa. A far, far more enjoyable route, however, starts in Petaluma, passes through Bodega Bay, and winds along a gorgeous stretch of Highway 1 before crossing the Russian River into Jenner (see "Getting There" in the Bodega Bay chapter).

About 3 miles north of Fort Ross is one of Ansel Adams' favorite places to photograph, Timber Cove.

hand to protect the seals (they give birth on land) from dogs, answer questions about the playful animals, and even lend out binoculars for a closer look.

  Russian Fort. A sinuous 12-mile drive north of Jenner on Highway 1 takes you to the mildly interesting Fort Ross State Historic Park, a semi-restored redwood fortress built by Russian fur traders in 1812. Plan to spend about an hour here should you decide to cough up the $5 parking fee, starting with a short history lesson at the million-dollar visitors center and finishing with a walk down to the cove and beach; (707)847-3286.

Story has it John Sutter of Gold Rush fame agreed to purchase Fort Ross from the Russians for $30,000. He stripped it of equipment and furnishings to improve his own fort in Sacramento, yet never paid a nickel toward the balance.

 Salt Point State Park. A great daytrip from Jenner is the scenic drive along Highway 101 to Salt Point State Park. There's all kinds of things to do here, including skin diving and tidepooling off rocky beaches, hiking through coastal woodlands' wildflower meadows, and poking around the 3,500-acre park for wild berries and mushrooms—simply pull the car over anywhere along Highway 1 and start walking. At the north end of the park on Kruse Ranch Road is the 317-acre Kruse Rhododendron Preserve, a forested grove of wild pink and purple flowers that grow up to 18 feet tall in the shade of a vast canopy of redwoods. Peak blooming time varies yearly, but April is usually the best time to see the world's tallest *Rhododendron californicum*; (707)847-3221.

RESTAURANTS

RIVER'S END ☆☆

Don't bother looking around for a better restaurant or bar in the area; for more than 20 years owner-chef Wolfgang

The entire coastal community contributed funds and materials to help sculptor Benny Bufano create the North Coast's towering monument to Peace. Erected in 1969 and completed shortly before his death, the 8-story totemlike statue is located a short walk seaward from the Timber Cove Lodge parking lot on Highway 1.

Gramatzki's oceanside establishment has been the local favorite. Who'd have guessed you could order roasted baby pheasant in tiny Jenner? Rum-roasted saddle of pork, a $53 rack of lamb for two, and straight-off-the-boat fish specials give you an idea of what to expect for dinner. Lunch is more down to earth: a burger with fries is under $6. Most tables have a wonderful view of the ocean, as does the small outside deck—the perfect spot for an apres-lunch glass of Sonoma County wine. *Just north of Jenner on Hwy 1; (707)865-2484; Hwy 1, Jenner; full bar; MC, V; no checks; lunch, dinner every day, June–Sept, call ahead other months; $$$.&*

SIZZLING TANDOOR ☆

 On a warm, sunny day you won't find a better place on the Sonoma Coast for lunch than the Sizzling Tandoor, an Indian restaurant perched high above the placid Russian River. The view, particularly from the outside patio, is fantastic, as are the inexpensive lunch specials—huge portions of curries and kabobs served with vegetables, soup, *pulao* rice, and superb *naan* (bread). Even if you don't have time for a meal, drop by and order some warm *naan* to go. *At the south end of the Russian River Bridge, south of Jenner; 707)865-0625; 9960 Hwy 1, Jenner; beer and wine; AE, MC, V; no checks; breakfast, lunch, dinner every day; $.&*

LODGINGS

MURPHY'S JENNER INN ☆

 When people say they stayed at the cutest little place in Jenner, they're talking about Murphy's Jenner Inn. There are only 13 guest rooms, each dispersed within a cluster of seven cottages and houses perched above the Russian River or the ocean. Most of the houses have been subdivided into suites that are rented out individually, and all have private baths, separate entrances, and antique and wicker furnishings; many units also have kitchens, fireplaces, hot tubs, and private decks or porches. The rose-covered Rosewater Cottage sits right beside the Russian River estuary and is warmed by a stone fireplace (or the king-sized bed). The adorable Pelican Suite is a honeymooners' favorite, with big bay windows overlooking the water. An extended continental breakfast, served in the main lodge, is included in the room rate, which ranges from $75 to $175 per night. In addition to the bed-and-breakfast accommodations, the inn rents out six private vacation homes located along the river, within Jenner Canyon, or overlooking the ocean. *1 mile north of the Hwy 116/Hwy 1 junction in downtown Jenner; (707)865-2377, (800)732-2377; 10400 Hwy 1, PO Box 69, Jenner, CA 95450; AE, MC, V; checks OK; $$.&*

THE
MENDOCINO
COAST

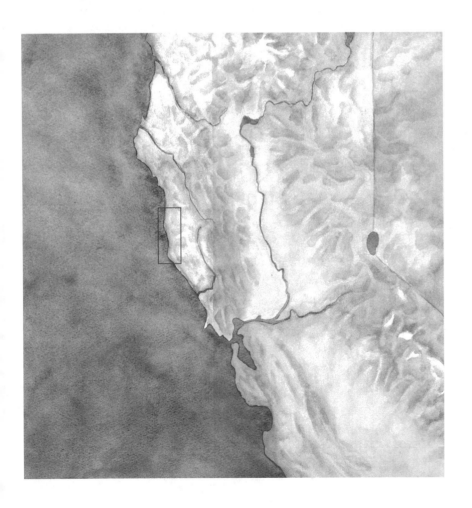

THE MENDOCINO COAST

A south-to-north sweep of the Mendocino County coastline, beginning at Gualala and ending at Westport.

There are four things first-time visitors should know before heading to the Mendocino coast. First, be prepared for a long, beautiful drive; there are no quick and easy routes to this part of the California coast, and there's no public transportation, so traveling by car is your only option. Second, make your hotel and restaurant reservations as far in advance as possible because everything involving tourism books up solid during summers and holidays. Third, bring warm clothing. You might as well forget about packing only shorts and T-shirts—regardless of how broiling it is everywhere else—because a windless, sunny, 80° day on the Mendocino coast is about as rare as affordable real estate. Fourth and finally, bring lotsa money and your checkbook. Cheap sleeps, eats, and even banks are few and far between along this stretch of shoreline, and many places don't take credit cards (though personal checks are widely accepted).

So where exactly is the Mendocino coast? Well, it starts at the county line in Gualala and ends a hundred or so miles north at the sparsely populated stretch known as the Lost Coast. The focal point is, of course, the town of Mendocino, but the main center of commerce—and the area's *only* McDonalds, if you can believe it—is in Fort Bragg, 15 miles up the coast. Compared to these two towns, every other part of the Mendocino coast is relatively deserted—something to consider if you're looking to escape the masses.

Spring is the best time to visit, when the wildflowers are in full bloom and the crowds are still sparse. Then again, nothing on this planet is more romantic than cuddling next to the fireplace on a winter night, listening to the rain and thunder pound against your little cottage as you watch the waves crash against the cliffs, so don't rule out a trip in the colder months, either. Actually, when you get down to it, any time you have a few days off is a good enough excuse to pack your bags and head for the coast, and remind yourself why you don't live in Idaho.

GUALALA

The southernmost town in Mendocino County, Gualala also happens to have the most mispronounced name in Mendocino County. Keep the G soft and you end up with "wah-LAL-ah," the

GETTING THERE

Since Greyhound has shut down all routes to the Mendocino coast and the closest Amtrack route is 40 miles inland, the only way to get here is by car or by chartering a private plane. There are six routes into Mendocino from Highway 101; the most popular and scenic is the freshly paved stretch of Highway 128 starting from Cloverdale, which passes through a gorgeous redwood forest before dumping you onto Highway 1 a few miles south of Mendocino. Slightly faster but far less stimulating is the Highway 20 link between Willits and Fort Bragg. A somewhat secret, rarely used route starts at the north end of Ukiah at Orr Springs Road and ends as the Comptche-Ukiah Road right outside Mendocino, a sneaky alternative if you're bored of Highway 128 or 20. The last two options—entering via Highway 1 from the north at Leggett or from the south at Jenner (via 116)—should be considered all-day adventures.

Story has it Gualala's original spelling was Walalla until the federal postal bureau decided to dephoneticize the town's moniker to its proper Spanish version.

Spanish version of *walali*, which is Pomo Indian patois for "water coming down place." The water in question is the nearby Gualala River, a placid year-round playground for kayakers, canoers, and swimmers.

Once an industrious, lively logging town, Gualala has tamed considerably since the days when loggers would literally climb the saloon walls with their spiked boots. Though a few real-life suspender-wearing lumberjacks still end their day at the Gualala Hotel's saloon, the coastal town's main function these days is providing gas, groceries, and hardware for area residents. On the outskirts, however, are several excellent parks, beaches, and hiking trails; combine this with the region's glorious seascapes, and suddenly poor little mispronounced Gualala emerges as a serious contender among the better vacation spots on the North Coast.

ACTIVITIES

Kayaking. One of the most enjoyable, healthy, and rewarding activities on the California coast is river and sea kayaking. It's the ultimate form of escapism, effortlessly paddling your safe, silent, and unsinkable craft anywhere you please, sneaking up on river otters and great blue herons. Placid Gualala River is ideal for beginner kayakers, and either Adventure Rents (707-884-4FUN) or Gualala Kayak (707-884-4705) will transport single and two-person kayaks to and from the river and provide all the necessary gear and instruction. (Adventure Rents also carries canoes, rafts, inflatable kayaks, and on- or off-road and tandem bicycles.) You don't need any experience for river kayaking, and all ages are encouraged, so why not give it a try?

 Scottish-style Links. Open to the public, the award-winning Sea Ranch Golf Links is a challenging Scottish-style course designed by Robert Muir Graves. Originally built as a 9-hole oceanside course, the Links will expand to a full 18 holes by August 1996. It's located along the Sea Ranch's northern boundary at the entrance to Gualala Point Regional Park. Open daily; (707)785-2468.

 Best Beach Access. Of the six public beach access points along Highway 1 between the south end of Sea Ranch and Gualala, the one that offers the most bang for the parking-fee buck is the 195-acre Gualala Point Regional Park. The park has 10 miles of trails through coastal grasslands, redwood forests, and river canyons, as well as picnic sites, camping areas, and excellent bird and whale watching along the mostly deserted beaches; (707)785-2377.

RESTAURANTS

ST. ORRES RESTAURANT ☆☆☆

In addition to St. Orres' fantastic accommodations (see Lodgings, below) the St. Orres Restaurant is one of Gualala's star attractions, and one of the main reasons people keep coming back to this region. Reserve a table for dinner when you make your room reservation; breakfast comes with the room, but dinner doesn't, and the restaurant is almost always booked. The constantly changing prix-fixe dinner menu focuses on wild game: dishes range anywhere from wild turkey tamales to tequila-marinated quail or sautéed medallions of venison. Self-taught chef Rosemary Campiformio's dark and fruity sauces and sublime soups are perfectly suited to the flavorful game, a distinctly Northern California rendition of French country cuisine. St. Orres' wine cellar stores a sizable selection of California wines. *2 miles north of Gualala on the east side of Hwy 1; (707)884-3335; 36601 Hwy 1, Gualala; MC,V for hotel guests only, otherwise no credit cards; checks OK; breakfast (guests only) every day, dinner every day; $$$.&*

THE OLD MILANO HOTEL RESTAURANT ☆☆

If you can get over the odd feeling that you're dining in somebody's former living room (which you are), you're bound to enjoy a candlelight dinner in the Old Milano's small, wood-paneled, Victorian dining room. Chef Madeleine Jordon stuffs her guests with tantalizing entrees such as spice-crusted rack of Sonoma spring lamb, herb-marinated tiger prawns, and a wonderful eggplant chèvre tart. Come early and spend some time basking on the sun porch overlooking the ocean. *Just north of the Food Company, ³/₄ mile north of Gualala; (707)884-3256; 38300 Hwy 1, Gualala; beer and wine; no credit cards; checks OK; breakfast (guests only) every day, dinner Wed–Mon (reservations required); $$$.*

THE FOOD COMPANY ☆

For fine dining in Gualala, go to the St. Orres Restaurant or Old Milano Hotel. For every other kind of dining, come here. Open every day all day, the Food Company is a cross between a deli, bakery, and cafe, serving fresh-baked breads, pastries, and sandwiches alongside an ever-changing menu of meat pies, pastas, quiches, tarts, meat loafs, stuffed bell peppers, Greek moussaka, enchiladas, and lord knows what else. It's sort of like coming home from school for dinner— you never know what's going to be on the table, but you know it's probably going to be good. On sunny afternoons, the cafe's garden doubles as a picnic area; throw in a bottle of wine from their modest rack, and you have the makings for a romantic—and inexpensive—alfresco lunch. *¹/₂ mile north of Gualala at the corner of Hwy 1 and Robinsons Reef Rd; (707)884-1800; 38411 Hwy 1, Gualala; beer and wine; MC, V; checks OK; breakfast, lunch, dinner every day; $.*

LODGINGS

ST. ORRES ☆☆☆

In the early '70s, a group of young architects and builders, inspired by the Russian architecture of the early Northern California settlers, took their back-to-the-land dreams to Gualala and created this dazzling copper-domed inn from redwood timbers scrounged from old logging mills and dilapidated bridges. Located just off Highway 1 and within walking distance of a sheltered, sandy cove, St. Orres consists of 8 small, inexpensive rooms in the main lodge (two with great ocean views and all with shared baths) and 11 private cottages scattered throughout the 42 acres of wooded grounds. Top choice for the cottages is the super-rustic and surprisingly affordable Wild Flower Cabin, a former logging-crew shelter furnished with a cozy sleeping loft, a real wood-burning stove (topped with cast-iron skillets), an adorable outside shower overlooking the woods, and even your own gaggle of wild turkeys waiting for handouts at your doorstep. Second honeymooners should book the gorgeous Sequoia cottage: tucked into the edge of the forest, this solid-timbered charmer comes with an elevated king-size bed, skylight, soaking tub, wet bar, private deck, and wood-burning fireplace. Start the day with a complimentary full breakfast (delivered to the cottages in baskets), spend the day lolling around the nearby beaches, have dinner at St. Orres' superb restaurant (see Restaurants, above), and end the day at your private dacha, snuggled in front of the fireplace listening to the distant roar of the ocean—not a bad vacation. *2 miles north of Gualala on the east side of Hwy 1; (707)884-3303; 36601 Hwy 1, PO Box 523, Gualala, CA 95445; MC, V; checks OK; $ (lodge), $$$ (cottages).*

THE OLD MILANO HOTEL ☆☆☆

 Overlooking the sea above Castle Rock Cove, this picturesque Victorian bed and breakfast, built by the Lucchinetti family in 1905, is featured on the National Register of Historic Places. If you can drag yourself away from the verandah with the knockout ocean view and through the front door, you'll find six small yet elegant bedrooms upstairs (all with shared baths) and a downstairs suite replete with antique furnishings and a private bath. All but one of the rooms (the Garden View Room) feature fantastic views of the sea. Elsewhere on the 3-acre estate are the Vine Cottage, located in the gardens and furnished with a brass bed, a reading loft, a wood stove, a small deck, and a private bath; the Caboose, a genuine railroad caboose converted into the quaintest, coziest, and most private room at the inn (if not on the coast); and a cliff-side hot tub for two. A full breakfast, included in the room rate, may be served in your room, on the garden patio, or by the fire in the parlor (see Restaurants, above). *Just north of the Food Company, ³/₄ mile north of Gualala; (707)884-3256; 38300 Hwy 1, Gualala, CA 95445; MC, V; checks OK; $$$.*

"People are trying to make Sea Ranch into a resort, but it's not. It's a community, a place where people live."
—Arlene Perry, owner, Sea Ranch Rentals

SEA RANCH ☆☆☆

 A sort of upper-middle-class ritual among Northern California families or groups of friends is renting a vacation home along the 9-mile coastal stretch of residential development called Sea Ranch. Begun in the 1960s by the land-hungry Castle and Cooke Company of Hawaii, Sea Ranch is undoubtedly one of the most beautiful seaside communities in the nation, due mostly to rigid adherence to environmentally harmonious (or "organic") architectural standards for its six- and seven-figure homes. Roughly 300 homes are available as vacation rentals, managed by eight or nine rental companies, with prices ranging from as low as $165 to $550 for two nights. There's also a lodge and restaurant within Sea Ranch, but neither are recommended, particularly when you can have your own house and full kitchen for only a few dollars more. *On Hwy 1 between Stewarts Point and Gualala; contact Sea Ranch Rentals at (707)785-2579; PO Box 88, The Sea Ranch, CA 95497; no credit cards; checks OK; $$$.*

The Sea Ranch made national news—even the National Enquirer—when one of its recently widowed residents had his $350,000 home confiscated by the Sea Ranch Homeowners Association management for owing $567 in back membership dues.

POINT ARENA

Fifteen miles north of Gualala is one of the smallest incorporated cities in California, Point Arena. Once a bustling shipping port, the 3-block-long city is now home to only 400 or so people, mostly transplants from larger cities who have set up shop along Main Street with neither the desire nor intention of making much money. They're just here to enjoy the quiet small-town life.

Since there is no direct inland road to Point Arena, few

tourists pass through, ensuring that the city will never become as overloaded as Mendocino. Yet this ain't no cow town either. It has one of the hottest restaurants on the North Coast, artistic (and historic) lodgings, and even poetry readings at the local bookstore. So if you're tired of the crowded Mendocino scene yet want to spend a relaxing weekend on the coast, there's no better alternative than little Point Arena.

ACTIVITIES

 Cafe & Bookstore. Sort of a cross between a bookstore, cafe, coffeehouse, and impromptu community center is Bookends, the dream-come-true of co-owner Alix Levine, an admitted bibliophile and town mother. Located within a beautifully restored Main Street edifice, Bookends is the perfect place to start your day, whether you're staying in Point Arena or just passing through. Breakfast—tofu scrambles, house-baked pastries—is served until 2pm on weekends, and an eclectic lunch menu ranging from croissant sandwiches to veggie stir-fry is served until closing time at 9pm. On sunny days, warm your bones on the outdoor patio; 265 Main Street, (707)882-2287.

 Lead Crystal Lens. Oh boy, yet another historic lighthouse and museum. Ho hum, right? Not this one. Even people who loathe tourist attractions end up enjoying a tour of the Point Arena Lighthouse. Built in 1870 after 10 ships ran aground here on a single stormy night, the fully operational lighthouse had to be rebuilt after the 1906 earthquake, but now it's solid enough for visitors to trudge up the 6-story tower's 145 steps for a standout view of the coast (that is, if the fog has lifted). The dazzling, 6-foot-wide, lead-crystal lens is worth the hike alone. The lighthouse is open 11am to 3:30pm weekdays, 10am to 3:30 weekends in the summer (11am to 2:30pm daily in the winter), and is located at the end of scenic Lighthouse Road, about 5 miles northwest of downtown Point Arena off Highway 1. Parking/tour/museum fee is $2.50; (707)882-2777.

A Pier for All Ages. In 1983, a mother of a storm wiped out Point Arena's century-old city wharf. Seven years and $2.2 million dollars later, the old pier was replaced by a 330-foot bullet-proof cement pier. Though it ain't pretty, it's still worth a stroll to watch the fishermen unload their catch or, if you're lucky, spy a gray whale migrating along the coast. Access to the pier is free, and no license is required for fishing. Take the Iversen Avenue turnoff west off Highway 1 at the south end of town.

On sunny summer Sundays, the parking lot of the Arena Pharmacy in downtown Point Arena is transformed into a farmers market; (707)882-3025.

 Tick Talk. After a walk through coastal forests or meadows, it's always a good idea to check for hitchhikers on your pant legs and socks. The western black-legged tick, bearer of the dreaded Lyme disease, awaits its prey at the tips of knee-high vegetation, then burrows its head into the victim's skin.

While there are dozens of old wives' tales on how to remove a tick (from dousing it in peanut butter to "unscrewing" it counterclockwise), the only real solution is to pull it straight out—without twisting or jerking—with tweezers. Grab the tick as close to the skin as possible and gently pull. If you have to use your fingers, be sure to use a tissue; afterward, wash your hands and the bite site with soap and water and apply an antiseptic.

Symptoms of Lyme disease include a bull's-eye marking or other rash around the bite, often accompanied by a fever or flu-like feeling anywhere from a week to months after the encounter. Since Lyme disease can be fatal, it's a good idea to call your doctor or the Infectious Diseases Branch of the California Department of Health Services in Berkeley (510-540-2566) if symptoms start to occur.

 Beach Bliss. Virtually isolated is the 5-mile sweep of shore, dunes, and meadows that comprise Manchester State Beach. Though several access roads off Highway 1 lead to the beach, the closest one to Point Arena also happens to be the best—the 10- to 15-minute walk across the dunes from the parking lot is a leg-burner, but it's a small price to pay for your own private beach. Take the Stoneboro Road exit west off Highway 1, 2 miles north of the turnoff to Point Arena Lighthouse; (707)882-2463 or (707)937-5804.

RESTAURANTS

PANGAEA ☆☆☆☆

After stints as the exalted chef of St. Orres and Old Milano Hotel Restaurants, Shannon Hughes recently opened her

*Locals know that
Point Arena has
some of the best
surfing waves on
the North Coast.*

*That little AT&T
shack at the end of
Kinney Road at
Manchester State
Beach is the trans-
Pacific fiber-optic
cable station—the
U.S. mainland link
for all undersea
telephone, data,
and video
communication to
Hawaii and the Far
East. The station
was placed here
because this is the
West Coast's closest
point to Hawaii.*

own place in tiny Point Arena to the relief of every innkeeper in the city ("*finally*, a restaurant in town I can recommend," says one). Although it's been open less than a year, Pangaea is already the talk of the North Coast, particularly when Hughes goes off on one of her international tangents and astounds patrons with exotic theme-cuisine nights à la Indonesia or Nigeria. Not that she's above chicken and dumplings (free-range Rocky Range chicken stewed in savory sage gravy) or even a good ol' American burger (beef from Marin County's Niman-Schell Farms, fresh-baked buns, Thai chile sauce, organic greens, and homemade ketchup). Even the restaurant's neo-bronze decor and hand-blown Mexican glassware are bloody works of art. Go Shannon. *In downtown Point Arena across from Bookends; (707)882-3001; 250 Main St, Point Arena; beer and wine; no credit cards; local checks only; dinner Wed–Sun (call ahead in winter); $$.&*

LODGINGS

COAST GUARD HOUSE ☆☆

 Poised high above Arena Cove, this historic Cape Cod cottage was originally built by the Life-Saving Service in 1901 to lodge crew members. Beacon lamps, anchors, and a sea captain's hat tossed haphazardly on a table evoke memories of Point Arena's seafaring past, but the inn's Arts and Crafts interiors, designed by innkeepers Richey Wasserman and Merita Whatley, remain simple and uncluttered. The six guest rooms have all-cotton linens and fluffy down comforters, as well as organic soaps, shampoo, conditioner, and body lotion. The Surfman Cove Room, with windows on three sides, has a beautiful view of the ocean and cove, a wood-burning stove, and a sunken Japanese tub. Top choice is the separate Boathouse Cottage, a replica of the original Generator House (except for the spa tub for two, Swedish wood-burning stove, and private patio overlooking Arena Cove). An ocean-view hot tub is available for guests, and breakfast is included with the room. *Off Iversen Ave, 1 mile west of town; (707)882-2442, (800)524-9320; 695 Arena Cove, PO Box 117, Point Arena, CA 95468; MC, V; checks OK; $$.*

KOA KAMPING KABINS

Who would have guessed that Manchester Beach's Kampgrounds Of America would make *Northern California Coast Best Places?* Well, KOA's Kamping Kabins are just too adorable to pass up. Inside each of the little one- or two-room log cabins are a log-frame double bed and bunk beds with mattresses (cabins sleep 4 to 6 people), a heater, and a light bulb. Outside are a small porch with log swing, a barbecue, and a picnic table. Basically all you need to bring are kitchen utensils, charcoal, and bedding. Hot showers, clean rest rooms, laundry facilities, and a small store and pool are nearby (as is the beach). *On Kinney Rd off Hwy 1, 6 miles north of Point Arena; (707)882-2375; PO Box 266, Manchester, CA 95459; AE, DIS, MC, V; no checks; $.&.*

Never turn your back on the ocean while walking along the beach. Deadly gigantic waves known as rogues periodically sneak in along the North Coast and have been known to wash people out to sea.

ELK

Formerly known as Greenwood, this tiny former logging town was renamed Elk by the postal system when was it discovered there was already a town called Greenwood in California. For a such a small community—population 250—it sure has a booming tourist trade: six inns, four restaurants, and one authentic Irish pub. Its close proximity to Mendocino, a mere 30-minute drive up the coast, is one reason. Elk's paramount appeal, however, is its dramatic shoreline; the series of immense sea stacks create one of the most awesome seascapes on the California coast.

RESTAURANTS

HARBOR HOUSE RESTAURANT ☆☆☆

 The four-course prix-fixe dinners at the Harbor House Restaurant change nightly, but they always begin with a small, hot-from-the-oven loaf of bread that's perfect for sopping up the delicious soups such as the tomato-basil or Indian spice–spinach. The salad, made from homegrown vegetables, might be a combination of greens tossed with an herb vinaigrette or sprouts mixed with olives, water chestnuts, and a toasted sesame-seed dressing. The seafood is harvested from local waters, and the meats and cheeses come from nearby farms. Expect to find entrees such as free-form ravioli of crab, fennel, and shiitakes in a Pernod cream or seared sea scallops on roasted-yellow-pepper rouille with Spanish basmati pilaf. Many of the fine wines offered are locally produced. To take full advantage of the restaurant's spectacular view, request a window table. The only seating—very limited when the inn is full—is at 7pm and reservations are required. *At the north end of Elk; (707)877-3203; 5600 Hwy 1, Elk; beer and wine; no credit cards; checks OK; dinner every day; $$$.*

GREENWOOD PIER CAFE ☆

Part of the Greenwood Pier Inn, the cafe gives full rein to innkeepers Isabel and Kendrick Petty's penchant for baking, gardening, and artistic design. Most of the herbs and vegetables are straight from the elaborate gardens behind the cafe, and all the breads and pastries are baked on-site. Try the walnut-corn waffle for breakfast and the black bean chili with polenta for lunch. Dinner items range from baked salmon in a puff pastry to fresh summer veggies with baked polenta. Prices are very reasonable, and the ambience is pleasingly informal and relaxed. *In the center of town; (707)877-9997; 5926 Hwy 1, Elk; beer and wine; AE, MC, V; local checks OK; breakfast, lunch, dinner every day; $$.*

BRIDGET DOLAN'S DINNER HOUSE ☆

Adjoining the Griffin House B&B is innkeeper Leslie Lawson's Irish pub, complete with a great selection of imported beers on tap that you won't find anywhere else on the coast. The pub is open daily at 3pm, but dinner—ranging from locally caught seafood specials to Irish stew and corned beef sandwiches—doesn't start until 5pm. Those in the know never leave the bar for dinner, ordering from their stools a half-dozen mussels in garlic broth, sourdough bread, and a side of garlic and herb pasta, all for only $10. *In the center of Elk; (707)877-1820; 5910 Hwy 1, Elk; beer and wine; MC, V; checks OK; dinner every day; $$.*

LODGINGS

HARBOR HOUSE INN ☆☆☆

 In 1985, Helen and Dean Turner converted this palatial redwood house—perched on a bluff above Greenwood Landing—into the Harbor House Inn, adding six guest rooms, four cottages, and an exceptional restaurant. Top picks are the Harbor Room, a romantic suite with a fireplace and breathtaking view of the cliffs and surf, and the Lookout Room, a smaller, less expensive unit with a small private balcony that overlooks Cuffey's Cove. Any old room will do, however, since most of your time will be spent relaxing in the fabulous rose garden or down at the private beach. Breakfast and dinner (see Restaurants, above) are included in the room rates. *At the north end of Elk; (707)877-3203; 5600 Hwy 1, PO Box 369, Elk, CA 95432; no credit cards; checks OK; $$$.*

The curvaceous stretch of Highway 1 between Elk and Little River is locally known as Dramamine Drive.

GREENWOOD PIER INN ☆☆☆

What separates this cliff-top wonder from the dozens of other precariously perched inns along Highway 1 are the rooms' fantastic interiors and the brilliant flower gardens gracing the property. The inn offers 11 guest rooms, including three detached cliff-hanging suites (Cliffhouse and the Sea Castles) and the separate Garden Cottage. Many of the units have private or shared decks with stunning views of Greenwood Cove, and all guests have access to a hot tub on the cliff's edge. The whimsical, avant-garde decor and the tile and marble detailing in most of the rooms are the work of proprietor/artists Isabel and Kendrick Petty. Some units also feature Kendrick's colorful airbrush collages, and all of the rooms have private baths, fireplaces or wood stoves, and stereos. The elegantly rustic Cliffhouse is a favorite, with its expansive deck, marble fireplace, Jacuzzi, and Oriental carpets. While the suites and castles are rather expensive, the rooms in the main house are moderately priced. All rates include a continental breakfast delivered to your doorstep, and you can also opt to have dinner from the Greenwood Pier Cafe (see Restaurants, above) brought to your room. *In the center of Elk; (707)877-9997; 5928 Hwy 1, PO Box 36, Elk, CA 95432; AE, MC, V; local checks OK; $$$.*

GRIFFIN HOUSE BED AND BREAKFAST ☆☆

Each of innkeeper Leslie Griffin Lawson's seven cottages is named after a colorful figure who settled this part of the coast in the 1800s—characters like Charlie Li Foo, the one-legged town barber, and Gunderson, a Norwegian ship captain known for his swimming prowess. For fabulous views of the rocky coastline, ask for one of the cliff-top cottages, but no matter which cottage you choose you'll find a wood stove, a private bath, and a split of Anderson Valley wine. You'll also discover that Lawson is a charming host, warm and friendly without being the least bit intrusive as she delivers a fresh-baked breakfast (such as wild-rice waffles or a spicy Mexican soufflé with chiles, cheddar cheese, avocado, and salsa) to your cottage door. Adjoining the B&B is Bridget Dolan's Pub (see Restaurants, above). *In the center of Elk; (707)877-3422; 5910 Hwy 1, PO Box 172, Elk, CA 95432; MC, V; checks OK; $$.*

Albion was named in 1853 by Captain W.A. Richardson—builder of the first lumber mill at the mouth of the Albion River—after the high, pale cliffs of his British homeland.

ALBION

A renowned haven for pot growers until an increase in police surveillance and property taxes drove most of them away, Albion is more of a community or free-spirited ideal than an actual town. You know you're there when you cross a white wooden bridge; the last of its kind on Highway 1, it was built in 1944 (steel and reinforced concrete were unavailable during World War II).

RESTAURANTS

THE LEDFORD HOUSE RESTAURANT ☆☆

Listen to live jazz nightly at the bar of the Ledford House Restaurant.

 It's rare when an ocean-view restaurant's food is as good as the view, but owners Lisa and Tony Geer manage to pull it off, serving Provençal-style cuisine in a terribly romantic cliff-top setting. The menu, which changes monthly, offers a choice of bistro dishes—such as Antoine's cassoulet, a juxtaposition of lamb, pork, garlic sausage, and duck confit slowly cooked with white beans—or more familiar entrees including rack of lamb and roast duckling. With a view like this, a window table at sunset is a must. *Take the Spring Grove Rd exit west off Hwy 1; (707)937-0282; 3000 Hwy 1, Albion; full bar; AE, MC, V; checks OK; dinner Wed–Sun; $$$.*&

ALBION RIVER INN RESTAURANT ☆☆

 Chef Stephen Smith presides over the Albion Inn's ocean-view dining room, where fresh local produce complements dishes such as braised Sonoma rabbit, grilled sea bass, or rock shrimp pasta. The wine list has a good selection of hard-to-find North Coast labels. Arrive before nightfall to ooh and aah over the view. *On the northwest side of the Albion*

bridge; (707)937-1919; 3790 Hwy 1, Albion; full bar; AE, MC, V; checks OK; dinner every day; $$$.&

LODGINGS

ALBION RIVER INN ☆☆☆

 After a long period of ups and downs, this modern seaside inn, poised high above Albion Cove where the Albion River meets the sea, is now one of the finest on the California coast. All 20 of the individually decorated New England–style cottages are equipped with antique and contemporary funishings, private baths, queen- and king-size beds, fireplaces, and a bodacious array of potted plants. The clincher, though, is the private Jacuzzi tub that overlooks the headlands and ocean. (While all rooms have the same ocean view, not all of them have the Jacuzzis, so be sure to request one that does; it's well worth the added expense.) Rates include breakfast at the inn's restaurant (see Restaurants, above). *On the northwest side of the Albion bridge; (707)937-1919, (800)479-7944; 3790 Hwy 1, PO Box 100, Albion, CA 95410; AE, MC, V; checks OK; $$$.*&

LITTLE RIVER

Once a bustling logging and shipbuilding community, Little River is now more like a precious suburb of Mendocino. The town does a brisk business handling the tourist overflow from its neighbor two miles up the coast, and is centered around Van Damme State Park, one of the finest state parks on the Mendocino coast. Vacationers in the know reserve a room in serene Little River and make forays into Mendocino only for dining and shopping.

ACTIVITIES

Little River's Secret Sinkhole. Known by locals as the Little River Cemetery Sinkhole, this almost perfectly circular sinkhole is simply amazing. At low tide you can walk through the wave-cut tunnel to the tide pools at the bottom of the bluff; at high tide, you can sit on the tiny sandy beach and look at the tunnel as the waves blast through. Either way, the

Budget lunch tip: The Little River Market, located across from the Little River Inn on Highway 1, has a great little deli serving inexpensive sandwiches, bagels, tamales, and even an assortment of just-baked breads from the famed Mendocino eatery Cafe Beaujolais. Three small tables in the back overlook a gorgeous view of the bay. (Open 8am– 7pm daily; 707-937-5133.)

COMFORT CAMPING

Do you like to camp along the coast but hate the hassle of pitching tents, lighting lanterns, and picking grains of sand out of your food? Here's the solution: Call North Coast Trailer Rentals at (619)648-7509 and ask them to set up one of their self-contained, fully equipped trailers for you and your friends. You select the seaside campground (it must be in the Fort Bragg–Mendocino area), and they take care of the rest. There's a two-night minimum rental requirement, and prices start at about $65 a night—a real deal for beachfront property.

feeling of being within this natural phenomenon is borderline sacred. To get here, park across from the Little River Cemetery on Highway 1, walk to the southwest corner of the cemetery, and look for a small opening in the chain-link fence. The sinkhole is only a few dozen yards down the trail, but be prepared to enter and exit the hole on all fours or you might end up buried alongside it.

Van Damme State Park. A few miles south of Mendocino off Highway 1 is Van Damme State Park, a 2,072-acre preserve blanketed with ferns and second-growth redwoods. The park has a small beach, a visitors center, and a campground, but its main attraction is the 15 miles of spectacularly lush trails—ideal for a stroll or a jog—that start at the beach and wind through the redwood-covered hills. Fern Canyon Trail is the park's most popular, an easy and incredibly scenic 2½-mile hiking and bicycling path that crosses over the Little River. You can also hike or drive (most of the way) to Van Damme's peculiar Pygmy Forest, an eerie scrub forest of waist-high stunted trees. To reach the Pygmy Forest by car, follow Highway 1 south of the park and turn up Little River Airport Road, then head uphill 2¾ miles; (707)937-5804.

Plane Rides. For the ultimate romantic vacation—or if you can't stand the long drive to the coast—charter a Coast Flyers pilot to pick you up at the airport of your choice and fly you directly to Mendocino. Sure, it's big bucks, but for a group it just might be worth it. Coast Flyers also provides coastal tours, whale watching trips, introductory student pilot flights, and even car rentals from the Little River Airport; (707)937-1224.

RESTAURANTS

HERITAGE HOUSE RESTAURANT ☆☆☆

 While the cuisine doesn't quite match up to the spectacular view and decor, this is still one of the premier restaurants on the Mendocino coast. Dinner is served in several elaborate dining rooms, many reminiscent of a swank men's club; but the most spectacular is the main dining area, a domed room featuring a pastel fruit-and-flower fresco painted by local artist Stefan Kehr. Chef Deagon Williams-Geney's prix-fixe menu changes seasonally but may include such appetizers as spinach-and-rabbit ravioli or ginger-braised duck salad. Main-course selections vary from seared breast of Sonoma duckling in raspberry sauce to a simple bell-pepper risotto with balsamic-grilled summer vegetables. Sommelier Joseph Stein's wine list ranks among the top in the country. Reservations are required for dinner. *South of Van Damme State Park; (707)937-5885, (800)235-5885; 5200 Hwy 1, Little River; full bar; MC, V; checks OK; breakfast, lunch Mon–Fri, dinner every day, brunch Sat and Sun (closed for parts of the winter, call ahead); $$$.*&

LODGINGS

HERITAGE HOUSE ☆☆☆

 Immortalized as the ultimate bed-and-breakfast lodge in the movie *Same Time, Next Year*, Heritage House has a history well suited to Hollywood melodrama: its secluded farmhouse was used as a safe house for smugglers of Chinese laborers during the 19th century, for rumrunners during Prohibition, and for the notorious bandit "Baby Face" Nelson during the '30s. Since 1949, however, the Dennen family has opened the three guest rooms in the main building, the 68 cottages, and the detached 1877 farmhouse to a considerably tamer crowd. Heritage House sits on a cliff overlooking a rocky cove, surrounded by 37 acres of cypress trees, bountiful flower and vegetable gardens, and expansive green lawns. The best rooms are the cliff-hanging Same

Time and Next Year cottages with their king-size beds, fireplaces, and extraordinary ocean views (the Jacuzzi tub in the Next Year cottage explains the extra $20 cost, but at $300 a pop, who's counting). All room rates include breakfast and dinner at the Heritage House Restaurant (see Restaurants, above). The lodge is closed for parts of the winter, so call ahead and be sure to make reservations far in advance. *South of Van Damme State Park; (707)937-5885, (800)235-5885; 5200 Hwy 1, Little River, CA 95456; MC, V; checks OK; $$$.*&

GLENDEVEN INN   ☆☆☆

A few years ago Glendeven was named one of the 12 best inns in America by *Country Inns* magazine, and rightly so. Jan and Janet deVries' stately 19th-century farmhouse resides among 2½ acres of well-tended gardens and heather-covered headlands that extend all the way to the blue Pacific. The 10 spacious rooms and suites feature an uncluttered mix of country antiques and contemporary art that show off Janet's interior-design skills and Jan's fine carpentry work. For ultimate luxury, stay in the Pinewood or the Bayloft suite in the Stevenscroft Annex—each has a sitting parlor, a fireplace, and a partial view of the ocean. The cozy East Farmington room, with its private garden deck and fireplace, is another good choice. Above the Glendeven Gallery, the inn's fine-arts boutique, sits the fabulous Barn House Suite, a two-story, redwood-paneled house ideal for families or two couples. After breakfast—included with your room—walk to the beautiful, fern-rimmed canyon trails in nearby Van Damme State Park. *2 miles south of Mendocino; (707)937-0083, (800)822-4536; 8221 Hwy 1, Little River, CA 95456; AE, MC, V; checks OK; $$$.*

Glendeven Gallery is one of the premier contemporary galleries on the Mendocino coast, with an exquisite selection of ceramics, prints, and jewelry. It's open daily 10am to 5pm and is located 1¹/₂ miles south of Mendocino on Highway 1.

STEVENSWOOD LODGE   ☆☆

Stevenswood Lodge is for people who want the comforts of a modern hotel—cable television, telephone, refrigerator, honor bar—without feeling like they're staying at a Holiday Inn. As it works out, not many Holiday Inns are surrounded on three sides by a verdant 2,100-acre forest, or located just a quarter-mile stroll from the Mendocino shoreline, or embellished with sculpture gardens and contemporary-art displays throughout the grounds. Built in 1988, the lodge's one wheelchair-accessible room and nine suites are outfitted with handcrafted burl-maple furniture, large windows with striking vistas (some with a partial ocean view), private bathrooms, and access to several shared decks. The Pullen Room has a particularly pleasant view of the forest and gardens. The lodge plans to expand to include a restaurant, tennis courts, and additional rooms by June 1996. A full breakfast is included in the room rate. *2 miles south of Mendocino; (707)937-2810, (800)421-2810; 8211 Hwy 1, Little River, CA (PO Box 170, Mendocino, CA 95460); AE, DIS, MC, V; checks OK; $$$.&*

LITTLE RIVER INN AND RESTAURANT ☆☆

 Set on a 225-acre parcel of ocean-front land, the Little River Inn is an ideal retreat for those North Coast travelers who simply can't leave their golf clubs or tennis rackets at home (it's often jokingly referred to as the poor man's Pebble Beach). Susan McKinney operates the inn and restaurant, while her brother Dan Hervilla oversees the nine-hole golf course, driving range, and putting green, as well as the two lighted championship tennis courts. All of the estate's 65 rooms and cottages offer spectacular ocean views, many feature fireplaces, and some also have Jacuzzis. The antique-filled rooms in the main Victorian house are preferable to the north wing's motel-style cottages, which suffer from uninspired decor.

The Little River Inn's restaurant is a casual place for breakfast or dinner, but, oddly enough, is the only room at the inn without an ocean view. Chef Curt Gore maintains the house tradition of using mostly local products—fresh fish from nearby Noyo Harbor; lamb, beef, and potatoes from Comptche; and greens and vegetables from local gardens. For breakfast try the popular Ole's Swedish Pancakes. *Across from the Little River Market and Post Office, south of Mendocino; (707)937-5942; 7751 Hwy 1, Little River, CA 95456; full bar; MC, V; checks OK; breakfast, dinner every day; $$$.&*

RACHEL'S INN ☆☆

Strategically sandwiched between Van Damme State Park and the Mendocino headlands is Rachel Binah's 1860s Victorian farmhouse, one of the best bed and breakfasts on the Mendocino coast. All nine immaculate rooms and suites have queen-size beds with fluffy comforters, private baths, fireplaces, and original artwork (including some by Rachel). The newly renovated Parlor Suite is the most luxurious and

RACHEL'S
CONGRESSIONAL WALK

Innkeeper and environmentalist Rachel Binah calls it her Congressional Walk: a ¼-mile trail leading to the ocean that Rachel deftly uses to lobby visiting members of Congress on the need for the coast's permanent protection from offshore oil drilling. "Works every time," she says. What's so special about it? See for yourself by parking in the small dirt lot on the south side of Rachel's Inn (2 miles south of Mendocino on Highway 1), then walking 49 steps up Highway 1 from Rachel's gravel driveway to a small opening in the fence—the beginning of the end for offshore oil.

spacious of the lot, although it's subject to highway noise and the hubbub of people eating breakfast on the other side of its French doors (not a good combo for late sleepers). A quieter unit is the Blue Room, with a balcony overlooking the back garden, meadow, and trees. The inn's main attraction, actually, is Rachel, a vivacious innkeeper who spends her time campaigning to protect our nation's coastline from offshore oil drilling when she's not busy welcoming her guests, catering a wedding, or preparing one of her grand breakfasts. *2 miles south of Mendocino; (707)937-0088; 8200 Hwy 1, Little River, CA (PO Box 134, Mendocino, CA 95460); no credit cards; checks OK; $$$.&*

THE INN AT SCHOOLHOUSE CREEK   ☆☆

 Whereas most small inns along the Mendocino coast have to make do with an acre or less, the Inn at Schoolhouse Creek has the luxury of spreading its six private cottages and seven ocean-view rooms amidst 10 acres of beautiful flower gardens, meadows, and cypress groves. The result is a sense of seclusion and tranquility the instant you pull into the driveway, a feeling that you *know* you're going to enjoy your stay here. Splurge an extra $30 per night for one of the turn-of-the-century cottages, particularly the super-quaint Cypress Cottage with its own private yard graced by an inviting pair of Adirondack chairs. *Just south of Little River; (707)937-5525; 7051 Hwy 1, Little River, CA 95456; MC, V; checks OK; $$.&*

FOOLS RUSH INN   ☆

Not only is Fools Rush Inn the most cleverly named accommodation in the area, it wins the prize for being the best-all-around budget lodging along the Mendocino Coast. Imagine this: your own private cottage (such as the Gualala House) perched high above the Pacific in a secluded grove of redwood, pine, and cypress trees. Through one window you see the distant ocean glimmering, and through the other you see a dense, inviting forest. As the wood-burning fireplace roars to life, you make a pot of coffee in the kitchen, contemplating your options for the day. Hiking along the fern trails of nearby Van Damme State Park, golfing at the adjacent nine-hole course, relaxing at the beach, or perhaps making the 2-mile drive into Mendocino to do a little shopping? Yep, life is rough. . . . *Just south of Van Damme State Park; (707)937-5339; 7533 Hwy 1, PO Box 387, Little River, CA 95456; no credit cards; checks OK; $.*&

MENDOCINO

The grande dame of Northern California's coastal tourist towns, this refurbished replica of a New England–style fishing village—complete with white-spired church—has managed to retain more of its appealing village-esqe allure than most North Coast vacation spots. Motels, fast-food chains, and anything hinting of development are strictly verboten here (even the town's only automated teller is subtly recessed into the historic Masonic Building), resulting in the almost-passable illusion that Mendocino is just another quaint little coastal community. Try to find a parking space, however, and the illusion quickly fades; even the four-hour drive fails to deter hordes of Bay Areans.

Founded in 1852, Mendocino is still home to a few fishermen and loggers, although writers, artists, actors, and other urban transplants now far outnumber the natives. In fact, Mendocino County is rumored to have the highest percentage of Ph.D.s of any rural county in the country. Spring is best time to visit, when parking spaces are plentiful and the climbing tea roses and wisteria are in full bloom. Start with a casual tour of the town, end with a stroll around Mendocino's celebrated headlands, and suddenly the long drive and inflated room rates seem a trivial price to pay for visiting one of the most beautiful places on earth.

Mendocino's only automated cash cow is at the northwest corner of Lansing and Ukiah Streets.

The Gallery Bookshop at the corner of Main and Kasten Street in Mendocino has "story time" daily at noon.

ACTIVITIES

 Shop & Eat. To tour Mendocino proper, lose the car and head out on foot to the Tote Fête Bakery near the corner of Albion and Lansing Streets (10450 Lansing Street; 707-937-3383). Fuel up with a double capp and cinnamon bun, throw away your map of the town, and start walking—the shopping district of Mendocino is so small it can be covered in under an hour, so why bother planning your attack? Two must-see shops are the the Gallery Bookshop, which features a wonderful selection of books for kids, cooks, and local-history buffs (at Main and Kasten Streets, 707-937-BOOK); and Robert's Jams & Preserves, a town landmark that offers free tastings—à la cute little bread chips—of its luscious marmalades, dessert toppings, mustards, chutneys, and other spreads (440 Main Street, 707-937-1037).

 Arts & Crafts. The Mendocino Art Center offers various art classes and workshops—storytelling, sculpture, ceramics, gardening, textiles, jewelry, crafts, and more—to the public, including annoying tourists. Either call for a free brochure of future classes, or drop by 45200 Little Lake Street at Williams Street and crash a class already in session. The center also has multiple art exhibits on display and a retail art shop; (707)937-5818.

Headlands & Parks. As with many towns that hug the Northern California coast, Mendocino's premier attractions are provided by Mother Nature and the Department of Parks and Recreation, which means they're free (or nearly free). Mendocino Headlands State Park, the small grassy stretch of land between the village of Mendocino and the ocean, is one of the town's most popular attractions. The park's flat, 3-mile-long trail winds along the edge of a heather-covered bluff, providing spectacular sunset views and good look-out points for seabirds and California gray whales. The headlands' main access point is at the west end of Main Street, or skip the footwork altogether and take the scenic motorist's route along Heeser Drive off Lansing Street.

About two miles north of Mendocino off Highway 1 is the worst-kept secret on the coast: Russian Gulch State Park, a veritable paradise for campers, hikers, and abalone divers. After paying a $5 entrance fee, pick up a trail map at the park entrance and find the path to Devil's Punch Bowl—a 200-foot-long, sea-carved tunnel that has partially collapsed in the center, creating an immense blowhole particularly spectacular during a storm. Even better is the 5½-mile round-trip hike along Falls Loop Trail to the Russian Gulch Falls, a misty 35-foot waterfall secluded in the deep old-growth forest; (707)937-5804.

 Botanical Gardens. If you have a passion for plants and flowers, blow a few dollars on the admission fee to the Mendocino Coast Botanical Gardens, located 2 miles south of Fort Bragg, at 18220 Highway 1. The nonprofit gardens feature 47 acres of native plants—ranging from azaleas and rhododendrons to dwarf conifers and ferns—as well as a picnic area, retail nursery, and restaurant (see Restaurants, below); (707)964-4352.

Coastal Trail. The black sheep of Mendocino hiking trails is Jug Handle State Reserve's Ecological Staircase Trail. Maybe it's because it's free and "educational" that people think it's not worth the effort, but this 5-mile round-trip trail gets surprisingly little traffic for such a wonderful hike. The attraction is a series of naturally formed, staircase-like bluffs—each about 100 feet higher and 100,000 years older than the one below it—that differ dramatically in ecological formation: from beaches to headlands to an amazing pygmy forest filled with waist-high, century-old trees. The trail entrance is located on Highway 1, 1½ miles north of the town of Caspar between Mendocino and Fort Bragg; (707)937-5804.

Whale Watching & Fishing. Between December and April, the migrating California gray whale and humpback whale make their annual appearances along the North Coast. Although they're visible from the bluffs, you can meet the 40-ton cetaceans face to face by boarding one of the whale-watching boats in Fort Bragg. The *Tally Ho II* charter offers two-hour tours for about $20, departing from The Old Fish House on North Harbor Drive in Fort Bragg; (707)964-2079. Another great way to get out on the ocean is to book a trip on one of the numerous fishing charters that depart from Noyo Harbor. For approximately $55 per person, which includes rod, bait, and a one-day

Ricochet Ridge Ranch offers guided horseback rides (English- and Western-style) along the Mendocino coast and into the redwoods; (707)964-PONY.

To rent mountain bikes for exploring nearby Van Damme and Russian Gulch State Parks, or to rent a kayak, canoe, or outrigger for a leisurely paddle up the Big River, head to Catch a Canoe & Bicycles, Too!, a rental shop located at Stanford Inn by the Sea. On Highway 1 at Comptche-Ukiah Road, ½ mile south of Mendocino; (707)937-0273.

fishing license, Anchor Charter Boats will take you on a five-hour salmon- or bottom-fishing trip. No experience is necessary, and gear, instruction, and fish-cleaning services are provided; (707)964-4550.

Golf & Tennis. The North Coast has never been famous for its golf courses or tennis courts, but if you get the urge to smack a ball across the range or over the net, the only show in town is the Little River Inn Golf and Tennis Club. Located a few miles south of Mendocino on Highway 1, the club has a regulation nine-hole course, driving range, lighted tennis courts, and a pro shop, all open to the public; 7750 Highway 1, Little River; (707)937-5667.

Drinks & Dancing. After dinner, why not top off the evening with a little nightcap and music? If you appreciate classical tunes and warm snifters of brandy, take a stroll down Mendocino's Main Street to the elegant bar and lounge at the Mendocino Hotel and Restaurant (45080 Main Street; 707-937-0511). If blue jeans and baseball caps are more your style, hang out with the guys at Dick's Place, which has the cheapest drinks in town and the sort of jukebox-'n'-jiggers atmosphere you'd expect from this former logging town's oldest bar (45080 Main Street, next to the Mendocino Hotel; 707-937-5643). For a rowdy night of dancing and drinking, head a few miles up Highway 1 to the Caspar Inn, the last true roadhouse in California where everything from rock and jazz to reggae and blues is played live Thursday through Sunday nights starting at 9:30pm. Take the Caspar Road exit off Highway 1 between Mendocino and Fort Bragg; (707)964-5565.

Birdwatching. Papa Birds, a nature gift store on Albion Street between Lansing and Kasten Streets, sponsors free bird-watching walks along the Mendocino headlands every Saturday morning at 10am (rain cancels it). The 1½-hour tour, which starts at the gift store, is given by expert birder Steve Cardwell, who recommends that you bring warm clothing and binoculars; (707)937-2730 or (800)845-0522.

 A Walk on the Edge. This has to be one of the most beautiful seaside trails on the California coast. The trail-

If the house on the
corner of Little
Lake and Ford
Streets in
Mendocino looks
strangely familiar,
that's because it's
the set for the hit
TV show "Murder,
She Wrote,"
starring Angela
Lansbury.

WHERE EVERY DAY IS SUN-DAY

When the fog refuses to lift for days—even weeks—at a time during Mendocino summers, locals are sure to be found a few miles inland at the perpetually sunny "3.66 Beach" on the Navarro River. The small golden-sand beach fronts a placid pool of cool green river water that's ideal for swimming. To get here, head south from Mendocino on Highway 1, turn inland at the Highway 128 junction, and look for the 3.66 mile marker. Park along the road and take the short, well-worn path down to the beach.

 head starts ³/₁₀ of a mile down road 500D, the first left turn off Highway 1 north of the Lansing Street exit in Mendocino (park across from the red-and-white "No Parking 10pm–6am" sign). Veer left at the trailhead to see an enormous sinkhole linked by a wave-cut tunnel, then backtrack and veer right to start the coastal trail. When the trail loops back to the road, turn left, walk up the road (away from your car) a few hundred feet to the dead end, and start the second half of the trail, which is even better than the first. The total walk is about one hour.

RESTAURANTS

CAFE BEAUJOLAIS   ☆☆☆

Cafe Beaujolais started out as the finest little breakfast and lunch place in Mendocino. Then, over the years, owner Margaret Fox (author of two best-selling cookbooks, *Cafe Beaujolais* and *Morning Food*) and her husband, Chris Kump, managed to turn this modest little Victorian into one of the most-celebrated restaurants in Northern California (recently, however, there have been complaints from regular customers that the food, while still quite good, isn't as fantastic as it used to be). Breakfast, served only on weekends, is one of the cafe's specialties. You won't be disappointed with the moist and fluffy omelet filled with sautéed mush-

Docent-led tours of
the Point Cabrillo
Light Station, built
in 1908 to protect
schooners hauling
lumber to San
Francisco, are
offered on summer
weekends from May
through October.
The tour starts at
the light station's
main gate, located
on Point Cabrillo
Drive, 1¹/₅ miles
north of the
Russian Gulch State
Park entrance. Call
for specific
departure times;
(707)937-0816.

*Cafe Beaujolais'
renowned "brickery
breads" are sold
daily from noon
until they're sold
out at the
to-go window on
the west side of the
restaurant.*

*Budget Lunch Tip:
Tote Fête Bakery
has a divine little
carry-out booth
located on the
corner of Albion
and Lansing Streets
in Mendocino;
(707)937-3383.
Choose from
inexpensive items
such as pesto pizza
by the slice, twice-
baked potatoes,
house-made
focaccia bread, and
foil-wrapped
barbecued-chicken
sandwiches, then
take your loot
to the bakery's
garden patio
around the corner
or head to the
headlands for an
impromptu picnic.*

rooms and herbed cream cheese, the wonderful waffles made from buttermilk and cornmeal, or the Mexican tofu scramble with black bean chili and fresh vegetables. Chef Kump takes charge of the kitchen in the evening; his dinner menu might feature such entrees as a roast free-range chicken with red country mole sauce, soft polenta, and garlic sautéed greens. Try to avoid sitting in the bustling bench section, which has itsy-bitsy tables, and when the weather is warm and the back deck is open, by all means dine among Cafe Beaujolais's lovely, fragrant gardens. *Ukiah St at Evergreen St on the east end of town; (707)937-5614; 961 Ukiah St, Mendocino; beer and wine; no credit cards; checks OK; dinner every day (call in winter), breakfast, lunch Sat and Sun; $$$.*

MACCALLUM HOUSE RESTAURANT ☆☆☆

Using fresh, locally grown ingredients, chef Alan Kantor offers a great combination of traditional favorites—broiled New York steak with shiitake mushrooms and roasted-garlic polenta—and more contemporary California cuisine, such as his roasted salmon with saffron-pistachio risotto and arugula pesto. Lighter and less expensive pasta and bistro dishes, including a nightly summer special for under $10, are served at the adjoining Grey Whale Bar & Cafe, a nice alternative for those who wish to forgo a formal dinner in the elegant dining room. *Between Kasten and Lansing Sts; (707)937-5763; 45020 Albion St, Mendocino; full bar; MC, V; checks OK; dinner Fri–Tues; closed Jan–mid-Feb; $$$.*

955 UKIAH STREET RESTAURANT ☆☆☆

This relatively unknown Mendocino restaurant is described by local epicureans as "the sleeper restaurant on the coast." The powers behind the restaurant's doors are Jamie and Peggy Griffith, who have managed to turn 995 Ukiah into a serious (and slightly less expensive) rival to its more famous neighbor, Cafe Beaujolais. The dramatic interior, with its split-level dining room, 20-foot ceilings, rustic wood-trimmed walls, and elegant table settings, sets the mood for the haute cuisine, which might include seared pork loin stuffed with prosciutto, crispy duck served with ginger–apple brandy sauce, and a thick swordfish steak resting in a red chile–tomatillo sauce. The upstairs section can get cramped and a little noisy, so try to sit downstairs—

preferably at the corner window table—where the vaulted ceiling imparts a comfortable sense of space. *Next to Cafe Beaujolais; (707)937-1955; 955 Ukiah St, Mendocino; beer and wine; MC, V; checks OK; dinner Thurs–Sun; $$$.*&

THE MOUSSE CAFE　　☆☆

Rising triumphantly from its ashes—literally—this small, popular cafe has made an amazing comeback after burning to the ground a few years back. Formerly known as the haunt for Mendocino's confessed chocoholics, the Mousse has switched to a more substantial (read: healthier) menu that makes the most of local and organic meats, herbs, and vegetables (the caesar salad, fashioned with a perfect balance of Parmesan and a robust smack of garlic, is particularly good). The result? Make a reservation, because there's usually a waiting list for dinner. Of course, dessert is as good as it ever was. *Corner of Albion and Kasten Sts; (707)937-4323; 390 Kasten St, Mendocino; beer and wine; no credit cards; checks OK; lunch, dinner every day, brunch Sun; closed in Jan; $$.*

MENDOCINO CAFE　　☆

The Mendocino Cafe is one of the last vestiges of the Mendocino of the '60s. Everyone from nursing mothers to tie-dyed teenagers to Gap-clad couples queue up for the cafe's eclectic mix of Asian and Mexican specialties, served fresh and fast. The hands-down winner is the Thai burrito, a steamed flour tortilla filled with brown rice, sautéed vegetables, a healthy dash of the cafe's fresh chile sauce, and a choice of smoked chicken, pork, or beef. The hot Thai salad, spicy nachos, and barbecued half chicken are also good bets. If the weather's mild, grab a table on the deck. *Corner of Lansing and Albion Sts; (707)937-2422; 10451 Lansing St, Mendocino; beer and wine; MC, V; checks OK; lunch, dinner every day; $.*

LODGINGS

AGATE COVE INN　　☆☆☆

 Completely renovated in 1995 with light pine furnishings and "casual country" decor, the cottages at Agate Cove offer the seclusion, privacy, and views that the in-town B&Bs just can't match. All but one of the 10 cottages have good views

One of the best burger-and-fries combos in California is at Mendo Burgers, located behind the Mendocino Bakery & Cafe at 10483 Lansing Street in Mendocino; (707)937-1111.

For a quick, healthy bite to eat while touring Mendocino, keep an eye peeled for Lu's Kitchen on Ukiah Street between Lansing and Ford Streets (look for a small shack with a few plastic tables around it). The mostly Mexican menu—burritos, tacos, salads, and quesadillas—is all vegetarian, organically grown, and a real deal at under $6; (707)937-4939.

of the ocean, king- or queen-size beds, TVs with VCRs (and a free video library), fireplaces or wood stoves, and private decks. In the morning on your doorstep you'll find the *San Francisco Chronicle*, which you can peruse at your leisure over breakfast in the enclosed porch of the main house. *½ mile north of downtown Mendocino; (707)937-0551, (800)527-3111; 11201 N Lansing St, PO Box 1150, Mendocino, CA 95460; AE, MC, V; checks OK; $$$.*

CYPRESS COVE ■ CYPRESS HOUSE ☆☆☆

 Hidden among the cypress trees that encircle the bluff across the bay from Mendocino is the Cypress House, Pamela Williams' spacious garden cottage that is as hard to forget as it is to find. After Pamela gets you situated, you're on your own: light a fire, insert a relaxing tape into the cassette deck, pour a glass or two of brandy from the decanter, slip into the thick white robes, and head for the private hot tub. In the morning, after reluctantly surfacing from underneath the down comforter, descend from the loft, sit in the fully stocked kitchen, and munch on the fresh fruit and breakfast breads while the coffee brews. In fact, the cottage's only flaw is a lack of an ocean view.

A second option is reserving one of the two new Cypress Cove suites adjacent to the cottage. Each is lavishly appointed with a fireplace, Jacuzzi, stereo, and TV with a VCR, and while the modern two-story duo of suites doesn't afford the space or privacy of Cypress House, the view from the large bay windows is one of the best on the Mendocino coast. *Off Hwy 1 at the south end of Mendocino Bay (call for directions); (707)937-1456; PO Box 303, Mendocino, CA 95460; no credit cards; checks OK; $$$.*

JOSHUA GRINDLE INN ☆☆☆

The most authentic of Mendocino's many New England–style B&Bs, this masterpiece was built in 1879 by the town's banker, Joshua Grindle. Startlingly white against a back-drop of wind-whipped cypress trees, the two-story beauty has lovely bay windows and a wraparound front porch trimmed with gingerbread arches. There are five Early American rooms in the clapboard house, two in the cottage, and three in an old-fashioned water tower set back in the trees. Top picks are any of the cute water-tower rooms or the Library room with its country-pine furnishings, four-poster bed, 19th-century hand-decorated tiles, and fireplace. All of the rooms have sitting areas and private baths. The large front lawn and garden, equipped with a pair of Adirondack chairs, is an ideal place to relax in the sun. *East end of Little Lake Rd; (707)937-4143, (800)GRINDLE; 44800 Little Lake Rd, PO Box 647, Mendocino, CA 95460; AE, MC, V; checks OK; $$$.*

THE STANFORD INN BY THE SEA
BIG RIVER LODGE ☆☆☆

 Hats off to Joan and Jeff Stanford, the environmentally conscious couple who turned this parcel of prime coastal property and the former Big River Lodge into something more than a magnificent resort. It's a true ecosystem, a place where plants, animals, and people coexist in one of the most unforgettable lodging experiences in California. Upon entering the estate you'll see several tiers of raised garden beds, where a wide variety of vegetables, herbs, spices, and edible flowers are organically grown for local grocers and restaurants. Watching your every move as you proceed up the driveway are the Stanfords' extended family of 14 curious llamas, which, besides providing an endless source of entertainment, do their part in fertilizing the gardens. Guests may also bring along their own menagerie of critters, be it a pet dog, cat, parrot, or iguana—it's all part of the Stanfords' commitment to animal equality. Also on the grounds is a gigantic, plant-filled greenhouse that encloses a grand swimming pool, sauna, and spa. And if all this doesn't provide you with enough diversions, there's also a mountain-bike and canoe shop on the property; you can borrow a bike and pedal along several tree-lined trails or slip into a canoe and paddle through the Big River's pristine estuaries.

The inn's 23 rooms and 4 suites display a mixture of styles, from units with dark-wood walls, deep-burgundy furnishings, and four-poster beds to sun-streaked suites with pine-wood interiors, country antiques, and sleigh beds topped with down comforters. All of the rooms feature decks with ocean views, fireplaces or Waterford stoves, TVs, VCRs, telephones, and sitting areas. The old renovated barn is a big, private space where kids and their pets can romp freely. The isolated, utterly romantic River Cottage sits right on the water's edge—an ideal honeymooners' hideaway. A buffet champagne breakfast, afternoon snacks, and evening wine and hors d'oeuvres are included in the price. *At Hwy 1 and Comptche-Ukiah Rd, ¼ mile south of Mendocino; (707)937-5615, (800)331-8884; PO Box 487, Mendocino, CA 95460; AE, CB, DC, DIS, MC, V; checks OK; $$$.*

JOHN DOUGHERTY HOUSE ☆☆

This classic saltbox is a wonderful example of why so many movies supposedly set in New England (*The Russians Are Coming, Summer of '42*) are actually filmed in Mendocino. The John Dougherty House features authentic Early Americana throughout: stenciled walls, Early American furniture, and all-cotton linens on the beds. Innkeepers Marion and David Wells have given each of the six rooms touches of individual charm, but your first choice should be one of the spacious two-room suites: the Starboard Cottage, Port Cottage, or everyone's favorite, Kit's Cabin—a small private cottage hidden in the flower garden. All the rooms have private baths, and most have a TV, a small refrigerator, and a wood stove. An expansive breakfast including homemade bread and scones is served next to a crackling fire. *Just west of Kasten St; (707)937-5266; 571 Ukiah St, PO Box 817, Mendocino, CA 95460; MC, V; checks OK; $$$.*

MENDOCINO FARMHOUSE ☆☆

Once you emerge from deep within the redwood forest surrounding Marge and Bud Kambs' secluded estate, you know you're going to be very happy here. First to greet you is one of the Kamb's friendly farm dogs, followed by their can't-pet-me-enough cats, and finally the instantly likable Kambs themselves. All five rooms—filled with antique furnishings and fresh flowers from the surrounding English gardens—have private baths, queen- and king-size beds, fireplaces, and, if you listen carefully, echoes of the nearby ocean. A real country breakfast (straight from the chicken coop) is served each morning at tables-for-two in the sitting room, after which the dogs give free lessons in the meadow on how to loll around in the sunshine. *From Hwy 1 just south of Mendocino, turn east on Comptche-Ukiah Rd, drive 1³/₄ miles to Olson Ln, and turn left; (707)937-0241, (800)475-1536; 43410 Comptche-Ukiah Rd, PO Box 247, Mendocino, CA 95460; MC, V; checks OK. $$.*

MENDOCINO HOTEL AND RESTAURANT ☆☆

 Selected as the best small hotel in Northern California by *San Francisco Focus* magazine in 1992, the Mendocino Hotel, built in 1878, combines modern amenities— telephones, full bathrooms, room service—with turn-of-the-century Victorian furnishings to create a romantic yesteryear setting with today's creature comforts. The hotel's 51 accommodations—all decorated with quality antiques, patterned wallpapers, and old prints and photos—range from inexpensive European-style rooms with shared baths to elaborate garden suites with fireplaces, king-size beds, balconies, and parlors. Suites 225A and 225B, on the hotel's third floor, have wonderful views of Mendocino Bay from their private balconies. Other favorites are the deluxe rooms with private baths, particularly rooms 201, 213, and 224, which face the water. Breakfast and lunch take place downstairs in the verdant Garden Room; at dinner, Chef Colleen Murphy's California-style cuisine—pan-seared ahi, double-baked pork chops, prime rib au jus—are served at the adjacent Mendocino Hotel Restaurant. Budding sommeliers should enquire about the hotel's Winemaker Dinners, featured one Sunday a month from October through May. *Between Lansing and Kasten Sts; (707)937-0511, (800)548-0513; 45080 Main St, PO Box 587, Mendocino, CA 95460; full bar; AE, MC, V; checks OK; breakfast, lunch, dinner every day; $$$.*

JUG HANDLE CREEK FARM AND NATURE CENTER

Getting next to nature has never been more fun and financially feasible. For a mere $12 to $20 per night, you can afford to shack up the whole family in this glorious old 1860 Victorian farmhouse (saving one of the private rooms or cabins for yourselves, of course). Cook breakfast in the huge,

Geologists speculate that within the next 50 to 150 years, a sudden shift in the Pacific Northwest's offshore subduction zone could cause an earthquake anywhere between Mendocino and Vancouver Island that would far surpass the strongest ever recorded in the mainland United States.

MENDOCINO'S
SECRET BEACH

There couldn't possibly be a cuter, more secluded little beach on the California coast than this one. Naturally there are no signs pointing the way and it requires a little effort to get there, but my-oh-my is it worth the walk. First you need to find the Pine Beach Inn along Highway 1 between Fort Bragg and Mendocino. Take the Ocean Drive exit next to the hotel's giant sign, park across from the tennis courts, and look for the trailhead you just passed at the curve in the road. A five-minute walk trough scrub pines rewards you with a billion-dollar view of the coast. Keep heading straight toward the narrowing bluff and you'll spot the little white-sand beach to your right and a larger one to your left.

fully equipped kitchen, then trek around the center's 39 wild acres or venture into the adjacent 1,000-acre State Reserve with its Ecological Staircase trail. Though the baths are shared, and pitching in for an hour of chores—chopping wood, weeding the garden, etc.—is part of the deal, most guests come to feel that all the money in the world couldn't buy such a positive communal experience. *Off Hwy 1 across from the Jug Handle State Reserve exit (look for a small white sign on the east side of the highway); (707)964-4630; PO Box 17, Caspar, CA 95420; no credit cards; checks OK; $.&*

FORT BRAGG

Even Fort Bragg, Mendocino's bad-boy cousin to the north, hasn't been able to escape the relentless approach of gentrification. Originally built in 1855 as a military outpost to supervise the Pomo Indian Reservation, it's still primarily a logging and fishing town, proud of its century-old timber-and-trawler heritage. But not a year goes by in Fort Bragg without yet another commercial fishing vessel being converted into a whale-watching boat (the ultimate insult) or an unemployed logger trading his chain saw for a set of carving knives.

Fort Bragg's two largest festivals best exemplify the sociological split: Paul Bunyan Days on Labor Day weekend features a big Labor Day parade, log-cutting races, and a demolition derby (of all things), while the annual Whale Festival, held the third Saturday of March, includes ranger-led talks about the cetaceans, a Whale Run, and a beer and chowder tasting. Whether this is progress or not is debatable, but hey, at least you have a choice.

ACTIVITIES

Theater. Before the Warehouse Repertory Theatre opened its performance loft at the corner of Redwood and Harrison Streets in Fort Bragg, there was little in the way of quality evening entertainment in Mendocino County. What possessed this gaggle of professional actors and producers—most of whom came from much bigger cities with much bigger salaries—to make the pilgrimage to the Mendocino Coast? Ashland II: If a stupid little town on the Oregon border can become world-renowned, they figured, surely Mendocino can. Call the box office at (707)964-5159 for a listing of performances ranging from modern comedies to Shakespeare classics. It's $10 well spenteth.

Seal Watching. One of the prettiest—and largest—public beaches on the Mendocino coast is MacKerricher State Park, located 3 miles north of Fort Bragg off Highway 1. The 8-mile shoreline is the perfect place to while away an afternoon, and it's free admission to boot. The highlight of the park is the Laguna Point Seal Watching Station, a fancy name for a small wood deck overlooking a gaggle of harbor seals sunning themselves on the rocks below; (707)937-5804.

Shopping. If you've visited all of Mendocino's boutiques and still haven't shrugged the shopping bug, head over to downtown Fort Bragg, which has enough shops and galleries—all within walking distance of each other—to keep you entertained for hours. Another dangerous place for a credit card is the Fort Bragg Depot, a 14,000-square-foot marketplace with more than 20 shops and restaurants, as well as a historical logging and railroad museum. At 401 Main Street at Laurel Street, Fort Bragg; (707)964-6261.

On the first Friday of each month, Fort Bragg has an open house of sorts in all its downtown galleries. The free wine starts flowing around 6:30pm and has been known to keep flowing all night long.

"It's great to have the Warehouse Repertory Theatre here in Fort Bragg. Now I no longer have to drive to Ashland to see a good play."— Melinda Kerry, Fort Bragg therapist

Bored and hungry? Chew on cod cheeks-'n'-chips from the deep fryers of Eureka Fisheries Inc. at Fort Bragg's Noyo Harbor while watching the sea lions vie for dock space. Open daily 11am–6pm; (707)964-1600.

Lettuce Rejoice. Long before "pesticide free" became the mantra of California growers, organic gardening was the modus operandi of local Mendocino farmers, who for years have catered to the desires of health- and quality-conscious clients such as Mendocino's Cafe Beaujolais. Although the produce is pricey, you can pay less for your luscious pesticide-free strawberries, asparagus, melons, and other goodies if you skip the middleman and buy directly from the growers. From May through October, they sell their wares to the public at the Mendocino Farmers Market on Friday, noon to 2pm (Howard Street, between Main and Ukiah Streets), and at the Fort Bragg Farmers Market on Wednesday, 3:30pm to 5:30pm (Laurel Street, between Franklin and McPherson Streets); Mendocino (707)937-3322, Fort Bragg (707)964-0536.

Train Ride. If you've dragged your feet up and down too many coastal trails this vacation, give your tired dogs an extended rest aboard Fort Bragg's popular Skunk Train (so named because the odoriferous mix of diesel fuel and gasoline once used to power the train allowed you to smell it before you could see it). Depending on which day you depart, a steam-, diesel-, or electric-engine train will take you on a scenic 6- to 7-hour round-trip journey through the magnificent redwoods to the city of Willits and back again (or you can take the 4-hour round-trip excursion to Northspur). Reservations are recommended, especially in summer. At 100 Laurel Street Depot, Fort Bragg; (707)964-6371.

RESTAURANTS

GARDENS GRILL ☆☆

If the perpetually packed parking lot is any indicator, the new Gardens Grill within the Mendocino Coast Botanical Gardens is a huge success. The romantic alfresco seating on the elevated deck overlooking the flower gardens is the main attraction. Though the lengthy lunch menu leans heavily toward salads and sandwiches, it's the Gardens Fajita that takes first prize. Dinner entrees range from fresh local fish—pan-seared ling cod with fennel ragout—to vegetarian dishes and good ol' New York steak served with mashed potatoes. *On Hwy 1 south of Fort Bragg; (707)964-7474; 18220 Hwy 1, Fort Bragg; beer and wine; MC, V; checks OK; lunch Mon–Sat, dinner Thurs–Tues, brunch Sun; $$.*&

NORTH COAST BREWING COMPANY ☆

If Norm Peterson of "Cheers" died and went to heaven, he'd end up here, permanently hunched over the bar within easy reach of his own ever-flowing tap of the North Coast Brewing Company's Scrimshaw Pilsner (a Gold Medal winner at the Great American Beer Fest, the Super Bowl of beer tastings). To his right would be a bowl of the brewery's "no-nonsense Texas-tradition Competition Chili," on his left a basket of fresh Pacific red-snapper fish 'n' chips (made with Scrimshaw-beer batter), and in front of his brewski a fall-apart-in-your-hands, country-style pile of Carolina barbecued pork. *Just south of the Grey Whale Inn; (707)964-3400; 444 N Main St, Fort Bragg; beer and wine; DIS, MC, V; checks OK; dinner Tues–Sun; $$.*&

THE RESTAURANT ☆

One of the oldest family-run restaurants on the coast, this small, unpretentious Fort Bragg landmark is known for its good dinners and Sunday brunches. The eclectic menu offers dishes from just about every corner of the planet: blackened New York strip steak, sweet-and-sour stir-fry, Livorno-style shellfish stew, and even shrimp rellenos. The comfortable booth section is the best place to sit if you want to keep an eye on the entertainment—courtesy of ebullient chef Jim Larsen—in the kitchen. *1 block north of Laurel St; (707)964-9800; 418 N Main St, Fort Bragg; beer and wine; MC, V; checks OK; lunch Thurs and Fri, dinner Thurs–Tues, brunch Sun; $$.*

VIRAPORN'S THAI CAFE ☆

When Viraporn Lobell opened this tiny Thai cafe in 1991, Asian-food aficionados on the North Coast breathed a communal sigh of relief. Born in northern Thailand, Viraporn attended cooking school and apprenticed in restaurants there before coming to the United States. After moving to the North Coast with her husband, Paul, she worked for a time at Mendocino's most popular restaurant, Cafe Beaujolais. A master at balancing the five traditional Thai flavors of hot, bitter, tart, sweet, and salty, Viraporn works wonders with refreshing Thai classics such as spring rolls, satays, lemon-

Fort Bragg's North Coast Brewing Company gives free tours of its brewery across the street at 455 N Main Street. Register at the brewery shop in advance of the daily 1:30pm tour.

At Schat's BBQ, located a few miles south of Fort Bragg at 24521 Highway 1, you can buy a mess of beef or pork ribs with beans & bread for only $6 during lunch hours; (707)964-7237.

At Lost Coast Adventures in Fort Bragg you can rent an ocean kayak to explore the coastline, coastal rivers, or—along with a guide— nearby sea caves; (800)961-1143 or (707)961-1143.

grass soup, and a wide range of curry dishes. *Across from PayLess off Hwy 1; (707)964-7931; 500 S Main St, Fort Bragg; no credit cards; local checks only; lunch, dinner every day; $.*

LODGINGS

GREY WHALE INN ☆☆

The wide doorways and sloped halls are the only vestiges of this popular inn's previous life as the town hospital. Owners Colette and John Bailey have successfully transformed this stately four-story building into one of the more comfortable and distinctive inns on the coast. Decorated with quilts, heirlooms, and antiques, the 14 large guest rooms have private baths and wonderful views of the town or the sea. Opt for one of the two penthouse rooms: Sunrise offers a view of the town, pretty wicker furniture, and a double whirlpool bath, while Sunset opens onto a private deck overlooking the ocean. Another good choice is the spacious Campbell Suite, which comes with a marble gas-log fireplace, a TV with VCR, a microwave oven, and a refrigerator. There's also a large rec room with a pool table and a TV. The full buffet breakfast (with trays for carrying your food back to bed, if you prefer) is included in the rates. *At Fir St and Hwy 1; (707)964-0640, (800)382-7244; 615 N Main St, Fort Bragg, CA 95437; AE, DIS, MC, V; checks OK; $$.&*

WESTPORT

If you've made it this far north, you're either lost or determined to drive the full length of Highway 1. If it's the latter, then you'd best stock up on a sandwich or two at the Westport Community Store & Deli, because you still have a loooong way to go.

LODGINGS

DEHAVEN VALLEY FARM
AND RESTAURANT ☆☆☆

This remote 1875 Victorian farmhouse, with its sublime rural setting and access to a secluded beach, comes complete with a barnyard menagerie of horses, geese, sheep (including one that thinks it's a horse), goats, llamas, and donkeys. If the animals aren't enough to keep you amused, try a game of croquet or horseshoes, or just soak in the hot tub set high on a hill overlooking the ocean. The inviting parlor has deep, comfortable couches, while the six guest rooms in the house and the two nearby cottages are decorated with colorful comforters and rustic antiques. In the morning, you'll wake to such treats as fried apples or baked pears, chocolate sour-cream coffee cake, and potato-artichoke frittata or cornmeal pancakes. The small DeHaven Valley Farm Restaurant offers a commendable four-course prix-fixe menu that might include such entrees as roasted pork tenderloin with apple horseradish and pasta primavera with Italian sausage. *1½ miles north of Westport; (707)961-1660; 39247 Hwy 1, Westport, CA 95488; beer and wine; AE, MC, V; checks OK; dinner Thurs–Sat; closed in Jan; $$.*

HOWARD CREEK RANCH ☆☆☆

This isolated 40-acre ranch, located off a remote stretch of Highway 1 near the tiny town of Westport, appeals to travelers who *really* want to get away from it all. You'll revel in the peace and quiet of this rustic retreat, which Mendocino County has designated as a historic site. For more than two decades, proprietors Sally and Charles Grigg have been renting out three cabins and the seven guest rooms in the farmhouse and in the renovated railroad barn. Set back just a few hundred yards from an ocean beach, the farmhouse and barn are on opposite sides of Howard Creek, connected by (among other routes) a 75-foot-long swinging footbridge. The rooms in the farmhouse feature separate sitting areas, antiques, and homemade quilts, while the barn units—each one handcrafted by Charles Grigg, a master builder with a penchant for skylights—have curly-grain redwood walls and Early American collectibles. The separate Beach House, with its freestanding fireplace, skylights, king-size bed, large deck, and Jacuzzi tub, is a great romantic getaway. A hot tub and sauna are perched on the side of a hill, as are Sally's pet cows and sheep. In the morning, Sally rings the breakfast bell to alert her guests that it's eatin' time—and the fare is definitely worth getting out of bed for. *3 miles north of Westport; (707)964-6725; 40501 Hwy 1, PO Box 121, Westport, CA 95488; AE, MC, V; checks OK; $$.*

"I worked all over the world as an Ocean Engineer, then decided one day I needed a career change and, well, here I am."—Charla Ledesma, manager, DeHaven Valley Farm

"One of my favorite things to do on a Saturday afternoon is take a leisurely drive along Highway 1 to DeHaven Valley Farm in Westport, have an early dinner, and follow the sunset back home."—Bob Richmond, Mendocino resident

THE
REDWOOD
COAST

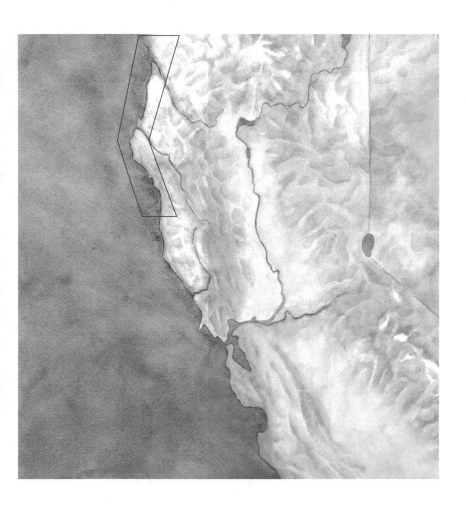

THE REDWOOD COAST

A south-to-north sweep of the Humboldt and Del Norte County coastlines, beginning at the Lost Coast and ending at the Oregon border.

Considering that California's Redwood Coast contains *the* most spectacular coastal forests in the world—including the world's tallest tree—it's surprising how few tourists care to venture north of Mendocino to get there. Perhaps it's the myth that the upper coast is permanently socked in with rain and fog, and that the only places to stay or eat are cheap motels and greasy diners.

Like most myths, of course, this isn't true (at least it's no *longer* true). Granted, the coastal weather can be miserable, but the fog usually burns off by the afternoon, and the rain—well, bring an umbrella; it's the price you pay for vacationing among the thirsty redwood giants. And while there are no Hyatts or Hiltons this far north, the Redwood Coast offers something even better: a wealth of small, personable inns and bed and breakfasts run by proprietors who bend over backwards to make your stay as enjoyable as possible. The food? Combine the northern region's penchant for organic gardening with a year-round supply of just-off-the-boat seafood, and you have the ingredients for remarkably fresh—and healthy—gourmet cuisine.

The reason for the Redwood Coast's recent upswing in fine dining and accommodations is that an increasing number of Bay Area baby boomers are migrating northward for a little more elbow room. Among the pilgrims are a number of noted chefs and innkeepers who have pulled up their big-city stakes and relocated in small towns such as Eureka and Arcata to open their own restaurants or inns. This, combined with the region's beautiful scenery and absence of crowds, has made the Redwood Coast one of the premier—and relatively unknown—tourist destinations in California.

THE LOST COAST

If you build it, they will come. And if you don't build, they won't come. What wasn't built between Ferndale and Rockport was a coastal road: the geography of the 90-mile stretch—steep mountain ranges abutting rocky shore—wouldn't allow it. The result is the last untamed and undeveloped region of the California coast, a place where two cars following each other are considered a convoy and there are more cows lying on the beach than people (seriously). Popular with campers, backpackers, and fishers, the Lost Coast is beginning to see a hint of gentrification at its only seaside town, Shelter Cove. Otherwise, the land is mainly inhabited by ranchers, retirees, and aging hippies, the latter of which have made the Lost Coast one of the most productive pot-growing regions in the world.

ACTIVITIES

 Scenic Drive. The Lost Coast makes for a fantastic day trip by car. Of the three entrance points into the region—Garberville, Humboldt Redwoods State Park, and Ferndale—the most scenic route is through the state park. Take the State Park turnoff on Highway 101 and follow the Mattole Road all the way to Ferndale and back onto Highway 101. The 3- to 4-hour, 75-mile drive is incredible, transporting you through lush redwood forests, across golden meadows, and along miles of deserted beaches (well, if you don't count the cows). Be sure to start with a full tank, and bring a jacket if you plan to venture anywhere on foot.

 Avenue of the Giants. Touristy to no end but always worth the detour is the 31-mile stretch of old Highway 101 known as the Avenue of the Giants. The narrow, paved road—which runs parallel to Highway 101 between Phillipsville and Pepperwood—winds through the world's largest concentration of coastal redwoods. Described by John Steinbeck as "ambassadors from another time," some of these trees have been around for 1,500 years, growing to heights of 350 feet. The best roadside attraction along the Avenue is Founders Grove, 4 miles north of the visitors center; (707)946-2263. Take the half-mile, self-guided loop trail that passes by the Dyerville Giant, which, before it fell on March 24, 1991, was considered the "champion" coastal redwood at 364 feet tall, 53 feet in circumference, and weighing in at nearly a million pounds. That's one big tree.

RESTAURANTS 🍴

PELICAN'S LANDING ☆☆

 At the north end of a small runway for private planes, this rather exclusive Shelter Cove restaurant—selected by

"Grow pot, mostly. And collect welfare. I'll deliver four, five checks to a single address."—Petrolia postman, when asked what people do around here for a living.

Two of the best-selling items at Lost Coast hardware stores are plastic piping and camouflage netting.

Private Pilot magazine as one of the nation's premier fly-in lunch spots—is situated in an A-frame beach house with two-story-high picture windows and a spectacular view of the Lost Coast. The menu's offerings are limited, but the food is well-prepared: charbroiled steak cut to order, Cajun-style fresh fish (we're talking right out of the water), grilled chicken, and piles of fresh shellfish. All meals are served with a creamy clam chowder, a shrimp or simple green salad, and fresh, crusty sourdough bread. Desserts range from fresh fruit pies (snatch a slice of the wonderfully tart wild huckleberry if it's available) to chocolate mousse and a house-made cheesecake. *On Wave Dr off Lower Pacific Dr; (707)986-7793; Wave Dr, Shelter Cove; full bar; MC, V; checks OK; lunch, dinner Thurs–Mon (Thurs–Sun in winter); $$.*

LODGINGS

SHELTER COVE OCEAN INN ☆☆

Snoozing seals, grazing deer, and migrating whales are just some of the sights you'll see in Shelter Cove, the Lost Coast's only oceanside community. Once you leave Highway 101 in Garberville, prepare to navigate along 24 miles of steep, twisting tarmac that passes through rocky grasslands and patches of forest before reaching the cove (good brakes are a must). At the end of the journey you'll reach the Shelter Cove Ocean Inn, a handsome Victorian-style facility built smack-dab on the shoreline. The inn offers two spacious suites with sitting rooms and Jacuzzi tubs, and two smaller rooms upstairs with balconies overlooking the ocean—all rooms have an ocean view, but the panorama from the suites is definitely worth the added expense. Since the B&B is in such a remote location, proprietor Don Sack will deliver a home-cooked breakfast, lunch, and dinner to your room on request (an ex-commercial fisherman who knows these waters better than anyone, Don will do triple-duty as your host, personal sportfishing guide, and chef, preparing your catch for the evening's dinner). Serious R&R is the theme here: lie on the sun deck overlooking the ocean, play a round of golf across the street, or walk to the nearby black sand beach—ain't nothin' to do around here except relax. *From Shelter Cove Dr, turn right on Lower Pacific Dr, then left on Dolphin Dr; (707)986-7161; 148 Dolphin Dr, Shelter Cove, CA 95589; MC, V; checks OK; $$$.&*

LOST INN   ☆

As you wind along the Mattole Road towards sleepy Petrolia, keep a lookout for an old green tractor with a hand-painted sign that reads, "Welcome! You have found the Lost Inn." Once you've spotted it, park in the circular driveway, and run the friendly gauntlet of cats, dogs, chickens, flowers, fruit trees, and antique knickknacks that line the driveway leading up to Gail and Phil Franklin's remote country inn. There is only one guest room here, a large two-room suite with a double bed, kitchen (bring your own grub), glassed-in porch, and private entrance. Solitude is this inn's selling point—you can't *get* any more away-from-it-all without a backpack—and it sells for a very reasonable price. *On Old Mattole Rd, one block west of the general store; (707)629-3394; PO Box 161, Petrolia, CA 95558; no credit cards; checks OK; $$.*

The Lost Coast community of Petrolia was named for California's first commercial oil well, drilled 3 miles east of town in the 1860s.

FERNDALE

Even if Ferndale isn't on your itinerary, it's worth a detour off Highway 101 to stroll for an hour or two down its colorful Main Street, browsing through the art galleries, gift shops, and cafes that are strangely reminiscent of Disneyland's "old town." Ferndale, however, is for real, and hasn't changed much since it was the agricultural center of Northern California in the late 1800s. In fact, the entire town is a National Historic Landmark because of its abundance of well-preserved Victorian storefronts, farmhouses, and homes. What *really* distinguishes Ferndale from the likes of Eureka and Crescent City, however, is the fact that Highway 101 doesn't pass through it: the difference—no cheesy motels, liquor stores, or fast-food chains—is remarkable.

ACTIVITIES

The Way It Was. For a trip back in time, view the village's interesting memorabilia—working crank phones, logging equipment, a blacksmith shop—at the Ferndale Museum, 515 Shaw Street at Third Street; (707)786-4466. Not officially a museum but close enough is the Golden Gate Mercantile at 421 Main Street. Part of the general store hasn't been remodeled (or restocked) in 50 years, giving you the feeling that you're walking through some sort of time capsule or movie set. Far less historic but equally engrossing are the previous pedal-powered entries in the World Championship Great Arcata to Ferndale Cross-Country Kinetic Sculpture Race on display at the Kinetic Sculpture Museum, 580 Main Street at Shaw Street. The dusty, funky museum is unlike anything you've ever seen.

 Coastal Drive. Reserve an hour of your day in Ferndale for a leisurely drive along scenic Centerville Road. The 5-mile excursion starts at the west end of Main Street downtown and passes through several ranches and dairy farms on the way to the Centerville Beach County Park. If you continue beyond the park and past the retired Naval Facility, you'll be rewarded with an incredible view of the Lost Coast, to the south. On the way back, keep an eye out for Fern Cottage, a restored 1865 Victorian farmhouse built by the late state senator Joseph Russ, one of the first Ferndale settlers. Tours of the farmhouse are by appointment only; call caretaker Greg Martin (who's also an accomplished organic gardener) at (707)786-4835.

 On the Boards. In keeping with its National Historic Landmark status, Ferndale has no movie theaters. Rather, it has something better: the Ferndale Repertory Theatre. Converted in 1972 from a movie theater, the 267-seat house—located at 447 Main Street downtown—hosts live performances by actors from all over Humboldt County. The revolving performances run pretty much year-round and range from musicals to comedies, dramas, and mysteries. Tickets are $10 and, due to the popularity of the shows, reservations are advised; (707)725-2378.

RESTAURANTS

CURLEY'S GRILL ☆☆

Longtime restaurateur and Ferndale resident Curley Tait decided it was finally time to open up his own business, so in April of '95 he filled the 460 Main Street vacancy—left when the Bibo and Bear Restaurant owner split town—with Curley's Grill, and it's been a hit ever since. The reason? Curley doesn't fool around: the prices are fair, the servings are generous, the food is good, and the atmosphere is bright and cheerful. Sure bets are the grilled polenta with Italian sausage, fresh mushrooms, and sage-heavy tomato sauce, or the moist tortilla-and-onion cake served with a tangy onion salsa. On sunny afternoons, request a seat on the shaded back patio. *On Main St between Washington and Brown Sts; (707)786-9696; 460 Main St, Ferndale; beer and wine; DIS, MC, V; checks OK; lunch and dinner daily; $.&*

STAGE DOOR CAFE ☆

Ferndale's top soup 'n' sandwich shop is the tiny Stage Door Cafe, run by Barbara and Jerry Murry. Barbara does most of the cooking, while Jerry—a real character—takes the orders and directs traffic. The daily specials are placed in the window, and if one of them happens to be Orange Wonder soup, it's sort of a Ferndale tradition that you have to order it. If no chairs are vacant, order your food to go and dine alfresco on one of the town's many benches lining the main drag. *On Main Street in the Ferndale Theatre; (707)786-4675; 451 Main St, Ferndale; no credit cards; checks OK; breakfast, lunch Fri–Tues; $.*

LODGINGS

THE GINGERBREAD MANSION ☆☆☆

The awe-inspiring grande dame of Ferndale, this peach-and-yellow Queen Anne inn is a lavish blowout for Victoriana buffs. Gables, turrets, English gardens, and gingerbread galore have made it one of the most-photographed buildings in Northern California. The mansion has been through several reincarnations since 1899, including stints as a private residence, a hospital, a rest home, an apartment building, and even an American Legion hall before Ken Torbert converted it into a B&B in 1983. All 11 guest rooms have queen- or king-size beds and private baths. The Fountain Suite boasts a grand view of Ferndale and the garden, twin claw-footed tubs for his-and-hers bubble baths, a canopied bed, a fireplace, and a fainting couch. The corner Rose Suite has a wonderful view of Ferndale village through a cut-out gingerbread verandah, stained-glass windows, two fireplaces, hanging plants, and a vast, mirrored bathroom that's as big as the bedroom. For the ultimate in luxury, though, reserve the new Empire Suite, an orgy of marble and columns with twin fireplaces and a lavish bathing area. In the morning all guests awaken to a sumptuous breakfast in the formal dining room that overlooks the garden. Afternoon

Ferndale's own little forest, Russ Park, has miles of nature trails leading through groves of fir and Sitka spruce. From the southwest end of Main Street, take Ocean Avenue southeast ¹/₂ mile to the gravel trailhead parking area; a few yards up the trail is a map of the park.

Local advice: Diane's Cafe at 553 Main Street in downtown Ferndale bakes the best breads, muffins, and pastries in the county (her hot-out-of-the-oven strawberry-rhubarb cobbler is to die for).

One of the finest examples of Victorian architecture anywhere is the gabled and turreted Carson Mansion, built in 1885 for lumber baron William Carson and now the home of a snooty private men's club. Mere commoners, however, are allowed to gawk from the sidewalk at the most-photographed Victorian house in America. Corner of 2nd and M Streets in Old Town Eureka.

tea is served in one of five parlors, each handsomely furnished with Queen Anne, Eastlake, and Renaissance Revival antiques. *Corner of Berding and Brown Sts, one block south of Main St; (707)786-4000 or (800)952-4136; 400 Berding St, PO Box 40, Ferndale, CA 95536; AE, MC, V; checks OK; $$$.*

THE SHAW HOUSE
BED AND BREAKFAST INN ☆ ☆ ☆

This Carpenter Gothic beauty—built in 1854 by Ferndale founder Seth Louis Shaw, and listed on the National Register of Historic Places—is modeled after the titular manse of Hawthorne's *House of the Seven Gables*. Meticulously restored by owners Norma and Ken Bessingpas, the oldest house in Ferndale is filled with books, photographs, baskets, antiques, and all manner of memorabilia; the couple also added a gazebo and a fish pond to the inn's well-tended acre. Each of the six rooms has a private bath (although three of the bathrooms are down the hall), and most have bathtubs and showers. Three units—the Honeymoon Suite, the Garden Room, and the Wisteria Room—have balconies overlooking the garden, and the Shaw Room, under the central gable, features the original bed Shaw and his bride slept in during their honeymoon. In the morning, guests feast on Norma's homemade breakfast, which may include oven-baked Dutch babies and cheddar French toast served with dried-fruit syrup specked with apricots and currants. After breakfast, ride around town on a vintage bicycle from Ken's collection. *On Main Street in downtown Ferndale; (707)786-9958 or (800)557-SHAW; 703 Main St, PO Box 1125, Ferndale, CA 95536; AE, MC, V; checks OK; $$$.*

EUREKA

One can only wonder what the city's founders were thinking of when they named this town after the popular gold-mining expression "Eureka!" (Greek for "I have found it!"). They certainly never found any gold in these parts. Perhaps the Eureka of yesteryear offered more to get excited about, but nowadays the North Coast's largest city has little to offer the visitor except a slew of cheap (and mostly dingy) motels, fast-food restaurants, gas stations, and a somewhat entertaining Old Town garnished with stately Victorian homes and storefronts. Most travelers take advantage of Eureka's budget prices and bunk down for the night, then head north to Arcata and the Lost Coast for more stimulating explorations. There are, however, a handful of exceptional hotels, restaurants, and shops here, particularly the Carter Hotel and its restaurant. Otherwise, you're better off spending your time up the road in Arcata, which is about half the size of Eureka but has twice the appeal.

Eureka's fishing industry provides about 90 percent of California's catch of Pacific shrimp and Dungeness crab.

ACTIVITIES

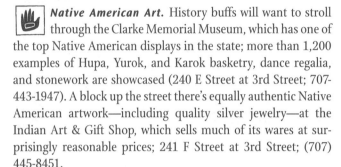

Native American Art. History buffs will want to stroll through the Clarke Memorial Museum, which has one of the top Native American displays in the state; more than 1,200 examples of Hupa, Yurok, and Karok basketry, dance regalia, and stonework are showcased (240 E Street at 3rd Street; 707-443-1947). A block up the street there's equally authentic Native American artwork—including quality silver jewelry—at the Indian Art & Gift Shop, which sells much of its wares at surprisingly reasonable prices; 241 F Street at 3rd Street; (707) 445-8451.

If you need a good book at a great price, stop by the Booklegger, a marvelous Old Town bookstore where thousands of used paperbacks (especially mysteries, westerns, and science fiction) are stocked, as well as children's books and cookbooks; 402 2nd Street; (707)445-1344.

Beet of a Different Grower. If purple potatoes, cylindrical beets, and other fancy foods are on your shopping list, then you're in luck, because you'll find them at the farmer's markets held weekly May through October in Eureka and Arcata. Most of the produce is grown along the local Eel and Trinity Rivers, and it's sold at bargain prices at Arcata Plaza on Saturday from 9am to 1pm, at Eureka Mall (on Highway 101 at the south end of Eureka) on Thursday from 10am to 1pm, and at Eureka's Old Town on Tuesday from 10am to 1pm.

Better yet, why not beet them to the punch and spend the day picking produce directly from the North Coast's small farms. Call the North Coast Growers Association at (707)441-9699 for a free copy of the Farmers Market Directory & Farm Trails Guide, a map and listing of 13 local family-run farms that encourage visitors to drop by and purchase their products—vegetables, fruit, herbs, teas, flowers, plants, etc.—directly from the dirt.

Bay Cruise. For a surprisingly interesting and amusing perspective on the history of Humboldt Bay, take a bay cruise on skipper Leroy Zerlang's *Madaket*, the oldest passenger

Thirsty? Stroll over to the Lost Coast Brewery for a fresh pint of Alleycat Amber Ale and a $1.75 rock cod taco. At 617 4th Street, between F and G Streets, in downtown Eureka; (707)445-4480.

vessel on the Pacific coast. The 75-minute narrated tour departs daily from the foot of C Street in Eureka, and gets progressively better after your second or third cocktail. For more information, call Humboldt Bay Harbor Cruise at (707)445-1910.

 Wildlife Refuge. More than 200 species of birds feed, rest, or nest in the Humboldt Bay National Wildlife Refuge, a bird-watcher's paradise that is open to the public year-round for hiking, bird-watching, boating, and fishing. The 2,200 acres of wetlands, marshes, mud flats, and open bay are accessible by two short, easy foot trails. To get there, take the Hookton Road exit off Highway 101 south of Eureka and turn west on Ranch Road. A free guide to the refuge is available at the Ranch Road entrance. For more information, call (707)733-5406.

RESTAURANTS

RESTAURANT 301   ☆☆☆

The highly acclaimed Restaurant 301 (formerly known as the Carter House Restaurant), located on the first floor of Hotel Carter, is orchestrated by owner Christi Carter, who also doubles as the chef. Diners, seated at windowside tables overlooking the bay, can choose either the regular or the prix-fixe five-course dinner menu; the accompanying wine list features more than 350 varietals. A meal might begin with a delicate Dungeness crab cake appetizer followed by a rich beef bourguignon with sautéed wild mushrooms; a garden-fresh salad topped with warmed chèvre, roasted hazelnuts, and a pear vinaigrette; and an entree of grilled duck breast served with a seasonal fruit and zinfandel sauce. Finish the evening with Christi's fresh rhubarb tart with lemon-curd sauce and you'll understand why most of her clientele are repeat customers. *Corner of 3rd and L Sts in Old Town; (707)444-8062; 301 L St, Eureka; beer and wine; AE, DC, DIS, MC, V; checks OK; breakfast (by reservation only) every day, dinner every day; $$$.*&

LAZIO'S SEAFOOD RESTAURANT   ☆

While definitely not on a par with the Hotel Carter's Restaurant 301, Lazio's has nonetheless enjoyed a longtime reputation—over half a century—for serving good seafood at reasonable prices. Chef Ron Garridoa, formerly of Domaine Chandon restaurant in the Napa Valley, offers a wide variety of fresh fish with your choice of cooking styles—sautéed, grilled, poached, or oven roasted—topped with yet another choice of nine sauces (the best combo is the spicy Asian black bean sauce on grilled sole). Lazio's is also famous for its pricey yet palate-pleasing bouillabaisse and elaborate oyster selection. *On 2nd between D and E Sts in Old Town; (707)443-9717; 327 2nd St, Eureka; full bar; MC, V; checks OK; lunch Mon–Sat, dinner every day; $$.&*

LOS BAGELS ☆☆

Simply put, Eureka's best bagel shop. For more details, see the Los Bagels review in the Arcata chapter. *Corner of 2nd and E Sts in Old Town; (707)442-8525; 403 2nd St, Eureka; no alcohol; no credit cards; local checks only; breakfast, lunch Wed–Mon; $.&*

TOMASO'S TOMATO PIES ☆

This family-style Italian pizza parlor reeks so divinely of baked garlic and olive oil that you can smell it a block away. Top of the list of Tomaso's favored fare are the calzone and the spinach pies, both guaranteed to make garlic lovers (and their dining partners) swoon. Other popular plates include the chicken cannelloni and the square pizza with a whole-wheat crust. Be prepared for a 30-minute wait—it's the price you pay for such fresh ingrediants. For a proper Italian finale, order a Cremosa: a blend of milk, soda water, and whipped cream infused with a fruity Torani Italian syrup). *Between 2nd and 3rd Sts in Old Town; (707)445-0100; 216 E St, Eureka; beer and wine; AE, DIS, MC, V; local checks only; lunch Mon–Sat, dinner every day; $.&*

SAMOA COOKHOUSE

Visiting the Eureka area without a stop at the Samoa Cook-house is like visiting Paris without seeing the Eiffel Tower. This venerable dining spot is the last surviving cook house in the West (it's been in operation for more than a century) and a Humboldt County institution, where guests are served lumber-camp-style in an enormous barnlike building at long tables covered with checkered cloths. Few decisions are required—just sit down, and the food will come until you say uncle. Breakfast typically features sausages, biscuits, scrambled eggs, potatoes, and French toast or pancakes.

Lunch and dinner include potatoes and the meat-of-the-day, which might be ham, fried chicken, pork chops, roast beef, barbecued chicken, or fish. Mind you, the food isn't great (except for the delicious bread, which is baked on the premises), but there's plenty of it. And just when you think you're about to burst, along comes the fresh-baked pie. After your meal, spend a few minutes waddling through the adjoining logging museum. *From Hwy 101 take the Samoa exit (R St) in downtown Eureka, cross the Samoa Bridge, turn left on Samoa Rd, then left on Cookhouse Rd; (707)442-1659; Cookhouse Rd, Samoa; no alcohol; AE, DIS, MC, V; checks OK; breakfast, dinner every day, lunch Mon–Sat; $.*

LODGINGS

CARTER HOUSE, HOTEL CARTER, AND CARTER HOUSE COTTAGE   ☆☆☆☆

What is now considered one of the finest accommodation-and-restaurant complexes on the North Coast started serendipitously in 1982, the year Eureka residents Mark Carter and his wife Christi officially converted their newly built dream home—a four-story, five-bedroom Victorian reproduction—into an inn. Not only did they turn out to be some of the area's best hosts, but the Carters actually reveled in their newfound innkeeper roles. Once word got around that the Carter House was *the* place to vacation, they were flooded with folks who wanted a room. In 1986 Mark, a former builder, added the 23-room Hotel Carter across the street (its design is based on the blueprints of a historic 19th-century Eureka hotel), and four years later he refurbished the Carter House Cottage, an adjacent three-bedroom Victorian mansion built in 1890.

The trio of inn, hotel, and cottage offers a contrasting array of luxury accommodations, ranging from rooms with classic Victorian dark-wood antique furnishings in the house and cottage to a softer, brighter, more contemporary decor in the hotel. Amenities, which vary from room to room, include marble fireplaces, imported antiques, two-person whirlpool bathtubs with views of the marina, immense four-poster beds, double-headed showers, entertainment centers, kitchens, baskets filled with wine and specialty foods, concierge services, overnight dry cleaning

Guests and nonguests are invited to tour the Hotel Carter's 10,000-square-foot organic garden, where more than 300 varieties of herbs, vegetables, fruits, and edible flowers are grown exclusively for the hotel restaurant. Tours are generally from 4 to 6pm daily and advance notice is required; call (707)444-8062.

and shoe shining, a videotape and CD library, tea-and-cookie bedtime service, and wine and hors d'oeuvres in the evening. Also included in the room rate is an outstanding full breakfast which includes fresh-baked tarts, muffins, cinnamon buns, breads, fresh fruit, juices, and strong coffee. *Corner of 3rd and L Sts in Old Town; (707)444-8062 or (800)404-1390; 301 L St, Eureka, CA 95501; AE, DC, DIS, MC, V; checks OK; $$$.* &

Get 24-hour recorded information on Redwood National Park by calling (800)423-6101.

AN ELEGANT VICTORIAN MANSION   ☆☆☆

This 1888 Victorian is a jewel—a National Historic Landmark lovingly maintained by owners Doug "Jeeves" Vieyra and Lily Vieyra. Each of the four guest rooms upstairs has furnishings reflecting a different period, place, or personage. The light-filled Lillie Langtry Room, named for the famed 19th-century chanteuse who once sang at the local Ingomar Theatre, has an impressive four-poster oak bed and a private bath down the hall. The French country–style Governor's Suite sleeps up to three (the side room is ideal for a child), has a private bath, and offers a distant view of the bay. The Vieyras have an incredible array of old (1905–1940) movies and a collection of popular music from the same era, which guests often watch and listen to in the common room. Then there's Doug's obsession with antique autos—he's frequently seen motoring (with guests on board) in his 1928 Model A Ford or one of his other two old Fords. Doug and Lily are incredibly attentive hosts; they'll lend you bicycles, show you the way to their Finnish sauna, pore over road maps with you, and make your dinner reservations. Lily, trained as a French chef (and Swedish masseuse), prepares a morning feast. *Corner of 14th and C Sts; (707)444-3144; 1406 C St, Eureka, CA 95501; MC, V; checks OK; $$.*

BAYVIEW MOTEL

The Bayview Motel is Eureka's top budget motel and so squeaky clean you could eat off the floor. Each of the 14 rooms has a private bath, remote-control TV, and queen-size bed. Perched on a knoll high above noisy Highway 101, the Bayview does have a view of the bay, but you have to look *real hard* past the industrial park to see it. The motel's best views are actually of the lovely, meticulously manicured lawn and garden. *From Hwy 101, take the Henderson St exit at the south end of town; (707)442-1673; 2844 Fairfield St, Eureka; AE, DIS, MC, V; no checks; $.*

*That handsome
1857 brick
storehouse at
the southwest
corner of Arcata
Plaza is Jacoby's
Storehouse, a fully
restored California
State Landmark
that houses several
shops, offices, and
restaurants.*

ARCATA

Home to the California State University at Humboldt, a liberal arts school, Arcata is like most college towns in that everyone tends to lean towards the left. Environmentalism, artistry, and good beads and bagels are indispensable elements of the Arcatian philosophy, as is a cordial disposition towards tourists, making Arcata one of the most interesting and visitor-friendly towns along the North Coast. The heart of this oceanside community is Arcata Plaza, where a statue of President McKinley stands guard over the numerous shops and cafes housed in Arcata's historic buildings. It's been said that a walk around the plaza—with its perfectly manicured lawns, ubiquitous hot dog vendor, and well-dressed retirees sitting on spotless benches—is enough to restore anyone's faith in small-town America.

ACTIVITIES

Community Forest. A two-minute drive east of downtown Arcata on 11th Street will take you to Arcata's beloved Redwood Park, a beautiful grass expanse—ideal for a picnic—complemented by a fantastic new playground that's guaranteed to entertain the tots. Surrounding the park is the Arcata Community Forest—600 acres of lush second-growth redwoods favored by hikers, mountain bikers, and equestrians. Before you go, pick up a free guide to the forest's mountain-biking or hiking trails at the Arcata Chamber of Commerce, 1062 G Street at 11th Street in downtown Arcata; (707)822-3619.

Bird-Watching. On the south side of town is the Arcata Marsh and Wildlife Preserve, a 154-acre sanctuary for hundreds of egrets, marsh wrens, and other waterfowl. A free self-guided walking tour of the preserve, which doubles as Arcata's integrated wetland wastewater treatment plant, is available at the Chamber of Commerce. Each Saturday at 8:30am the Audubon Society gives free one-hour guided tours at the cul-de-sac at the foot of South I Street; (707)826-7031.

Baseball. The best way to spend a summer Sunday afternoon in Arcata is at the Arcata Ballpark, where $3.50 buys you nine innings of America's favorite pastime hosted by the Humboldt Crabs semipro team. With the band blasting and the fans cheering, you'd swear you were back in high school. Most games are played Wednesday, Friday, and Saturday evenings June through July, with an occasional double-header thrown in. The ballpark is located at 9th and F Streets in downtown Arcata, but don't park your car anywhere near foul-ball territory. Visit the Arcata Chamber of Commerce for schedule information at 1062 G Street at 11th Street, or call (707)822-3619.

 Bicycling. Rent a 21-speed mountain bike or classic cruiser at Revolution Bicycle Repair, 7th and F Streets in downtown Arcata. Open Tues–Sat 9am–6pm; (707)499-9877.

Movies. For first-run and classic college flicks, queue up at the Arcata or the Minor Theatre, both of which offer a wide range of films at starving-student prices (the daily matinees are particularly cheap). Arcata Theatre: 1036 G Street at 10th Street; (707)822-5171; Minor Theatre: 1013 H Street at 10th Street; (707)822-5171.

Kinetic Kontraptions. Arcata is a festival-happy town, and its wackiest event of the year is the World Championship Great Arcata to Ferndale Cross-Country Kinetic Sculpture Race. The three-day event, held every Memorial Day weekend, draws more than 10,000 spectators who come to watch about 50 crazy competitors try to slog through 38 grueling miles of sand, swamp, and salt water in their custom-made, people-powered amphibious crafts. Contestants start in Arcata Plaza, pass though Eureka, and finish (if they're lucky) in the town of Ferndale. Cheating and bribery are part of the rules, provided they're done with "proper style and panache." The zaniest "sculptures" are showcased in the Kinetic Sculpture Museum at 780 Main Street in Ferndale. For more information about the race, call Hobart Brown at (707)725-3851.

"The Arcata Marsh and Wildlife sanctuary is a must see. It's a great place to go for a walk or jog, particularly during sunset or for some early morning bird watching."
—Arcata's former mayor, Sam Pennisi

"Baseball's a big tradition in Arcata; it's been around for 50 years. It's a really neat family activity . . . something to get the whole family out, young and old."—Shandra Grobey, Arcata Ballpark ticket seller

RESTAURANTS

ABRUZZI   ☆☆

Named after a region on the Italian Adriatic, Abruzzi is located on the bottom floor of the 140-year-old Jacoby Storehouse, an old brick complex that's been converted into the historic Arcata Plaza shopping mall. If you have trouble

Need a new read?
Tin Can Mailman,
located at the
corner of 10th
and H Streets in
downtown Arcata,
is a terrific used-
book store with
more than 130,000
hard- and soft-
cover titles,
including a few
collector's items;
(707)822-1307.

finding the place, just follow your nose: the smell of garlic and fresh bread will soon steer you to Chris Smith and Bill Chino's friendly spot, where you'll be served an ample amount of food, artfully arranged. Meals begin with a basket of warm bread sticks, focaccia, and a baguette, followed by such highly recommended dishes as the pasta carbonara, linguine *pescara* (prawns, calamari, and clams tossed in a light Sicilian tomato sauce), or any of the fresh seafood specials. The standout dessert is the chocolate *paradiso*—a dense chocolate cake set in a pool of champagne mousseline. Smith and Chino also own the Plaza Grill on the third floor of the same building—a great place for lunch or to finish off the evening by sipping a glass of wine and listening to live music. *At the corner of H and 8th Sts in Arcata Plaza; (707)826-2345; 791 8th St, Arcata, CA; full bar; AE, DIS, MC, V; checks OK; lunch Mon–Fri, dinner every day; $$.*♿

FOLIE DOUCE ☆☆

To say Folie Douce just serves pizza is like saying Tiffany's just sells jewelry. *Designer* pizza is more like it. Try the Thai chicken pizza—marinated bits of breast topped with fontina, mozzarella, bean sprouts, and mushrooms—which is cooked in a wood-fired oven. Other toppings you won't find in your standard Pizza Hut include spicy shrimp, chèvre, Brie, and wild mushrooms. If pizza doesn't set your heart aflutter, indulge in the filet mignon (brandy-flambéed and topped with Roquefort cheese and green peppercorns) or the moist Monk's Chicken (a full boneless breast sautéed in butter, flambéed in brandy, and simmered in white wine, mustard, and cream). Locals love this festive, brightly painted place, so reservations—even for early birds—are strongly recommended. *Between 15th and 16th Sts; (707)822-1042; 1551 G St, Arcata, CA; beer and wine; DIS, MC, V; checks OK; dinner Tues–Sat (Sunday in summer); $$.*♿

You can see (and touch!) 3-billion-year-old fossils and view various California flora and fauna exhibits at Humboldt State University's Natural History Museum at 13th and G Streets in downtown Arcata; (707)826-4479.

LOS BAGELS ☆

In 1987 bagel companies all over the country sent their doughy products to NBC's "Today Show" to vie for the title of Best Bagel. The verdict: the best bagel outside of New York City was made by Los Bagels in Arcata. This emporium is a popular town hangout, where you'll see lots of folks scanning the morning paper while they munch. If you're feeling particularly adventurous, try a poppyseed bagel topped with jalapeño jam and cream cheese, or perhaps the multigrain bagel smeared with hummus or guacamole. Also available to eat here or to take out are smoked salmon, albacore, and cod, as well as empanadas, corn-rye bread, and fresh-baked challah. Owing to Los Bagels' brisk business, the owners have opened a second location in Eureka (see Eureka chapter for location). *Between 10th and 11th Sts; (707)822-3150; 1061 I St, Arcata; no alcohol; no credit cards; local checks only; breakfast, lunch Wed–Mon; $.&*

At TJ's Classic Cafe on H Street at 11th you can order two eggs with pancakes, French toast, or potatoes for only $2.50 Monday through Friday between 7am and 10am. Darn good onion rings, too; (707)822-4650.

LODGINGS

THE LADY ANNE ☆☆

Just a few blocks from Arcata Plaza in a quiet residential neighborhood, this exquisite example of Queen Anne architecture has been painstakingly restored by innkeepers Sharon Ferrett and Sam Pennisi (who, by the way, was once Arcata's mayor). There are five large and airy guest rooms, each decorated with antiques, burnished woods, English stained glass, Oriental rugs, and lace curtains. Romantics should book the Lady Sarah Angela room, which boasts a four-poster bed and a beautiful bay view. Families often request the Cinnamon Bear room, which is chock-full of teddy bears and will sleep up to four with its king-size and trundle beds. The inn's two parlors are stocked with several games, as well as a grand piano and other musical instruments that you're welcome to play. When the weather is warm, relax on Lady Anne's verandah or head out to the lawn for a game of croquet. Breakfast (beg for the Belgian waffles) is served in the grand dining room, which is warmed by a roaring fire during the chilly months. *Corner of 14 and I Sts; (707)822-2797; 902 14th St, Arcata, CA 95521; MC, V; checks OK; $$.*

Heaven is a full pitcher of Red Nectar Ale at the Humboldt Brewing Company in downtown Arcata. For tour information, call (707)826-BREW or just show up at the corner of 10th and I Streets.

FAIRWINDS MOTEL

Aside from the Arcata Crew House dormitory, the Fairwinds Motel is the only budget accommodation in downtown Arcata. Located two blocks from Humboldt State University, it has 27 plain-but-pleasant rooms, all with direct-dial phones, cable TV, and double, queen, or king-size beds.

Although the hotel has been around for a few decades and its age-lines are showing, the interiors have been completely remodeled with new beds and modern furnishings. *Corner of 17th and G Sts; (707)822-4824; 1674 G St, Arcata, CA 95521; AE, MC, V; no checks; $.*

TRINIDAD

In the early 1850s Trinidad was a booming supply town with a population of 3,000; now it's one of the smallest incorporated cities in California, a small rocky bluff that a handful of fishermen, artists, retirees, and shopkeepers call home. A sort of Mendocino in miniature, cute-as-a-button Trinidad is known mainly as a sportfishing town: trawlers and skiffs sit patiently in the bay, awaiting their owners or tourists willing to part with a Grant for an afternoon of salmon fishing. Scenery and silence, however, are the town's most desirable commodities; if all you're after is a little R&R on the coast, Trinidad is among the most peaceful and beautiful areas you'll find in California.

ACTIVITIES

 Oceanside Park. Five miles north of Trinidad, off Patrick's Point Drive, is Patrick's Point State Park, a 640-acre oceanside peninsula laden with lush, fern-lined trails that wind through foggy forests of cedar, pine, and spruce. The park was once a seasonal fishing village of the Yurok Indians. Nowadays it's overrun with campers in the summer, but it's still worth a visit to stroll down Agate Beach (keep an eye out for the semiprecious stones), climb the stone stairway up to the house-size Ceremonial Rock, and admire the vistas from Rim Trail—a 2-mile path along the cliffs where you can sometimes spot sea lions, harbor seals, and gray whales. In 1990 descendants of the original Indian settlers reconstructed an authentic Yurok village—open to the public—within the park. A map and guide to all the park's attractions is included in the $5-per-vehicle day-use fee; (707)677-3570.

 Forest Trail. If the long drive on Highway 101 has you feeling cramped, unwind for a spell at Trinidad's Demonstration Forest. The self-guided trail—virtually unknown and almost always deserted—leads through a lush, peaceful redwood forest and takes about 20 minutes to complete. A picnic area hidden near the parking lot is the perfect spot for a leisurely lunch in the cool shade. Take the Trinidad exit off Highway 101 and head north on Patrick's Point Drive for about a mile.

A great way to start your day in Trinidad is with a hefty omelet at the Seascape Restaurant (707-677-3762), followed by a shoreline stroll along Trinidad Head Trail. You'll find the restaurant at the foot of Trinidad Pier and the trailhead at the southeast corner of the pier's parking lot.

 Sinker Swim. More fun and easier than you think is a day spent sportfishing off Trinidad's bounteous coast. Simply drop your prerigged line, reel in when something's tugging on the other end, and throw it in the burlap sack at your feet. For a small fee, the crew does all the dirty work of cleaning and cutting your catch, and Katy's Smokehouse (see margin) will take care of the rest. Trinidad's two sportfishing charter boats are the 36-foot *Jumpin' Jack* (707-839-4743 or 800-839-4744) and the 45-foot *Shenandoah* (707-677-3625). Both charters offer morning and afternoon trips daily from Trinidad Pier, and walk-ons are welcome. The 5-hour salmon and rockfish hunt runs about $55 per person, which includes all fishing gear. One-day fishing licenses can be purchased on board.

RESTAURANTS

LARRUPIN' CAFE ☆☆☆

The Humboldt State University Marine Laboratory, located at Edwards and Ewing Streets in downtown Trinidad, is open to the public Monday through Friday 9am to 5pm. The lab features various live marine life displays, including a touch tank and tide pool; (707)826-3671.

Trinidad's finest restaurant—looking very chic with its colorful urns full of exotic flowers—draws crowds for its creative seafood dishes and fantastic pork ribs doused with a sweet and spicy barbecue sauce. The oysters, mussels, and crab are often served the same day they're plucked from Humboldt Bay. Every meal comes with a red- and green-leaf salad tossed with a Gorgonzola vinaigrette and an appetizer board stocked with gravlax, pâté, dark pumpernickel, apple slices, and the house mustard sauce. For a starch, order the tasty twice-baked potato stuffed with locally made cheese, sour cream, and scallions. Finish off your feast with a slice of the pecan-chocolate pie topped with hot rum sauce. Dine on the patio in the summer months. Reservations are recommended year-round. *From Hwy 101, take the Trinidad exit and head north on Patrick's Point Dr; (707)677-0230; 1658 Patrick's Point Dr, Trinidad; beer and wine; no credit cards; checks OK; dinner Wed–Mon in summer (dinner Thurs–Sun in winter); $$.&*

LODGINGS

THE LOST WHALE BED AND
BREAKFAST INN ☆ ☆ ☆

 The Lost Whale isn't just a place to stay overnight, it's a destination in itself—particularly for families with small children. The traditional Cape Cod–style building, constructed in 1989, stands alone on a 4-acre grassy cliff overlooking the sea, with a private stairway leading down to miles of deserted rocky beach. Proprietors Suzanne Lakin and Lee Miller manage to give romancing couples lots of space and solitude, yet they have also created one the most family-friendly inns on the California coast. Five of the inn's eight soundproof rooms have private balconies or sitting alcoves with views of the Pacific, two rooms have separate sleeping lofts (to allow kids to escape from their parent's reach), and all have private baths and queen-size beds. Lakin and Miller also rent out furnished private homes that can accommodate up to six people—top choice is their spectacular farmhouse with views overlooking the ocean. After a day on the inn's beach or at neighboring Patrick's Point State Park, relax in the outdoor hot tub while listening to the distant bark of sea lions or looking out for whales. Kids can let loose in the playground—which has a small playhouse with its own loft—or run around with the menagerie of pygmy goats, ducks, and rabbits roaming the inn's 1½-acre plot up the street. Lakin and Miller take great pride in their huge breakfasts—casseroles, quiches, home-baked muffins, fresh fruit, locally smoked salmon served with vegetables from the garden—and provide plenty of snacks throughout the day and evening. *From Hwy 101 take the Seawood Dr exit and head north for 1¾ miles on Patrick's Point Dr; (707)677-3425 or (800)677-7859; 3452 Patrick's Point Dr, Trinidad, CA 95570; AE, DIS, MC, V; checks OK; $$$.*

TRINIDAD BED AND BREAKFAST ☆ ☆

 Perched on a bluff overlooking Trinidad's postcard-perfect fishing harbor and the rugged California coast, this Cape Cod–style inn is the dream house of innkeepers Carol and Paul Kirk, a couple of Southern California transplants who fell in love with the area while visiting Arcata a decade ago. There are four guest rooms to choose from, but the suites are your best option—both have private entrances, comfortable sitting rooms, spectacular views of Trinidad Bay, and breakfast-in-bed service. The Mauve Suite has a large brick fireplace, wraparound windows, and a king-size bed; the Blue Bay View Suite upstairs offers more privacy (its entrance is outside), a telescope for whale watching, a queen-size bed, and the best bay view in town. The Kirks' expanded continental breakfast features fresh and baked fruit, homemade breads served with lemon-honey and molasses butter, muffins (pear-ginger, cranberry-orange, fruit-bran), and locally made cheeses. *From Hwy 101, take the Trinidad exit to Main St, and turn left on Trinity St; (707)677-0840; 560 Edwards St, PO Box 849, Trinidad, CA 95570; MC, V; checks OK; $$$.*

ORICK

The burl capital of the world, Orick resembles more of a huge outdoor gift shop than a town. What's a burl, you ask? Well, take a sizable chunk of redwood, do a little carving here and there with a small chain saw, and when it resembles some sort of mammal or rodent, you have yourself a burl. There are thousands of burls to choose from here, ranging from the Abominable Burlman to Sasquatch and the Seven Dwarfs. Several roadside stands have viewing booths where mesmerized tourists watch the redwood chips fly. Orick is also regarded as the southern entrance to Redwood National Park; one mile south of town off Highway 101 is the Redwood Information Center, where visitors can pick up a free map of Redwood State Park and browse through the geologic, wildlife, and Native American exhibits. (Open daily 9am–5pm; 707-488-3461.)

ACTIVITIES

Canyon Trail. Up there with the natural wonders of the world is the spectacular Fern Canyon Trail in Prairie Creek Redwoods State Park. The half-mile trail winds through a narrow canyon whose 50-foot-high vertical walls are blanketed with lady, deer, chain, and five-finger ferns. Several footbridges allow you to cross the small stream that runs down the middle. Visit the canyon in the morning, then spend the day relaxing on Gold Bluffs Beach. From Highway 101, take the Davison Road

Redwood National Park, which stretches for 44 miles along the coast from Orick to Crescent City, was created in 1968 to protect 76,000 of the then-remaining 93,000 acres of old-growth forest—a forest that once covered a whopping 2 million acres of California and Oregon.

Prairie Creek Redwoods State Park has a fantastic 19-mile mountain-bike trail through dense forest, elk-filled meadows, and glorious mud holes. Parts of it are a real thigh burner, though, so beginners should sit this one out. Pick up a 25-cent trail map at the Elk Prairie campground ranger station.

exit (at Rolf's Park Cafe), which follows along Gold Bluffs Beach to the Fern Canyon parking lot. Day-use fee is $5. No motor homes or trailers more than 24 feet long; (707)488-2171.

 Chief Tenderfeet. Love nature but hate to hike? Then the Big Tree Trail is just for you. It's short (¼ mile), paved, and has a big finish; take the Big Tree turnoff along the Newton B. Drury Scenic Parkway. Even more popular among hill-haters is the Lady Bird Johnson Grove Trail, an easy self-guided tour that loops 1 mile around a glorious grove of mature redwoods; take the Bald Hills Road exit off Highway 101, ½ mile north of Orick. Then again, why leave your car at all? Cal-Barrel Road, a narrow, packed-gravel road located just north of the Prairie Creek Visitor Center off the Newton B. Drury Scenic Parkway, offers a spectacular 3-mile tour through an old-growth redwood forest (no trailers or motor homes).

 Tallest Tree. To see the world's tallest tree—we're talkin' 368 feet tall and 14 feet in diameter—you'll first have to go to the Redwood Information Center near Orick (see above) to obtain a free map and permit—only 35 issued per day—to drive to the trailhead of Tall Trees Grove. Another option is to pay $7 for a shuttle from the Information Center. Either way, you still have to walk a steep 1⅓ miles from the trailhead to the grove, but then you can tell your friends at home that, hey, you saw the tallest tree in the world. For more information, call the center at (707)488-3461.

RESTAURANTS

ROLF'S PARK CAFE   ☆

After decades of working as a chef in Switzerland, Austria, San Francisco, and even aboard the presidential ship SS *Roosevelt*, the trilingual Rolf Rheinschmidt decided it was time to semi-retire. He wanted to move to a small town to cook, and towns don't get much smaller than Orick— population 650. So here among the redwoods Rheinschmidt serves good bratwurst, wiener schnitzel, and crèpes Suzette. His specialty is the marinated rack of spring lamb, and he has some unusual offerings such as wild boar, buffalo, and elk steak (if you're truly adventurous, get a combo of all three). Each dinner entree includes lots of extras: hors d'oeuvres, a salad, vegetables, farm-style potatoes, bread, even dessert accompanied by a small glass of port or sherry. And ever since the debut of Rheinschmidt's German Farmer Omelet—an open-faced concoction of ham, bacon, sausage, mushrooms, cheese, potatoes, and pasta, topped with sour cream and salsa and garnished with a strawberry crêpe—breakfast in Orick has never been the same. *On Hwy 101 about 2 miles north of town; (707)488-3841; Hwy 101, Orick; beer and wine; MC, V; local checks only; breakfast, lunch, dinner every day in summer; closed Dec–Jan; $$.*&

A large old-growth redwood tree can be worth as much as $60,000 when sold for lumber.

KLAMATH

"For elk information tune to 1610 AM."—A roadside sign in Prairie Creek Redwoods State Park

The town of Klamath apparently hasn't recovered since it was washed away in 1964, when 40 inches of rain fell within 24 hours. All that remains are a few cheap motels, trailer parks, tackle shops, and boat rentals, which are kept in business solely by the gaggles of fishermen who line the mighty Klamath, one of the finest salmon and steelhead streams in the world. The scenery around Klamath, however, is extraordinary; smack in the middle of Redwood National Forest, the area has some incredible coastal drives and trails that even the timid and out-of-shape can handle with aplomb.

The Klamath is California's second-largest river, a 263-mile-long waterway fed by more than 300 tributaries.

ACTIVITIES

 Yurok Loop Nature Trail. A great way to spend an hour of your day is walking the Yurok Loop Nature Trail at Lagoon Creek, located 6½ miles north of the Klamath River bridge on Highway 101. The 1-mile self-guided trail gradually climbs to the top of rugged sea bluffs—with wonderful panoramic views of the Pacific—and loops back to the parking lot. If your partner's up to it, have him or her meet you at the Requa Trailhead (see below) and take the 4-mile coastal trail to the mouth of the Klamath. Dress warm, and bring some water and sunscreen.

 Coastal Overlook. As good a place to stretch your legs as any is the lofty Klamath Overlook, which stands some 600 feet above an estuary at the mouth of the Klamath River. A short but steep trail leads down to a second overlook that is ideal for whale-watching and photo ops. The coastal trail continues 4 miles north to the Yurok Loop trail at Lagoon Creek (see above). To get here, take the Requa Road turnoff from Highway 101, north of the Klamath River bridge.

  Forest & Coastal Drive. One of the premier coastal drives on the Redwood Coast starts at the mouth of the Klamath River and runs 8 miles south towards Prairie Creek Redwoods State Park. The narrow, partially paved drive winds through stands of redwoods, with spectacular views of the Pacific and numerous pull-offs for picture-taking (sea lions and pelicans abound) and short hikes. Keep an eye out for the World War II radar station, disguised as a farmhouse and barn. If you're heading south on Highway 101, take the Alder Camp Road exit just south of the Klamath River bridge and follow the signs to the Mouth of Klamath. North-bound travelers should take the Redwood National and State Parks Coastal Drive exit off the Newton B. Drury Scenic Parkway. Campers and cars with trailers are not advised.

LODGINGS

REQUA INN ☆

 The Requa Inn was established in 1885, and since then it has gone through several owners, three name changes, one relocation, and a major fire that burned it to the ground in 1914 (it was rebuilt the same year). But this venerable riverside inn is still going strong. Eight of the ten spacious guest rooms, modestly decorated with antique furnishings, come with private baths with showers or claw-footed tubs; four offer views of the lower Klamath River. The inn's main attraction is the cozy parlor downstairs, where guests bury themselves in the plump armchairs to read beside the wood-burning stove. If you're the outdoorsy type, there are plenty of enticements just outside: sandy riverside beaches, myriad hiking trails in nearby Redwood National Park, and, of course, fishing. Breakfast is included in the room rate. *From Hwy 101 take the Requa Rd exit and follow the signs; (707)482-8205; 451 Requa Rd, Klamath, CA 95548; beer and wine; AE, DIS, MC, V; no checks; breakfast, dinner every day (reservations required); $$.*

REDWOOD AYH HOSTEL–DEMARTIN HOUSE

 This turn-of-the-century logger's mansion was remodeled in 1987 to accommodate 30 guests dormitory-style (i.e., bunks and shared baths). What it lacks in creature comforts it makes up for in location—a mere 100 yards from the beach, and surrounded by hiking trails leading along the Redwood Coast. Family rooms are available with advance notice, and the hostel even takes reservations by credit card—strongly recommended in the summer. Showers, country kitchen, dining room, common room, wood stove, redwood deck, and bicycle storage are included in the $9-to $11-nightly rate. *Off Hwy 101 across from Wilson Creek Beach, about 7 miles north of Klamath; (707)482-8265; 14480 Hwy 101, Klamath, CA 95548; MC,V; checks OK; $.*&

A must-do detour along Highway 101 is the Newton B. Drury Scenic Parkway, which passes through dazzling groves of redwoods and elk-filled meadows before leading back onto the Highway 8 miles later.

RESTAURANTS

REQUA INN RESTAURANT ☆

 Besides being the only decent lodge in the greater Klamath area, the Requa Inn also has the only decent restaurant. The inn's dining area is simple yet dignified, with views overlooking the Klamath River and a wonderful parlor for sipping an after-dinner sherry by the fireplace. The no-nonsense double-digit menu of steak, chicken, and fresh seafood obviously caters to Klamath's more well-heeled fishermen. On Friday and Saturday summer nights, go with the seasoned prime rib and baked potato; the grilled salmon and halibut are also safe bets. Be sure to leave room for the fresh-baked blackberry cobbler and a side of vanilla ice cream. *From Hwy 101 take the Requa Rd exit and follow the signs; (707)482-8205; 451 Requa Rd, Klamath, CA 95548; beer and wine; AE, DIS, MC, V; no checks; dinner every day (reservations required); $$.*&

CRESCENT CITY

Because it's the northern gateway to the popular Redwood National Park, one might assume Crescent City would be a major tourist mecca, rife with fine restaurants and hotels. Unfortunately, it's not. Cheap motels, fast-food chains, and mini-malls are the main attractions along this stretch of Highway 101, as

Before touring Redwood National Park, pick up a free guide at the Redwood National Park Headquarters and Information Center at 1111 2nd Street (at K Street) in Crescent City. (Open daily 8am–5pm; 707-464-6101.)

Worth a gander is the vast fleet of stalwart fishing vessels docked in Crescent City Harbor off Highway 101. Watch the leathery crews unload their slimy catch and splay their massive nets to dry in the public parking lot, and you'll soon understand why Crescent City ain't no wimpy tourist town.

GETTING THERE

There's only one route along the Redwood Coast—Highway 101—and only one way to get there: drive. Greyhound (800-231-2222) offers limited bus service to Eureka and Crescent City but is next to worthless for exploring the coast, and Amtrak only runs inland along Interstate 5. A popular option among groups of couples is to rent a small motor home for wheels and book a series of rooms for sleeping; look in the Yellow Pages under "Motor Home—Renting & Leasing" for the nearest dealer.

if Crescent City exists only to serve travelers on their way someplace else. The city is trying, however, to enhance its image, and if you know where to go (which is anywhere off Highway 101), there are actually numerous sites worth visiting in the area and several outdoor-activity options that are refreshingly non-touristy. You won't want to make Crescent City your destination, mind you, but don't be reluctant to spend a day lolling around here, either; you'd be surprised what the town has to offer besides gas and groceries.

ACTIVITIES

Gone Fishin'. What's a trip to the coast without a little fishing thrown in? The captain and crew of the *Stinger*, a 30-foot Chris Craft, will take all comers on a half-day outing for ling cod, snapper, and even big ol' salmon. No experience is necessary, and all the rigging is provided. It's a great way to spend the day (unless you're prone to seasickness), and you even get to keep the fish you catch. Hint: Go on your last day of vacation, so you can brings the goods straight home. For reservations or information, call (707)464-3714. Average price is $50 per person, including rigging.

Sealife Under Glass. Crescent City's version of the Bay Area's popular Marine World–Africa USA is Undersea World, a painfully touristy attraction filled with sharks, eels, octopi, and various other caged creatures of the sea. Located on Highway 101 near the Crescent City Harbor (you can't miss it), it's best seen from the car window unless you have kids, who get a kick out of the petting pools. Oh, and don't forget to pick up a tiny shrink-wrapped seashell for only $4 at the glittery gift store. (Open daily 8am–8pm; 707-464-3522.)

 What to Do. Tennis: Lighted courts are available off Washington Boulevard near the Del Norte High School in Crescent City. Take Northcrest Drive off Highway 101 in downtown Crescent City and turn left on Washington Boulevard. Free.

Golf: Kings Valley Golf Course, a par-28 9-hole course, is at 3030 Lesina Road at the junction of Highway 101 and Highway 199, 3 miles northeast of Crescent City. Green fees under $10; (707)464-2886.

Swimming: Fred Endert Municipal Swimming Pool is at 1000 Play Street, directly behind the Crescent City Chamber of Commerce/Visitors Center. Fee; (707)464-9503.

Horseshoes: Pits are located on Beach Front Park near the visitors Center (BYO shoes). Free.

 Marine Mammal Center. Located at the north end of Crescent City Harbor at 424 Howe Drive in Beach Front Park is the North Coast Marine Mammal Center, a nonprofit organization established in 1989 to rescue and rehabilitate stranded or injured marine mammals. Staffed by local volunteers and funded by donations, the center is the only facility of its kind between San Francisco and Seattle, providing emergency response to environmental disasters and assisting marine researchers by collecting data on marine mammals. The Center is open daily year-round to the public, who are welcome to watch the volunteers in action, make a donation, and buy a nature book or two at the gift shop; (707)465-MAML.

 Pebble Beach Drive. To see the winsome side of Crescent City, take a shoreline cruise along Pebble Beach Drive from the west end of 6th Street to Point St. George. Along the way you're bound to see a few seals and sea lions at the numerous pullouts. End the tour with a short walk though a sandy meadow to Point St. George, a relatively deserted bluff that's perfect for a picnic or beach stroll. On a clear day, look out on the ocean for the St. George Reef Lighthouse, thought to be the tallest (146 feet above sea level), deadliest

Don't disturb any abandoned baby seals or sea lions you may encounter on California's beaches. The mom is probably out getting lunch, and she won't come back until you leave; in fact, you may be fined up to $10,000 for your good intentions. However, if a pup looks injured or in danger, call the Mammal Center at (707)465-MAML.

(several light-keepers died in rough seas while trying to dock), and most expensive ($704,000) lighthouse ever built.

 Crabbing & Fishing. Here's a hoot. Head to the B Street Pier in Crescent City (at the south foot of B Street), rent a crab net ($5) and fishing pole ($5 including tackle) from Popeye's bait shop (no phone), and do some fishing and crabbing off the city's 800-foot-long pier. Crabbing is simple: throw the pre-baited net into the water (don't forget to tie the other end to the pier or you bought it), wait about 10 minutes, then pull it up and see what's for supper. Because it's a public pier, you don't even need a fishing license.

 Wildlife Area. Crescent City's best kept secret is the Lake Earl Wildlife Area, a gorgeous habitat replete with deer, rabbits, beavers, otters, red-tailed hawks, peregrine falcons, bald eagles, songbirds (some 80 species), shorebirds, and migratory waterfowl who share 5,000 acres of the area's pristine woodlands, grasslands, and ocean shore. Hiking and biking are permitted, but you'll want to make the trip on foot with binoculars in hand to get the full effect of this amazing patch of coastal land. To get here, take the Northcrest Drive exit off Highway 101 in downtown Crescent City and turn left on Old Mill Road. Proceed 1½ miles to the park headquarters at 2591 Old Mill Road (if it's open, ask for a map) and park in the gravel lot. Additional trails start the end of Old Mill Road. For more information, call the Department of Fish and Game at (707) 464-2523.

 Picnic & Hiking. One of the prettiest picnic sites on the California Coast is along Enderts Road at the south end of Crescent City. Pack a picnic lunch at Alias Jones Cafe (see Restaurants, below), stop by a liquor store for a few bottles of Chianti, drive 3 miles south on Highway 101 from downtown, and turn right on Enderts Road (across from the Ocean Way Motel). Continue 2⅓ miles, park at the Crescent Beach Overlook, lay your blanket on the grass, admire the ocean view atop your personal 500-foot bluff, and relax. Type As can drive to the end of Enderts Road and take the short hiking trail to Enderts Beach. In the summer, free three-hour ranger-guided tide pool and seashore tours are offered when the tides are right, starting at the beach parking lot. For specific tour times, call (707)464-6101.

📷 **Through the Redwood Forest.** For car-bound cruisers who want to take a journey through an unbelievably spectacular old-growth redwood forest—considered by many one of the most beautiful areas in the world— there's a hidden, well-maintained gravel road called Howland Hill Road that winds for about 12 miles through Jedediah Smith Redwoods State Park. To get there from Highway 101, keep an eye out for the BP gas station at the south end of Crescent City; just before the station, turn right on Elk Valley Road, and follow it to Howland Hill Road, which will be on your right. After driving through the park, you'll end up at Highway 199 near the town of Hiouchi, and from there it's a short jaunt west to get back to Highway 101. Plan at least two to three hours for the 45-mile round- trip, or all day if you want to do some hiking or mountain biking in the park. Trailers and motor homes are not recommended.

🛶 **Kid-Friendly Kayaking.** For a mere six bucks, summer thrill-seekers can shoot the Smith River's wimpier rapids in an inflatable kayak. The 4-hour ranger-led outings include educational highlights covering local flora and fauna. Participants must: be at least 10 years old; sign up at least two days in advance; be under 220 pounds; be able to swim. The tour is limited to 12 kayakers, and spaces—as you would imagine—fill up fast, so reserve a spot (in person) as far in advance as possible at the Smith River Visitors Center in the town of Hiouchi, located 5 miles east of Highway 101 on Highway 199, 6 miles northeast of Crescent City. For more information, call (707)458-3134.

〰️ **Beach Seclusion.** For your very own private beach, take the Mouth Smith River Road exit (at Mandrake's Restaurant) on Highway 101 near the Oregon border. At the Mouth Smith River parking lot, turn right on S Indian Road and park at the small, flower-filled Brother Jonathan Cemetery—a memorial to the 213 ill-fated passengers of the ship *Brother Jonathan*, which crashed on a submerged rock off Point St. George on July 30, 1855. Take the foot path at the north end of the cemetery and voilà!, you'll come upon a secluded little beach overlooking majestic Prince Island (note the shanty built entirely of drift-

The average annual temperature along the Redwood Coast varies only 16 degrees.

Who says crime doesn't pay? Employing more than 1,500 people and pumping an annual $32 million into logging-starved Del Norte County's economy is Pelican Bay State Prison (affectionately referred to by locals as Slammer-by-the-Sea). The high-tech maximum-security facility, located 7 miles north of Crescent City on Lake Earl Drive, has become so profitable that a second prison is on the drawing board.

wood). On the way back to Crescent City, take the Lake Earl Drive turnoff for a brief, bucolic tour of the Smith River area before rejoining Highway 101 in town.

RESTAURANTS

ALIAS JONES ☆☆

Just when you were about to give up on Crescent City cuisine, along comes owner Sandy Kaufman's answer to "where's a good place to eat around here?" This small, lively cafe and bakery does just about everything right, serving savory sandwiches, salads, burgers, and breakfast items that never stray above the $6 mark. For breakfast, try the pesto omelet with herb cream cheese and mozzarella, washed down with a nonfat banana-berry tofu smoothie. A lunch favorite is the hot zucchini, mushroom, cream cheese, and tomato sandwich served on a roll. Bakery items are all made from scratch, and the espresso drinks are all standard doubles—zzzing! *On 3rd St between I and J Sts; (707)465-6987; 983 3rd St, Crescent City; no alcohol; no credit cards; checks OK; breakfast, lunch Mon–Sat; $.*

BEACHCOMBER RESTAURANT ☆

 Ever since the ever-popular Jim's Bistro closed down, it's been difficult for locals to recommend a good restaurant in town. The Beachcomber is the most-nominated spot, which, if you can get past its tired nautical theme and blue naugahyde booths, does a fair job of providing fresh seafood—halibut, red snapper, ling cod, chinook salmon—at reasonable prices. Situated right on the beach, the Beachcomber also specializes in flame-broiled steaks, cooked to your specification on an open- barbecue pit. Friday and Saturday are prime-rib nights. Ask for a booth by the window, and start the evening with the steamer-clam appetizer—1½ pounds of the North Coast's finest. *2 miles south of downtown on Hwy 101; (707)464-2205; 1400 Hwy 101, Crescent City; beer and wine; MC; checks OK; dinner Thurs–Tues; $$.*

LODGINGS

CRESCENT BEACH MOTEL

 Crescent City has the dubious distinction of being the only city along the coast without a fancy hotel or bed and breakfast. There is, however, an armada of cheap motels, the best of which is the Crescent Beach Motel. While the color scheme is a bit frightening—brown on yellow highlighted with orange—all but 4 of the 27 rooms (most with queen-size beds and color TVs) not only face the beach, but are within steps of it. The small lawn area and large sun decks overlooking the ocean are a major bonus, as is the convenience of have the Beachcomber Restaurant (see above) right next door. *2 miles south of downtown on Hwy 101; (707)464-5436; 1455 Hwy 101, Crescent City, CA 95531; DIS, MC, V; checks OK; $.&*

 Tenting it? Check out the relatively unknown Cifford Kamph Memorial Park, located 1 mile south of the Oregon border off Highway 101. It has several grassy campsites—with picnic tables—perched on a bluff overlooking the ocean. At $5 per night for beachfront access, it's a steal.

If you're bringing along the family or traveling in a group along the Redwood Coast, then ixnay on the motelay and rent a fully furnished home on the ocean or river's edge for as little as $80 a night. Call Redwood Coast Vacation Rentals for a free brochure at (707)487-8008.

INDEX

NORTHERN CALIFORNIA COAST BEST PLACES—A DESTINATION GUIDE
REPORT FORM

Know of a Northern California Coast restaurant or lodging that you consider a "Best Place"? Want to confirm, correct, or disagree with a review in this book? Have a tip on a great destination—a place, business, activity, or service—that should be included in this book? Send us your recommendations and evaluations. We value your input!

Name of establishment or destination (include address and telephone number if possible):

_____

_____

_____

_____

REPORT

Please provide a description and evaluation of the establishment or destination, based on your personal experience. Continue on the reverse side if necessary. Include the date of your visit.

_____

_____

_____

_____

I am not concerned, directly or indirectly, with the management or ownership of this establishment.

Signed: _____

Address: _____

Telephone: _____

Date:_____

Mail your report to:

Northern California Coast Best Places Destination Guide
c/o Sasquatch Books
1008 Western Avenue, Suite 300
Seattle, WA 98104

Or E-mail your report to us at:

books:@sasquatchbooks.com

Did you enjoy this book?

Sasquatch Books publishes high-quality books and guides related to the Pacific Northwest. Our books are available at bookstores and other retail outlets throughout the region. Here is a partial list of our current titles:

GUIDEBOOKS

Seattle Best Places
The most Discriminating Guide to Seattle's Restaurants, Shops, Hotels, Nightlife, Sights, and Outings. The original insiders guide—now in print for fifteen years with over 150,000 copies sold. Includes one-day to one-week itineraries, and pullout map.
Edited by Nancy Leson and Stephanie Irving

Northwest Best Places
The Definitive Guide to Restaurants, Lodgings, and Touring in Oregon, Washington, and British Columbia
Edited by Stephanie Irving and David Brewster

Portland Best Places
The Most Discriminating Guide to Portland's Restaurants, Shops, Hotels, Nightlife, Arts, Sights, and Outings
Edited by Kim Carlson and Stephanie Irving

Vancouver Best Places
The Most Discriminating Guide to Vancouver's Restaurants, Shops, Hotels, Nightlife, Arts, Sights, and Outings
Edited by Kasey Wilson and Stephanie Irving

Northwest Cheap Sleeps
Recommendations for the Budget Traveler in OR, WA, and BC
Edited by Stephanie Irving and Nancy Leson

Northern California Cheap Sleeps
Recommendations for the Budget Traveler
Rebecca Poole Forée

Back Roads of Washington
74 Trips on Washington's Scenic Byways
Earl Thollander

Back Roads of Oregon
82 Trips on Oregon's Scenic Byways
Earl Thollander

Earl Thollander's Back Roads of California
65 Trips on California's Scenic Byways
Earl Thollander

Earl Thollander's San Francisco
30 Walking and Driving Tours from the Embarcadero to the Golden Gate
Earl Thollander

FIELD GUIDES

Field Guide to the Bald Eagle
Field Guide to the Geoduck
Field Guide to the Gray Whale
Field Guide to the Grizzly Bear
Field Guide to the Humpback Whale
Field Guide to the Orca
Field Guide to the Pacific Salmon
Field Guide to the Slug

FOOD AND COOKING

The Encyclopedia of Country Living
An Old Fashioned Recipe Book
Carla Emery

Breakfast in Bed
The Best B&B Recipes from Northern California, Oregon, Washington, and British Columbia
Carol Frieberg

Pike Place Market Cookbook
Recipes, Anecdotes, and Personalities from Seattle's Renowned Public Market
Braiden Rex-Johnson

The City Gardener's Cookbook
Totally Fresh, Mostly Vegetarian, Decidedly Delicious Recipes from Seattle's P-Patches

GARDENING

Northwest Garden Style
Ideas, Designs and Methods for the Creative Gardener
Jan Kowalczewski Whitner

SASQUATCH BOOKS

1008 Western Avenue, Suite 300   Seattle, WA 98104   206-467-4300   1-800-775-0817